OPERATIONAL PHILOSOPHY

OPERATIONAL PHILOSOPHY

INTEGRATING KNOWLEDGE AND ACTION

By ANATOL RAPOPORT

Assistant Professor of Mathematical Biology
The University of Chicago
Author of "Science and the Goals of Man"

HARPER & BROTHERS PUBLISHERS

 NEW YORK ▪ 1954

OPERATIONAL PHILOSOPHY

*Printed in the United States of America
By The Haddon Craftsmen, Inc., Scranton, Pa.*

Library of Congress catalog card number: 53-8550

CONTENTS

v

PREFACE

The topics discussed in this book are as old as philosophy: How do we know what we know? How ought we to behave? What is it all about? The *approach* to these questions which we will use here is not old, certainly not more than a century old. Yet this approach, which we will call "operationalism," has roots stretching far back in the history of Western thought.

The nominalists of the twelfth century in their critique of the "reality of universals" carried the germ of the operational idea.[1] Roger Bacon (*ca.* 1212–*ca.* 1294), the earliest outspoken champion of the experimental method, appears as a prophet of the future philosophy of action among the scholasticists of his day. The line carries on through da Vinci, Galileo, Newton, and Huygens, through the English empiricists and the French Encyclopedists into the nineteenth century. Historically, operationalism has been the way of science. But in our day it has acquired a special significance. Today operationalism is *being aware* of the way of science— the philosophy of science.

The philosophy of science is a comparatively new field of inquiry. In the old days, science *was* philosophy. That is to say, the sort of knowledge which science has always pursued—knowledge of "general principles," of the "why" of things—was supposed to be embodied in the works of professional thinkers, philosophers. The other kind of knowledge which today goes under the name of "know-how," the knowledge of obtaining desirable results in specific, concrete situations, was practiced by a different class of people, the professional workers—artists, craftsmen, even slaves.

About the time of the Renaissance there occurred in Western Europe a union of these two—systematic thinking, recorded and accumulated, and purposeful activity toward preconceived desired ends. This union of "know how" and "know why" can be taken to be the beginning of our scientific age. It also marks the separation of science and philosophy, in which science switched its allegiance from "eternal truths" to immediate "brute facts."

Thereafter many philosophers turned their backs on science, impatient with its preoccupation with detail, and many scientists turned away from philosophy and forgot their heritage. They forgot that were it not for the intellectual fountainhead of philosophic thought, they would have nothing to investigate. As Alfred North Whitehead put it, scientists were living on the intellectual capital of the seventeenth century (109).

Near the end of the nineteenth century, this capital was nearing exhaustion. A new intellectual outlook was needed. It could not have come from the then existing philosophy, which had divorced itself from science. So science created its own philosophy, a reexamination of its own methods and foundations. This philosophy appears in the works of Whitehead (108, 109), of Poincaré (72), of Russell (86), of Vaihinger (104), and of many others all clustering in the first quarter of this century. All these works reflect a growing preoccupation of science with *itself*, an increasing self-awareness of science. Out of such self-awareness, particularly in the light of the new theory of meaning (semantics), operationalism has crystallized.

The newest developments, particularly in the United States, are attempts to extend operationalism so as to make it a method for dealing with human affairs. In particular, the school of thought founded by Alfred Korzybski (1879–1950) has had many followers. The impetus of Korzybski's ideas gave rise to numerous popularizations of operationalism (19, 20, 35, 43, 48, 77). Although the difficulties of scientific philosophy are largely passed over in these popularizations, they nevertheless have played an important part in establishing an intellectual climate in which such a philosophy can flourish. The existence of such a climate is of prime importance in our day when public opinion has much more weight than formerly in influencing educational policies.

Thus there is no dearth of literature on the subject of operationalism (the philosophy of science), both "technical" and "popular." There may, however, be a lack of works on the "middle" level, aimed, say, at the third- and fourth-year college population or at a public familiar with popular presentations but not trained to read technical works. It is to fill this gap that this book is offered.

The task here is to work with elementary ideas as much as possible but to lead into some of the technicalities of modern philosophy (symbolic logic, probability, statistical aspects of causality, mathematical notions of structure and order, etc.). We will begin with the modern theory of knowledge, which in operational philosophy cannot be separated from a theory of communication and meaning. The topics are standard: definition, causality, predictability, logic, probability, and the quantity-quality dichotomy. All of these topics have been treated elsewhere. For example, an extensive treatment of definition appears in Hayakawa's *Language in Thought and Action* (35), of causality and probability in Reichenbach's *The Rise of Scientific Philosophy* (81), of predictability in Bridgman's *Logic of Modern Physics* (11), and an excellent elementary exposition of logic (both Aristotelian and symbolic) is given in Lieber's *Mits, Wits, and Logic* (50).

This book was prompted not by a lack of literature but by a felt need to have both old and new ideas presented in a certain order and treated with more or less uniformity of style and from a definite point of view—the relation between ideas and action, between what we do and what we think. In old philosophy this was the problem of relating the "subjective" to the "objective."

In the light of this relation I go on to consider ethics. This was the main theme of my earlier book (77). Here, however, the relation of ethics to operational philosophy is made (it is hoped) more explicit. The critique of the relativist position, sketched in the earlier book, is extended. New material is offered in a classification of ethical systems and in a discussion of self-fulfilling assumptions and of action-directed goals. In its approach to ethics, operational philosophy leans heavily on the sociology of knowledge and on modern psychiatric theories. This approach is also apparent in a different form in Mannheim's *Ideology and Utopia* (57), in Fromm's *Man for Himself* (34), in Morris' *The Open Self* (63), in Overstreet's *The Mature Mind* (68), in Whyte's *The Next Development in Man* (110), in Dewey's *Reconstruction in Philosophy* (25), and in Popper's *The Open Society and Its Enemies* (73).

Finally, I attempt to survey the "frontiers" of operational philosophy. Most of the thinking on this subject seemed to me to stem from a critique of scientific philosophy in terms of its limitations rather than from attempts to extend scientific philosophy to regions still outside its scope. However, there is no lack of fresh, constructive ideas in the writings of the critics of scientific philosophy, particularly in the works of Whitehead (108, 109), Cassirer (18), Langer (47), and Burke (14). A late acquaintance with some of those ideas gave me the notion that philosophy can still permit itself to leave the safety of operational analysis and yet make *some* sense. There is, it seems, a borderland between what logical positivists[2] consider "legitimate" philosophy (the philosophy of science) and poetry. The recognition that the soil of this borderland may be fertile has led me to abandon the austere conservatism of pure logical positivism (represented, say, by Wittgenstein [113] and Ayer [4]), to which I previously subscribed.

Yet it is one thing to venture from the shores and another to be altogether at sea. I undertake to determine the conditions under which "wild speculations" may be safely engaged in. If there is to be discovery there must, of course, be venturesome speculations of the kind that burst, to use Whitehead's metaphor, through the current abstractions of our culture. And if speculations are to be venturesome, they cannot be expected to make much immediate sense.

The most difficult problem in writing this book is to decide how much to assume about the reader's background. Operational philosophy makes possible the extension of scientific evaluating habits to areas in which such habits do not prevail. The birthplace of operational philosophy is scientific practice, in particular the practice of that most scientific of scientific disciplines—mathematical physics. Thus, if our exposition is to be more than a mere verbal description of scientific evaluating habits, that is, if the origin and evaluation of these habits are to be looked into, we must talk about science (especially physics), its subject matter and history. In particular, it will be necessary to refer to certain physical laws (e.g., universal gravitation, conservation of energy, and degradation of energy) and to certain formal techniques, such as symbolic logic, quantification, and the mathematics of probability.

Obviously an adequate exposition of all these matters cannot be included here. Therefore the following expedient will be adopted. Whenever such subjects are discussed, references will be given to a bibliography of writings which offer information on them to the "layman." In addition, an attempt will be made to develop in greater detail the basic ideas in the notes placed at the end of the book. The numbers in parentheses throughout the text are the references to bibliographic entries. The superscripts are references to the notes. A similar purpose is assigned to the glossary at the end of the book. The reader will have, therefore, the opportunity to refer to the glossary for a more or less extended "definition" of a term as a reminder of its technical context, to the notes for a more explicit treatment of technicalities, and to the bibliography for access to further information.

The plan followed in the exposition is predominantly to let the main ideas of each chapter emerge from the discussion. Those who prefer to have the ideas stated first and then developed may start with the summaries placed at the end of some of the chapters.

I wish to acknowledge a debt to my students who played a vital part in the writing of this book. Most of the material is an outgrowth of courses I have given during the last two years at University College of The University of Chicago and in seminars arranged by the New York Society for General Semantics, the Chicago Chapter of the International Society for General Semantics, and the University of Denver. In their always lively and frequently penetrating discussions, the students provided me with indispensable "feedback" as guidance in presenting the material.

Similar guidance came from my family (father, mother, and wife) and from my old friend Sara Goldberg, who also typed the manuscript at a stage when it was especially difficult to read. My thanks also go to Professors Charles Morris, Russell Meyers, and Wendell Johnson for their critical reading of the manuscript. I am deeply grateful to S. I. Hayakawa, who took special pains in going over several successive drafts and made especially pertinent and valuable suggestions in matters of both content and presentation. Finally, I am indebted to Harper & Brothers, who have encouraged me in the writing of this book.

A. R.

Chicago, Illinois
April 1, 1953

Part I. OPERATIONAL KNOWLEDGE

INTRODUCTION

TRADITIONALLY, philosophy courses offered in universities have been concerned with the study of various philosophical systems. Such studies are sometimes purely descriptive (simply noting what each philosopher has said); sometimes they are historical (noting how the ideas of one system of philosophy have stemmed from those of another); sometimes comparative (noting how various systems of philosophy are like or unlike each other). What is usually lacking in the conventional academic approach to philosophy is an extensive inquiry into the relations between *thinking* and *doing*. How does the framework in which people think about the world influence what they do about the world and (what is even more important) vice versa?

There have been thinkers who were keenly concerned with such problems and who have offered theories to deal with them. One such thinker was Marx. He tried to show how what people do in the economic structure of their society influences (we are toning him down here—Marx actually believed *determines*) what they think about the nature of society, about right and wrong, and even about the physical world.

Another such thinker was Freud. He tried to explain the formation of the individual personality in terms of the individual's early "sexual" experience. It is natural to extend this point of view to a theory of the relation of a world outlook to primitive sexual experience.

And still another such thinker (although this has not been commonly recognized) was Einstein. He actually showed by mathematical reasoning how what one "does" determines what one "means." His investigations have been confined to simple kinds of meaning and action, and for this reason his results have been more lucid and precise than those of Marx and Freud. Einstein showed, for example,

3

that if our reasoning about events in time and space is to make sense, we must always keep in mind that "time" and "space" mean not what we *say* or *think* about them, but what we *do* about them— they acquire meaning from the operations we must perform in measuring them and have no meaning *apart* from these operations. Thus Einstein's contribution has to do with the relation between thought and action and as such has something in common with the contributions of Freud and Marx.

Marx, Freud, and Einstein are not often thought of as "philosophers," at least not in the same way as Plato, Hegel, and Bergson are. Perhaps this is so because Marx, Freud, and Einstein fixed their attention on "events" (such as "price fluctuations," "impotence," "propagation of electromagnetic waves") instead of on "ideas" (such as "the soul," "the Absolute," "the Vital Force") as the philosophers who are universally recognized as philosophers do. Yet there is an abundance of ideas in the theory of surplus value, in the notion of the Oedipus complex, and in the definition of space-time curvature. The difference between thinkers like Plato, Hegel, and Bergson on the one hand and Marx, Freud, and Einstein on the other is that one can trace the ideas put forward by the latter to some sort of *action* or some set of "operations," both with regard to where the ideas come from and to what can be done with them. Operational philosophy, the kind this book is concerned with, stems from an attempt to treat the sort of problems which occupied people like Marx, Freud, and Einstein.

One of the pioneers in operational philosophy was John Dewey. Dewey's interests were along the same lines as those of Marx, Freud, and Einstein: he was intent on discovering the relation between what people do and the way they think. He was primarily an educator, so it is easy to see why he was interested in this relation. That is, it is easy for us who are a generation or two removed from Dewey to see this. But when Dewey first put forward the idea that education should be "operational," that is, should be a process of integrating thought and action, the idea was regarded as revolutionary. And, as is so often the case with revolutionary ideas, it soon became altogether perverted, so perverted that Dewey was forced to abandon the term "pragmatism," which at first was associated with his attitudes.

In some quarters pragmatism became all but synonymous with opportunism. To illustrate, we will take two notions from Dewey's educational philosophy and see what became of them. One notion has to do with the definition of truth as "that which 'works.' " Without further qualification, this definition may well be taken to mean (and has been taken to mean) that truth is that which serves one's purpose, with obvious consequences in the world of politics and public relations. Without further explanation of what is meant by "works," pragmatism can be invoked in defense of outright quackery, as has been done, for example, by the adherents of "dianetics." Another notion has to do with motivation for learning. Dewey has maintained (23) that people will learn only the things that interest them, that learning and doing are inseparable. A perversion of that notion among the people of the United States has given rise to two delusions with regard to the educational process. In one delusion "education" is identified with "training." According to this notion, the sole purpose of study is to be able to perform certain (usually remunerative) activities. In the second delusion, on the contrary, education is sharply distinguished from training—or, as it is usually put, the "academic" is distinguished from the "practical."

The curricula of thousands of American high schools and colleges with their courses in car driving, public speaking, and dating etiquette testify to the effects of the first delusion on our educational system. The other side of this picture, somewhat contradicting the first, is the American's uneasy concern with the questionable "practicality" of education. If pinned down, he will usually admit that by "practical" he means "contributing to one's ability to get along." Getting along, in turn, usually means making money, but may also mean enjoying the approval of one's acquaintances. Thus the practicality of mathematics is evaluated in terms of how much mathematical knowledge one uses on one's job; while the practicality of English may be evaluated in terms of how "good English" may help one get a good job or be accepted in certain circles.

It is necessary to mention these distortions in order to bring out the true meaning of Dewey's ideas, that is, of operationalism. We will see how the operational definition of truth (that which "works") has been developed in a direction entirely different from that of opportunistic pragmatism. There is a broad humanitarian aspect to operationalism which leads to an educational philosophy different from that which pervades most of American education today.

Dewey's re-evaluation of the tasks of philosophy appears, among other places, in his book *Reconstruction in Philosophy* (25), which was published in 1920. Another book appeared at the same time by another man who was profoundly interested in the relation between thought and action. This was *Manhood of Humanity* by Alfred Korzybski (45). The theme of Korzybski's book is contained in the first sentence of Dewey's book: "Man differs from the lower animals because he preserves his past experiences."

Note that the sentence is, in a way, a definition of man. Korzybski's whole book *Manhood of Humanity* is an extended definition of man, a definition identical with Dewey's. Now, definitions of man have been given before, chiefly in terms of presumed differences between man and the lower animals. The usual definition in Christian theology emphasizes the possession of a "soul." Aristotle's definition hinges on the faculty of "reason." Descartes' definition brings out the possession of "free will," etc. We will note in passing that any three-year-old can distinguish a human being from a nonhuman, but that three-year-olds do not usually bother to search for a "soul," for "reason," or for "free will." That is to say, philosophers spent much thought trying to define man not because it is difficult to tell man from non-man but for entirely different reasons.

Philosophers are interested in what is *proper* for man (ethics). Some of them are also interested in what is going to happen to man (prophecy). They think they can solve these questions by uncovering the "nature" of man, and they think they can uncover this nature by studying some property of man which is crucial. The scheme is praiseworthy except for the fact that none of the properties cited ("soul," "reason," "free will") can be fruitfully studied because it is difficult to agree on what they stand for. But the Dewey-Korzybski definition is different. It is a definition from an operational point of view. It points to a "property" of man which can be fruitfully studied: the accumulation of personal and cultural experience. It is this shift of interest from what man *is* to what he *does* (the crucial orientation of operationalism) that Dewey called a reconstruction in philosophy and Korzybski called the manhood of humanity. From this operationally oriented definition of man arise the ethics of operational philosophy, as we shall see.

The problem of defining man, although a chronic one in philosophy, became acute for Western thinkers in the first quarter of our century. It is not hard to see why. We usually become conscious of problems only when something goes wrong, just as we become conscious of parts of our bodies when they start hurting. If everything goes smoothly, there are no problems. Things went comparatively smoothly for Western civilization for a whole century, from 1815 to 1914. There were, of course, wars, crises, revolutions, epidemics, famines, and disasters. But superimposed on all these ups and downs was something called "progress." In technology, invention followed invention, making more and more goods available to more and more people. In science discoveries multiplied at an ever-increasing rate, making possible the solution of nature's secrets and increasing man's ability to combat the elements and diseases. In politics it seemed that the privileges of the aristocracy, which up until the French Revolution were firmly entrenched in Europe, were gradually disappearing. Literacy was on the increase. Ideas on social welfare and on the responsibility of rulers to the ruled spread. There seemed to be no reason why this "progress" could not go on indefinitely, bringing more blessings within the reach of more people.

Suddenly came the shock of the First World War, which, when it was over, appeared to many to have been simply an outbreak of insanity. True, the nineteenth century had its prophets who kept warning the Europeans of the impending catastrophe. But the din of "progress" drowned these voices. The century was marked by a widespread conviction that the future would be a better time to live in than the past had been. This faith can be seen in the utopian novels of the nineteenth century, for instance those of Jules Verne and H. G. Wells. Jules Verne's novels were mostly about bold individuals endowed by inventive genius who, in spite of scoffing and ridicule by the mediocre, performed magnificent feats of technology —submarine navigation, aeronautics in heavier-than-air machines, space-ship travel, etc. Wells, on the other hand, pictured societies of the future as founded on scientific faith and practice. For both writers, science and technology were marvelously exciting and magnificent opportunities for the liberation of mankind.

Compare these with the "prophetic" novels of our own century, such as Aldous Huxley's *Brave New World* (40) and Orwell's *Nineteen Eighty-Four* (67). In them the future appears as a nightmare, and science is a principal agency of man's enslavement. This change of attitude toward the future (and toward science, with which the future is interlaced) is traceable to the shock of the First World War and to the revolutions which followed it.

The great hopes of the nineteenth-century humanitarians had been science and socialism. Science, they thought, would eventually make everyone rich, and socialism would make everyone free. In the first quarter of the twentieth century, it became evident that science could also mean mass murder and a socialist revolution could also lead to mass enslavement.

Following the end of the First World War, there was a decade of respite in which the Western world tried to return to what it had considered normal living. But only in the United States was the old-time optimism recaptured. Mass production began really to pay off in this country of still unlimited resources. Rolling off the assembly lines came not only an abundance of necessities to make life easy, but also wonderful toys to make an easy life bearable—automobiles in which to go joy-riding; radios, to provide a background of constant noise as an antidote to the boredom of satiety; movies, synthesized from prefabricated situations and peopled with stereotypes —all avenues of escape from dull daily routine, all effective in blunting the critical faculties. And so in the United States the "prosperity" of the twenties was taken uncritically. The stock market continued to rise. Politicans proclaimed that soon everyone would be rich, ride in two cars, and live on chicken. Then it happened again. Something went wrong. Everyone suddenly became poor and was getting poorer by the hour.

By the time the Second World War came along, no one was surprised. It had been expected for years. There were no cheering crowds of the kind that greeted each country's entry into the First World War. Instead, there was gloom and anxiety. For a while it was not even evident that there would be much fighting. For seven months the allied armies sat facing the Germans in the Rhine Valley with hardly a shot exchanged. Authorities in military science proclaimed that at last impregnable fortifications had made decisive battles impossible. But again the unexpected happened. The Germans advanced through the "impregnable" fortifications, and in a few weeks everything was over on the continent.

But then the leaders of the United States and of Great Britain spoke to the millions on the radio and said that the enemy must be resisted and destroyed. Once he was destroyed, they said, the world could be reconstructed on the basis of equality and justice. Again the vision of the nineteenth century was invoked—a sane, quiet, prosperous (Western) world with dignity and security for the Common Man and with continuous progress spearheaded by science. It turned out that the U.S.S.R., previously an outcast from the community of Western nations, also shared the vision. Only one thing stood in the way: the Axis powers, led by madmen and gangsters. The way to the future led over the ruins of the evil Axis.

And so the Axis was smashed. And again the vision promptly vanished. As this is being written (1953), everyone talks of the Third World War, and no one even dares to suggest that it will be the last. No one tells us any more how things will be after the next war. There is little talk of war aims aside from "smashing Communism."

War has ceased in the minds of men to be something that one does to gain something. It has become something that happens to you, like a plague or an earthquake. It is the same notion that people had about wars before wars started to be peddled as achievements of national glory.

The self-awareness of the Western world since the end of the Napoleonic wars appears, then, as a century of steadily rising hopes followed by two generations of disillusionment, trauma, and frustration, all the more keenly felt against a background of bright hopes. The pressure has kept increasing to re-examine the foundations of our thinking process. It seemed as if the Reason to which eighteenth-century writers had so eloquently appealed had betrayed us. The horrors of the twentieth century could not be blamed on illiteracy, superstition, and the despotism of monarchies (the scapegoats of the eighteenth). The new horrors were the by-products of scientific ingenuity and were often perpetrated in the name of democratic and humanitarian ideals. The incongruities between reality and rationalization became so flagrant that it appeared natural to ask whether people were not crazy.

Radical thinkers like Korzybski did maintain that most people are crazy most of the time and presented arguments to support this view. Others, like Dewey, put it somewhat more mildly. They place the blame for the present impasse of mankind on the inadequacy of traditional philosophy to cope with modern problems. One might question the relevance of this observation. Philosophers are seldom called upon to cope with practical problems; so it appears futile to blame them for the inability to solve them. However, if one goes deeper into Dewey's argument one becomes aware of its relevance. The point is that everyone is a philosopher. That is to say, everyone has a framework for organizing his experience. One does not usually make one's own framework. One gets a ready-made one from parents, teachers, and peers, just as they got theirs. If one traces the ancestry of these frameworks, which Westerners carry around with them, one comes to the carpenters who built them: Plato and Aristotle, Paul and Augustine. What these people wrote had a far-reaching influence on the "schoolmen" of the later Middle Ages, who founded the first universities in Europe. These universities were the fountainheads of the European educational system, which was in great measure responsible for the political development of Europe. European political ideas, particularly English and French, were brought to America together with certain currents of philosophy and theology, such as Calvinism and Puritanism. These are to a large degree responsible for the development of the American educational system. From the educational system and from the special circumstances of American history (such as an expanding frontier, heavy immigration, isolation) stems an American philosophy.

To the extent that certain beliefs are present in most Americans, one can speak of the beliefs of the "average" American. It is safe to say that this "person" does not believe in the divine right of kings, but he does believe in something he calls "free enterprise." He says he believes in God, but when he gets a toothache he relies on the dentist rather than on prayer. Nor does he attribute to God his own successes and failures. He thinks it is all right for people to sell almost any kind of services for money, but it is not all right for a woman to sell her favors for money. This transaction, however, is not altogether bad if it is legalized by marriage. He is apt to believe the assertions of a physicist about matter even if they seem to contradict what he holds as "common sense." But he is much less apt to believe the assertions of a social scientist about society if they contradict his beliefs. He thinks opinions on religious subjects are matters of individual preference, but he believes that some political opinions are "subversive."

All these beliefs constitute a philosophy, regardless of how articulate or inarticulate they happen to be. Moreover, such philosophies can be traced to the thinking of professional philosophers. And what is most important, such philosophies, being often badly out of date, are in a measure responsible for the "average man's" inability to help himself, to save himself from catastrophes which threaten him. These catastrophes are themselves the results of mixing up-to-date technology with out-of-date philosophy.

John Dewey, therefore, in that year of 1920, following the great catastrophe of the First World War, proposed a *Reconstruction of Philosophy* not just for professional philosophers, but for educators, political leaders, and everyone, since everyone is a philosopher. Korzybski's proposal for a re-evaluation of man's role in this world was of a similar nature.

The reconstruction foretold by Dewey in 1920 is now well on its way. It was launched when modern philosophy became rooted in scientific practice. The resulting intellectual revolution, reflected in the rise of operational philosophy, is now with us. It is this revolution and the postulated urgent necessity for pursuing it further that we intend to examine.

Chapter 1. THE PROBLEM OF DEFINITION:

"WHAT IS X?"

It is remarkable how frequently the same problems recur in the history of man. The most ancient myths, fairy tales, and proverbs often apply, with only slight modifications, to present-day events. In the old tales of malicious gods and demons one finds the perennial problem of human survival in the face of hostile nature. There are, in stories of invisibility gadgets, flying carpets, seven-league boots, and horns of abundance, dreams of technological miracles. There is incessant concern with guessing the future, as in tales of oracles and seers; with family relations, as in stories of the wicked stepmother or the disinherited youngest son; with the frailties of human nature, such as now are the concern of psychiatrists, as in the animal fables common to so many cultures; with rules of living, as in proverbs; with social problems, as in tales of the abuse of privilege by proud and wicked kings.

With one class of problems, however, our forefathers were not nearly as preoccupied as we are. These are problems of communication and understanding. The Genesis story of the Tower of Babel is a notable early exception. It may have had its roots in an actual crisis, a result of importing large numbers of workers or slaves from distant lands. On the whole, however, language awareness is largely absent in ancient folklore. When Aladdin (presumably a Persian) visits the Chinese princess, the question never arises as to how they are able to converse. They just do. Although the heroes of fairy tales do an enormous amount of traveling, interpreters are generally not mentioned. Communication with foreigners, gods, devils, sphinxes, and beasts, appears to encounter no linguistic obstacles whatever.

On rare occasions, one does find a folk tale which reveals insight into the problems of communication—sometimes an insight which goes far beyond the mere recognition, as in the Tower of Babel story, of linguistic differences. The following ancient anecdote is probably of Indian origin.

A blind man asked someone to explain the meaning of "white."
"White is a color," he was told, "as, for example, white snow."
"I understand," said the blind man. "It is a cold and damp color."
"No, it doesn't have to be cold and damp. Forget about snow. Paper, for instance, is white."
"So it rustles?" asked the blind man.
"No, indeed, it need not rustle. It is like the fur of an albino rabbit."
"A soft, fluffy color?" the blind man wanted to know.
"It need not be soft either. Porcelain is white, too."
"Perhaps it is a brittle color, then," said the blind man.

This story goes to the core of the matter. It illustrates the impossibility of communication between two people who have not shared a common *experience*. From the point of view of operational philosophy, this is perhaps the most fundamental philosophical problem.

LANGUAGE AS AN ORGANIZATION OF EXPERIENCE

I will begin to discuss the problem of communication by proposing a rather unconventional classification of languages. I will suppose that people are potentially able to speak the same language to the extent that they share certain areas of common experience. Let us see how that compares with the usual classifications (as made by linguists).

The fact that you and I both speak English means this: If we make a list of all the words you use in your speech from day to day and all the words I use from day to day, we will find that practically all the words each of us uses will be found in a standard English dictionary. Do we then speak the same language? We ordinarily assume that we do.

But look at it this way. To determine whether you and I speak the same language, let us leave the dictionary (a third party) out of it and compare our verbal outputs with *each other*. If we do, we will probably find that although our verbal outputs overlap, the correspondence is never exact. There will almost certainly be words which one of us uses and the other does not—and if our backgrounds differ markedly, the differences may be very great. The usual way of stating this fact is to say that we have different "vocabularies." But then one might ask at what point a difference in "vocabularies" amounts to a difference in "language."

Dr. X understands the *Journal of Cellular and Comparative Physiology*, but the *Racing Form* is a complete mystery to him. Mr. Y conducts his business with the aid of the *Racing Form*, but he may not understand a single line of the *Iliad*, even if it is in "English," which Mr. Y insists is his mother tongue. The fact that Dr. X, sitting next to Mr. Y at a lunch counter can ask Mr. Y to pass the mustard and be understood still does not establish that they speak the "same language." If it did, we would have to say that Mr. Y speaks the same language as Señor Z, who comes to see Mr. Y daily. However, Mr. Y would not understand a word of what Señor Z sings to Señorita Q out on the breakwater on a summer night.

There are, of course, explanations for these discrepancies. We say that the scientist's vocabulary is "specialized"; that the bookie speaks only "a little Spanish," just enough to do business with Señor Z, etc. But there is also another way to look at these matters, a more radical way. This is to recognize that the conventional division of languages into groups (Indo-European, Semitic), families (Teutonic, Slavic), and species (English, German) does not serve *all* purposes of communication study. Such classifications, although useful to the professional linguists, are not particularly helpful in the construction of a theory of communication—and a theory of communication is essential to a general theory of knowledge. The linguist's classifications do not, for example, deal with scientific, underworld, commercial, and other jargons which are based on specific areas of experiences shared by groups of people engaged in common activities.

The importance of jargons in the study of communication is beginning to be recognized. There have been serious and semiserious studies of slang, teen-age "jive," "legalese," and "federalese." With increasing frequency one reads in the press comments such as these: "In the jargon of Soviet officialdom this means. . . ." or "Translated from diplomatic parlance into plain English, this means. . . ." Periodically articles appear in scholarly and scientific journals deploring the mushrooming of specialists' jargons, which make communication between one scholar or scientist and another practically impossible. To complicate matters, jargons do not necessarily involve many artificial or unfamiliar words. The mathematician, for example, uses words like "group," "ring," "blanket," "loop," "lattice," "ideal," "normal," "singular," "measure" to denote matters which are almost as difficult to explain to someone who is not a mathematician as it is to explain the meaning of "white" to a blind man.

This discrepancy between the seeming simplicity of some kinds of words and the difficulty of communicating their meaning indicates that the meanings of words are not in the words themselves but in the experiences behind them. This sounds so obvious as to seem trite. Yet the fact remains that until recently the main efforts of the students of language have been directed to the analysis of its purely formal aspects, such as phonetics, grammar, and syntax. Only in the last half century or so, with the advent of semantics and metalinguistics,[3] has a concerted effort been made to study language as related to man's experience.

Studying the relation of language to human experience is a major concern of operational philosophy. Operational philosophy views any language as *a certain way of organizing experience*. This view emphasizes the psychological and cultural aspects of language rather than its formal aspects.

To regard languages as ways of organizing experience is to look at them from what is called a *metalinguistic* point of view, as contrasted with the point of view customary in traditional linguistics. In daily life, as in traditional linguistics, we say that the German mystic and the German empiricist "speak the same language"; metalinguistically speaking, we would have to say that they speak different languages, since they organize their experiences in entirely different ways. Similarly the Japanese physicist and the Swedish physicist, even if they have difficulty in asking each other to pass the mustard, may be said to "speak the same language" in their scientific communication, since they organize the same kind of experience in the same kind of way. From the point of view of metalinguistics, it is easy to understand why an American mathematician with a dictionary and a little effort can read a mathematical paper in a Russian journal; and why an English-speaking jazz enthusiast, speaking to an English-speaking lover of Viennese waltzes, cannot make himself understood. Important in the sense of this definition is not the repertory of symbols on which experiences are mapped (vocabularies) but the repertories of the experiences themselves and especially the way experiences are organized (orientation). Once one has had a certain experience or has succeeded in organizing one's experiences in a certain way, it is a simple matter to put a label on it. It is usually much more difficult to do the opposite, namely to enlarge one's experience to fit a label.

To illustrate, take the word *kis*. If you don't happen to know Hungarian, it means nothing. Once it is translated (*kis* means small) one more word is added to your vocabulary with very little effort on your part. But now take the term *standard deviation*. You may know the meaning of both English words which comprise the term, but unless you know quite a bit of mathematics and some rudiments of statistics, it might take you *months* to learn the meaning of this term in the sense of knowing how and when to use it. In the case of the (linguistically) foreign word "kis," you are only enlarging your vocabulary to cover a familiar experience. In the case of the (linguistically) nonforeign terms "standard deviation," you are enlarging your experience to fit words that are familiar in appearance only.

DEFINITION

The process of making a word usable is called *definition*. Obviously, if people speak the same language (the "same" in the strictest sense of the word, that is, sharing not only the same vocabularies but also the same experiences), the need for definition does not arise. The need for a definition becomes felt only if one's vocabulary is inadequate to name a new experience, or if one is faced with a word which does not occur in one's vocabulary. This need can be expressed in the question "What is X?"

Note that "What is X?" can have at least two different kinds of meaning. If X stands for "this," that is, refers to some object or situation, it is the *word* which is missing. Such are the questions of a child about the objects around him, the questions of a person examining the construction of a machine, or the questions of someone learning to speak a foreign language by pointing to objects and learning their names, as Gulliver did on his travels.

On the other hand, if X stands for a word, it is the *experience* (meaning) which is missing. Such are the questions of someone learning a foreign language by reading with the help of a dictionary.

Now the question "What is this?" is easily answered if "this" refers to something tangible. The answer is just the appropriate word. The question "What is X?" where X stands for a word is not so easy to answer effectively, that is, to relate the word to the experience of the questioner. We have seen how difficult, if not impossible, it is at times to extend or to reorganize someone else's experience. Even when there are no conceptual difficulties, that is, when words have simple referents, referents are not always at hand. One cannot exhibit a printing press, an iceberg, a diplomat, and a hippopotamus in one's living room in answer to a youngster's demand for definitions.

To get around this difficulty, there are verbal definitions. If the direct purpose of a definition is to link a word with an experience (either by naming an experience at hand or by letting the questioner experience what the word stands for), then verbal definitions are necessarily indirect. Verbal definitions, after all, link only words with words. They may be nonetheless effective if the defining words are somehow closer to the questioner's experience than the words defined. For instance, if someone learns French, his question "What is 'vie'?" refers to a foreign word. The answer "life," gives him the equivalent in English, and that is sufficient if the word "life" *is* linked with his experience, that is, *means* something to him. Similarly, if the weather is not right for a trip to the zoo, one may define the hippopotamus by a description.

In many cases such indirect definitions do the job. They lose their significance, however, if the words used in the definitions stand no closer to experience than the word defined. Such definitions preserve their form but lose their content. Webster's *New International Dictionary* (second edition), for example, defines *love* as "A feeling of strong personal attachment induced by that which delights or commands admiration, by sympathetic understanding, or by ties of kinship; ardent affection; as, the *love* of brothers and sisters."

Definitions that do *not* bring the word closer to the hearer's experience are not confined to dictionaries. They constitute a goodly portion of our formal education. "A peninsula is a body of land surrounded on all sides but one by water"; "A democracy is a form of government in which the people rule"; "A noun is a name of a person, place, or a thing" are all shabby but remarkably viable examples of classroom knowledge. The worship of verbal definitions stems from a tenacious notion that "to define a thing is to know it."

An operational philosophy of knowledge reflects certain attitudes toward these two separate meanings of the question "What is X?"

1. If X stands for an unnamed thing, the question can be taken to be a request to name it and nothing else. To supply a name commonly used to refer to the thing is to answer the question. The answer adds no knowledge beyond the knowledge of common usage. It enables the questioner to *refer* to the thing named.

2. If X refers to a word, the question can be taken for a request to describe or to elicit an *experience,* to which the word refers.

Obviously, then, verbal definitions which do not bring words closer to experience fail to achieve their purpose from the operational point of view. Why, then, does the notion that to "define something is to know it" persist? It persists because it has deep roots in our philosophy of knowledge, roots which stretch to the Middle Ages, when European universities were founded. According to this so-called Aristotelian philosophy of knowledge, to know means to *classify,* and a correct verbal definition *gives the appearance* of classifying the thing defined.

The view that knowledge is primarily a skill at classifying (as the knowledge of the collector undoubtedly is) implies that there is a third meaning to the question "What is X?" The question is then a request to inform about the *nature* of X, about what X is like. It is clear that from an operational point of view such information can be supplied only by some sort of experience with X. A classification, which is a purely verbal act, does not *by itself* supply such experience or add to experience already at hand. Thus defining murder as "malicious, premeditated homicide" does not in itself tell us anything about murder that we did not know before. The only way to find out more about murder is to study the circumstances under which it is committed, the persons who commit it, etc.

In all three cases, therefore, to answer the question "What is X?" from an operational point of view means to make some connection between a word and experience, not merely between a word and other words. Even if the answer is in terms of words alone, these words should be chosen according to the likelihood that they bring the term defined closer to the experience of the questioner.

Confusing one meaning of the question with another leads to frequent miscarriages of communication. For instance, a man contemplating a curious gadget may ask, "What is this?" His question may be taken as a request for a name, so that the answer "This is a parapetaculator" seems appropriate. However, the question might have been asked in another sense, for example, "What is this gadget *used* for?" in which case the answer given carries no meaning

at all. Such misunderstandings are not serious if they are cleared
up by further questioning.

Unfortunately, our educational system places such emphasis on
the importance of knowing names of things that our appetite for
knowledge (experience) with which we begin our lives is often
channelized into an appetite for names. All too often "This is a
parapetaculator" or its equivalent is taken to be the complete and
final answer to the question "What is this?"[4]

Failure to keep in mind that meaning means the link between
words and experience has been at the root of the sterility of most
traditional philosophy. The failure is a reflection of the long preoccupation of philosophers with the *formal* aspect of the question
"What is X?" that is, with the form of the answer rather than its
content (meaning).

A prescribed form for answering the question "What is X?" was
given by Aristotle in his rule for making definitions: name the class
to which the thing defined belongs and differentiate it from the
other members of its class. In this sense, the Webster Dictionary
definition of "love" is a valid definition, since love is classified as a
"feeling" and differentiated from other feelings.

The danger in such definitions is in that they *look* like definitions.
They purport to explain meaning without indicating any connection between things defined and experience. Similar definitions
(often enlarged into dissertations) constitute a great part of what
has gone under the name of philosophy. One finds in philosophy
discussions about the nature of space and time, of virtue and sin,
of causality and will, or the microcosm and macrocosm, of thesis
and antithesis. One searches usually in vain for indications of how
these words reflect common human experiences.

It is not necessary to look into books on philosophy to find
words without referents. Any commencement speech, sermon, newspaper editorial, or radio commercial follows the same philosophic
tradition of reinforcing the delusion that anything which is talked
about is real: success, charity, public opinion, and four-way indigestion relief. Indeed, nothing is easier than to "define" these noises
so as to make it appear that they mean something.

What is success? Success is the attainment of one's ideals.

What is charity? Charity is the practice of Christian attitudes.

What is public opinion? Public opinion is the prime mover of
public policy in a democracy.

What is four-way indigestion relief? Four-way indigestion relief is a gentle action which alkalizes the system, purifies the blood, activates the bile, and helps Nature to re-establish equilibrium.

Operational philosophy reflects an altogether different attitude toward the question "What is X?" We have already seen how the various meanings of that question are distinguished. Fundamental in that distinction is a recognition that the question "What is X?" is a particular kind of social act. It is a request *to share experience*. Now, experience can be shared only on the basis of a *common experience*. Therefore any definition must rest on a basis of common experience shared by the giver and the receiver of the definition. This interpretation of the question "What is X?" implies that the answer must be tailored to fit the experience of the questioner. The expression "as impossible as explaining colors to a blind man" reflects this point of view.

It follows that there can be no completely general rule for making definitions. The making of pedagogically or heuristically useful definitions is an "art" rather than a "science." That is to say, the choice of a good definition is more often guided by intuitive feelings about the needs of a particular situation rather than by application of well-defined principles.

Thus, if a child asks "What is time?" it is probably best to talk of days and nights, summers, and winters, to call his attention to the effects of age, to teach him how to cross days off on a calendar while waiting for chicks to hatch, etc. If an experimental physicist asks "What is time?" a good answer is "That which is measured by a clock." But if a theoretical physicist asks "What is time?" the most meaningful answer is "The independent variable in the differential equations of motion." Each definition is geared to a specific set of experiences.

In our discussion, there will be a great deal to say about the so-called operational definition, of which the experimental physicist's definition of "time" is an example. The importance of operational definitions became especially apparent in the beginning of this century when it seemed that some of the most established notions of the most firmly established branch of science (time, space, causality) were about to be overthrown. The preoccupation with operational definitions and their philosophical consequences (which logical positivists call "logical analysis") has marked the birth of modern operational philosophy and has determined its view toward the most fundamental of philosophical problems—the nature of reality.

Chapter 2. THE PROBLEM OF REALITY:

"IS X REAL?"

MOST of us have strong convictions that the world about us exists whether we look at it or not. We set a mouse trap at night. In the morning there is a mouse in it. We fill in what happened. It makes no difference that we were not there. It must have happened. We look at the records of the rocks and reconstruct events of long ago. No one looked at what was happening a billion years ago, but most of us are sure that the events were happening anyway.

This strong intuitive feeling of the *objectivity* of the existence of things extends also to our feeling about the "properties" of things. An object, we are sure, "has" a certain size, regardless of whether we measure it, and a certain weight regardless of whether we weigh it. On a more abstract level, we attribute "natures" to things, people, institutions, etc., natures which we suppose to be "there." For a long time it has seemed obvious that the search for knowledge and for truth is the search for whatever "is," and we still tend to assume that whatever is experienced (at least whatever *we* experience or think we have experienced) is "real," is "there," and that to know it means to discover its properties or nature, which are also "there."

The view that reality resides somehow in the things around us has been repeatedly challenged by philosophers. Plato, for example (71), maintained that the world we experience (trees, houses) is far from real. He argued that somewhere quite beyond human experience but within reach at least partially of human reason there must be a world of Ideas or Forms, where things and qualities exist in perfection. The things and qualities we observe, Plato taught, are only imperfect copies of those perfect Forms. Thus, he insisted, somewhere (in the mind of God, perhaps) there is a perfect Man, a perfect Tree, even a perfect Bed. The cypresses and beds of Athens and even Plato himself were only approximations.

The philosophical view that reality is not in objects but in ideas about objects is usually called idealism. The opposite view that reality is in the things themselves has gone under the name of materialism.

In the eighteenth century, George Berkeley (7) argued the idealist position in a way somewhat different from Plato's. He maintained that it was impossible to conceive anything existing except as it is reflected in our senses. One simply cannot imagine, Berkeley argued, a tree which no one has ever seen or a splash which no one has ever heard. Berkeley concluded, therefore, that reality resides not in things but in our sensations of things. The "mind of God" was again brought in, this time to account for the strikingly similar accounts people give of what they see—this agreement was supposed to be due to the fact that all individual sensations (excepting hallucinations, of course) were instances of what God himself was experiencing.

Neither Plato's nor Berkeley's notions of reality can be lightly dismissed if one takes seriously the views inherent in modern scientific method. Science offers explanations of events by summarizing many events under some general rule. If the rules are sufficiently general and well established, they are called "laws" (in old fashioned terminology "laws of nature"). Now the exactness of exact sciences (such as astronomy and physics) is in the exact formulation of their laws. For instance, the law of falling bodies can be stated as follows: "All bodies falling in vacuum near the surface of the earth suffer exactly the same acceleration." Note that the law does not say "approximately the same acceleration." It says "exactly the same." The fact is, however, that no one has ever seen this law obeyed. It is always disobeyed. Cannon balls fall faster than feathers.

"The answer is simple," says the physicist confronted with this evidence. "We don't live in a vacuum."

"Can you make a vacuum?" we can ask.

"We can make something very close to a vacuum," replies the physicist. "And the closer we get to a vacuum, the better is the law obeyed."

"Yes, but was there ever a perfect vacuum? Was the law ever perfectly obeyed?"

"No."

"Then what is your law talking about?"

"It is an idealization. It says how bodies *would* fall if there were a perfect vacuum."

The answer has a curious resemblance to Plato's discourse about an idealized reality. Of course Plato never performed any experiments, nor did he formulate any valid physical laws. But we are nevertheless aware of a trace of "Platonism" in the way modern physical laws are formulated.

Just as traces of Plato's notions about Forms and Ideas can be found in modern theoretical science, so Berkeley's "common sense" argument (no sensation—no existence) is to a certain extent inherent in the philosophy of experimental science. The assumption of experimental science is that the final result of experiment (that is, *observation*) is the final court of appeal in the quest for truth. The implication that reality (or truth) cannot be separated from the results of observation reminds us of Berkeley's brand of idealism.

However, we have come a long way from Berkeley's naive identification of reality with "sensations." We could not construct any coherent picture of the world if in offering proof for the existence of something we were limited to pointing to things immediately perceived by the senses. It is a simple matter to prove the existence of giraffes by exhibiting giraffes (the oft-quoted farmer's scepticism notwithstanding). But we cannot prove the existence of atoms, genes, gravity, heavy hydrogen, antisemitism, the Oedipus complex, inflation, or Communism by exhibiting them. One proves or tries to prove the existence of such things by pointing to their *effects*. If one stays on operational ground, appeal to the senses still plays a part in the proof, but *between what one observes and what one concludes there is a long and tortuous chain of reasoning, inference, and evaluation.*

If I were asked to summarize in a single sentence the most serious shortcoming of the theory of knowledge as it has been developed in traditional philosophy, I would put it thus: Traditional philosophy offered no well-defined criteria for evaluating the relevance and the importance of the different links in the chain of mental steps which leads from what one observes, perceives, or imagines to what one concludes about "what is." It is not surprising, therefore, that arguments about "what is real" should have been among the most fruitless intellectual pursuits of man.

Operational philosophy avoids the much-debated question of whether the "world exists independently of our observations." This debate could never be resolved, because the debaters had no commonly accepted criteria to apply to the question of reality. Instead of posing the question "What is real?" operational philosophy *seeks acceptable criteria of reality*. The operational philosopher asks: "To what sort of experience do people usually refer when they say something is 'real'?" He must therefore begin with intuitive notions of what is real (since intuitive notions are by their very nature acceptable), but he must not stop there, because intuitive notions often contain contradictions. Being a critical and analytic philosopher, he must pose the question, "How do these intuitive notions of reality arise?"

To fix ideas, let us suppose that the intuitive notions are those of materialistic philosophy, namely, that the things around us exist "objectively," and so do their "properties" and "natures." How, we ask, do such notions arise? To investigate this question, I shall introduce two concepts, both connected with meaning, namely "relativity of meaning" and "invariance."

If the meaning of a word is in the experience connected with it, there can be no "precise" meaning in this sense, simply because the experiences of no two persons are alike. For you the word "mouse" means all *your* experiences with actual mice, pictures of mice, and statements about mice; while for me it means all *my* experiences. The fact that we still understand each other for all practical purposes (what you call "mouse" I call "mouse") means that the experiences, though varied, still have a great deal in common. We feel we can communicate, *because* such common experiences exist and provide a common denominator for what we feel to be "real."

To refer to the variability of private experience inherent in the meaning of words, I shall use the term "relativity of meaning." On the other hand, to indicate the existence of the common bases of experience which make communication possible, I shall use the term "invariance." The term "invariant" (a noun) will be used to refer to something which indicates invariance in a particular situation. Relativity of meaning and invariance are, in a way, opposites, but they can be best understood in situations where they occur together, and this happens quite frequently.

If two men face each other, what is right for one is left for the other. This is relativity of meaning. But both men can agree on the meaning of "east." East is the same direction for both of them and is thus an invariant. Again, Americans think of Tokyo as being "west," and Russians think of it as being "east," but both can agree on the *longitude* of Tokyo. Here direction is relative, but longitude is an invariant. A March day in Chicago may seem cold to a Nigerian and warm to an Eskimo, but both can be taught to read the thermometer. They will agree on the invariance of 40°F. The notion of invariance is fundamental for understanding the central idea of the operational definition.

Let us see what an operational definition looks like when applied to a familiar "property." Let us take your weight. If you were to define it in the best Aristotelian tradition, you might say, "My weight is a certain property which I share with all heavy bodies and which insures that I stay on the ground instead of floating off into space." You might also add that this weight can be "measured" by appropriate instruments, and you might point out that the better the instruments the more precise are the measurements. In other words, if you are committed to the view that properties are in the things, not in the observations (in this case measurements), you will be convinced that you "have" a certain weight regardless of whether you choose to measure it or not. The operational definition of weight, on the contrary, implies that the notion "weight" cannot be separated from the operations which measure it. Different operations may give different results, but the "reality" of weight resides in certain invariants among these results. Here, then, is a possible operational definition of your weight. I have made it especially simple-minded for the sake of emphasizing the operational idea.

Look around in railway stations, drug stores, and other public places where people with some time on their hands congregate, and you will usually find small platforms surmounted by large dials with numbers ranging from zero to about 300. These devices are called "scales." Stand on a platform of the scale and deposit a coin in the slot as indicated. A pointer will swing from the zero position on the dial to some other position. Record the number indicated by the pointer. If you repeat this operation on several different scales, you will find that although the numbers indicated by the pointer will vary (relativity of meaning of weight with respect to the scale used), still the numbers will remain within a certain range, say between 150 and 155 (invariance). Then any number between 150 and 155 can be taken to be your weight in pounds.

To someone unaccustomed to operational definitions, this definition of weight will appear not only cumbersome and bizarre but also unnecessarily lacking in precision. Certainly it seems that such a fundamentally inherent property of bodies as weight should not depend on the erratic behavior of drug store scales! One feels that one's weight is an "objective fact" and ought to be independent of the way one measures it. One feels that the scale is one thing and weight quite another. Certainly our weight does not change if we tamper with the scale. Why then make the definition of weight depend on the existence of scales? Would it not be more sensible to define weight as a property of the body and then say that one can get an indication of how much of it there was in a body by *means* of a scale, the indication being more accurate the better the scale?

From the operational point of view, the sensible thing is to keep the referents of the words one uses constantly in mind or at least within calling distance. If the only way we can be aware of the amount of weight is by means of a scale, then the very definition of weight has to be in terms of the scale.

It must be admitted that the notion of the "property" called weight which exists apart from scales is not altogether unfounded. It stems from a conviction that nature is less erratic than drug store scales. But this conviction is, in turn, a reflection of the observation that better scales than drug store scales exist. That is to say, an operational definition of weight can be given in which the range of uncertainty (taken to be five pounds in our definition) can be considerably narrowed down. Such a definition would, of course, be more complicated, because it would have to include directions for either recognizing or making a rather precise scale. But when everything is said and done, weight will still have to be defined in terms of scale readings, which, to be sure, will have less variability than the readings of crude public weighing machines. The notion that there is a "true" weight to which scale readings are only approximations is an idealization of the actual state of affairs, a Platonic notion.

The rather uncomfortable actual state of affairs is that if you make a scale sensitive enough, it will not give the same reading in two consecutive weighings because it may, for example, record the minute loss of weight through perspiration or the changes in the buoyance of the air around you produced by air currents. One would then have to abandon the notion of *the* weight of an individual and speak of the "weight at a given instant." But how long is an instant? So long as it has any length at all, the weight (if recorded on a scale sensitive enough) will vary during that interval. And if the "instant" has no extension at all, there is no way to record what is happening at the "instant" on any instrument.

We are able to talk of "your weight" at all because we are willing to forgo precision to gain invariance. We could keep greater precision if we broke up the notion of "your weight" into a multitude of subnotions, such as "your weight on this scale," "your weight on that scale," "your weight in the valley," "your weight on the mountain," "your weight today," and "your weight yesterday." Such qualifications might be necessary in some situations, but the more qualifications there are, the less meaningful is the central notion.

The chief reason the croquet game in *Alice in Wonderland* is meaningless is because the expected invariances do not function. Live flamingoes and hedgehogs do not make good croquet sticks and balls because their behavior is not sufficiently invariant under the conditions of the game. Plainly speaking, they don't stay put.

The attempts to make less exact sciences (like psychology) more exact have been mainly attempts to find invariants with which to build operational definitions. The so-called intelligence quotient (I.Q.) is a familiar example. "Intelligence" is quite an old concept in psychology, but its usefulness has been questionable, because no operational definition of it has ever been given, so that one was never sure just what to observe to be aware of intelligence. The I. Q., on the other hand, is easy to define operationally: give such and such a test and compute the score. The meaningfulness of the I.Q., however, depends on its invariance. To the extent that it is invariant (and it is within limits), the I.Q. measures "something" and thus is at least meaningful. To the extent that the score enables a psychologist to predict *other* things about the individual, for example, the ease with which he will perform certain tasks *other* than those in the I.Q. test, the I.Q. is useful. But this usefulness is nothing but an extended meaningfulness. it points to more invariance of the I.Q., for example, the invariance of its connection with other types of performance.

The search for meaningfulness, then, is the search for invariance. More precisely, it is a search for invariance amid change, for order amid seeming chaos, for stability amid precariousness. Such a search is not confined to science. All people are concerned with it. What distinguishes the scientist's search for invariants is that it is conscious, critical, and often successful. Outside of science (in religion, in philosophy, in folk wisdom) significant invariances are sometimes observed. But without the tools of science their discovery is slow, success is erratic, and frequently the supposed invariances are misleading. Often the religious thinker becomes a dogmatist (claiming divine guidance), the philosopher becomes reactionary, and the folk sage is misled by nostalgia (since the past always seems more stable than the present). The great shortcomings of religions and of most systems of philosophy is that the invariances on which their meaningfulness depends are either not defined or defined in terms of experiences not readily reproducible.

The history of science, on the other hand, abounds in instances when the search for invariances was repeatedly rewarded. A significant invariant is one from which conclusions can be drawn which can be *repeatedly* checked by experience. That is, a significant invariant is a stable invariant. The discovery of stable invariants is the discovery of reality. Thus the chronic question of philosophy "Is X real?" acquires meaning if it is restated as "How stable is the invariant to which X refers?" In the sense of this question, one can discuss the "reality" of distance, time, mass, momentum, energy, entropy, gene, heredity, metabolism, adaptation, evolution, behavior, learning, motivation, adjustment, personality, culture, society, class, authority, value, price index, monopoly, etc. To determine the "reality" of each of these terms one must give an operational definition which connects the term (or its presumed effects) to commonly shared experience. The stability of the invariance involved (that is, the extent to which the experience can be shared) measures the meaningfulness of the term.

One measure of stability is invariance of *independent* experiences. If two witnesses tell an identical story *independently* of each other, each story corroborates the other. Evidence for the truth of the story is not nearly so strong if one witness heard what the other said. The reason I do not believe in ghosts is because I have never heard two *independent* accounts of how a particular ghost behaved in a particular situation. That is what I mean when I say "Ghosts are not real." When I say, "Atoms are real," I mean that if you assume the reality of atoms, you can arrive at explanations of several kinds of seemingly unrelated events, that is, there are several *independent* lines of evidence for the existence of atoms.

On the other hand, words that have become established by repeated usage, especially in political and journalistic discourse, can have no such claim to reality. We can see this if we try to design operational definitions for the most frequently used terms in political campaigns, such as Americanism, Communism, and patriotism.

A word of caution must be interposed. Meaningfulness from

the operational point of view is not synonymous with "concrete-ness," nor is meaninglessness synonymous with "abstractness." These terms only indicate whether the chain of reasoning which leads to the inference concerning the "reality" of a concept is short or long. The longer the chain, the more abstract is the concept. The concept "unicorn" is not particularly abstract: a unicorn can be imagined as easily as a horse. Nevertheless, the word "unicorn" has no referent (at least no animal referent). On the other hand, the concept "entropy" is exceedingly abstract. Entropy cannot be visualized at all. But there is a reality behind the concept because, plugged into a chain of reasoning, it leads to the observation of proper invariants.

Scientific abstractions point to invariants which ordinarily would not have been observed. For example, no amount of passive observation, no matter how astute, could have established the invariance underlying such seemingly diverse processes as respiration of animals, burning of substances, and rusting of iron. Yet there is a process underlying all of these—oxidation. On the basis of the discovery of such invariants, predictions can be made. The fulfillment of the predictions tests the stability of the invariant. For example, if it is known that neither life nor combustion can go on in the absence of oxygen, then on the basis of the invariant underlying respiration, combustion, and rusting we can predict that there will also be no rusting without oxygen, even though we have never performed the appropriate experiment. Similarly, on the basis of the known invariance of the laws of motion and the law of gravity, the astronomer can predict the course of a comet which he sees for the first time.

The notion of invariance, in terms of which reality is operationally defined, thus leads naturally to the notion of predictability. The importance of this notion will emerge more clearly in connection with the operational definition of "truth."

SUMMARY OF CHAPTERS 1 AND 2

We have seen that for the operational philosopher the question "What is X?" has a number of meanings, depending on what X stands for. The symbol X can stand for something in the world which is being pointed out (a thing, an event, a sequence of events). In this case, the question "What is X?" is accompanied by *exhibiting* X and thus is nothing but a request for a name. It is then (philosophically speaking) a trivial question and calls for a trivial answer

—the name usually applied to X. But sometimes more information is wanted: "What *about* X? What is X like? How should I behave toward X?" When this occurs, the operational philosopher turns the task of answering the question over to the scientist, whose business it is to look for significant invariants in X (classify the animals, record constancies in the sequences of events, etc.). To the extent that Aristotle understood the importance of observation in arriving at knowledge, this sort of conception of the question "What is X?" is not too different from Aristotle's. The departure from the Aristotelian conception is technical rather than conceptual. It is occasioned by the modern methods of hunting invariants, more refined and more effective than Aristotle's had been.

In one respect, however, the operational attitude toward the question "What is X?" differs radically from the traditional attitudes (including the Aristotelian). This comes to light when X stands for a *word*. For example, one can ask "What is truth?" "What is real love?" "What is justice?" or even "What is weight?" without pointing to anything. All too often, such questions are *taken for granted* to have meaning. It is supposed that "truth," "justice," or "weight" are given (that is, exist, are *real*) and that the question is the starting point of an investigation concerning the nature of these things.

For the operational philosopher, this context of "What is X?" is first of all a request for a definition. Sometimes the request is puzzling, because often the one who asks is the first to use the word, so that it should appear that the burden of definition should fall on him. However, the operational philosopher is not averse to join in the search for such a definition, provided attempts are made to make it operational. Thus, to the question, "What is virtue?" the operational philosopher might reply, "Well, let us see what we can possibly mean by it in terms of commonly shared experiences," or "Let us see to what experiences people usually refer when they use the word."

The important thing about operational definitions is that they tell *what to do* and *what to observe* in order to bring the thing defined or its (invariant) effects within the range of one's experience. The invariants pointed out in operational definitions are not assumed to be "there" to begin with, but rather our attention is called to the relative invariants which emerge *as a result of operations.* In this way, the thing or quality defined is not assumed to exist *a priori.* Rather its existence or reality follows from the operations performed and resides in the invariants observed.

Chapter 3. THE PROBLEM OF VERIFICATION:

"IS X TRUE?"

To RESTATE the fundamental difference between the traditional and the operational approaches to philosophic questions: The traditional philosopher (especially the metaphysician) asked, "What is the nature of things? What is reality?" The operational philosopher asks instead, "What kind of answers do people want when they ask 'What is X?' or 'Is X real?' Under what conditions do such answers have meaning, that is, when are they rooted in experience, or when can they lead to specific action aimed at answering the question?"

Similarly, the old philosophic question "What is truth?" becomes, in operational philosophy, "What are acceptable criteria for truth?"

It seems there are three kinds of criteria, and all of us have used all three at one time or another. We are likely to believe an assertion on three grounds:

1. We trust the author of an assertion (the assertion is credible). *Example*: "Net weight 14 oz." (on a package of a product marketed by a reputable firm).

2. We have an experience to which an assertion refers (the assertion is empirically true). *Example*: "Snow is white." (We look and see that it is indeed white.)

3. We cannot deny the assertion without contradicting ourselves (the assertion is logically valid). *Example*: "If John is the husband of Mary, Mary is the wife of John."

Failure to agree on the truth of an assertion can often be traced to confusions among the various kinds of "truth." For example, we often assert that something is "true" without specifying that we have used only the credibility criterion in establishing the truth (father said so or the editorial in our favorite newspaper said so). What is credible to us may not be credible to our opponent in a discussion. But since our philosophical tradition (again reaching back to Plato) recognizes the existence of The Truth in a vague sort of way, we often fail to realize that we are arguing merely about credibility (a subjective criterion) and as a result come to question each other's honesty or sanity.

Operational philosophy defines the reality of concepts in terms of the invariants associated with them. Therefore truth, too, must be so defined. This leaves out credibility altogether, since it is universally observed that credibility is a relatively subjective matter. What is credible to Tom is not credible to Dick. The important question is whether we can find criteria more invariant than credibility, so that even Tom and Dick can agree on what is true regardless of what is credible.

We see immediately that what we called "empirical truth" is indeed such a criterion. If Tom believes the inscription "Net wt. 14 oz." and Dick does not, the thing to do is to weigh the contents.

It is tempting to suggest that thereby the whole problem of "truth" is solved, that arguments about truth are nothing but disagreements inherent in the relativity of meaning—what is credible to you is not credible to me—which can be resolved by appealing to the invariance of empirical truth. Unfortunately, the situation is not nearly so simple. If it were, then the argument about the shape of the earth would have to be resolved in favor of the conclusion "The earth is flat," as anyone can see by looking at it. Only the simplest assertions ("It is raining," "The name of this book is *Operational Philosophy*") can be unambiguously verified by simple observations. In most cases, difficulties arise as soon as verification is attempted.

To begin with, different attempts at verification may lead to different results.

Example: "Is there a singer concealed in the phonograph?" The sounds of singing issuing from the phonograph certainly indicate that there may be a singer inside. Inspection shows no singer there. Of course we now believe our eyes rather than our ears. But not so long ago, when the first phonographs were demonstrated, people were not at all sure. They doubted what they saw. It was easier to conclude something about a "conjurer's trick" than to imagine that sounds could be recorded on a cylinder of wax.

Second, there arise sometimes conflicts between logical validity and empirical truth.

Example: "If all criminals are untrustworthy and this man is a criminal, then this man is untrustworthy" is logically valid, but the conclusion may be empirically false, that is, actual tests may show that the man is trustworthy in many situations.

Third, the most serious difficulty of all lies in the fact that procedures for verification are not often implicit in the assertions. If we say, "It is raining," the verification procedure is obvious—look out of the window. If, however, we say, "The universe is finite," or "God is love," or "Mr. X is disloyal," the verification procedures are far from obvious.

The operational definition of truth is an attempt to get around all these difficulties; it forms, in fact, the cornerstone of operational philosophy. Actually, it is not "truth" that is defined but the meaning of the statement "Assertion X is true." As an example, take the assertion "Benares exists." About this assertion we can make another, namely, "The assertion 'Benares exists' is true." An operational definition of truth is really a definition of what is meant by such assertions about assertions.

To begin with, two distinct kinds of truth are recognized in operational philosophy, each characterized by the verification procedure associated with it.

1. If verification involves looking at things other than the assertion itself or other assertions, we are dealing with truth proper.

2. If verification involves looking at assertions only, we are dealing with validity.

Thus to verify the truth of "Snow is white," we look at snow, not at the assertion. But to verify the validity of the assertion "If John is the husband of Mary, Mary is the wife of John," we do not look at John and Mary; we look at what the assertion says.

Sometimes we can test both the validity and the truth of an assertion. Take for example the assertion contained in the famous Theorem of Pythagoras: "The square of the hypothenuse of a right triangle equals the sum of the squares of the other two sides." We can test its validity by checking whether it follows logically from other assertions of geometry. We can also check its truth by measuring the sides of right triangles. To take another example, if you go shopping with twenty dollars and if, having added the amounts of your purchases, you find you have spent $11.82, you can make the assertion, "I have $8.18 left." Now when you check your arithmetic, you are checking the validity of your assertion, but when you look into your purse to see whether there are $8.18 there, you are checking the truth of your assertion.

In this chapter I will discuss the operational approach to truth proper, leaving the discussion of validity to Chapter 4.

If truth depends on verification, one cannot say anything about the truth of an assertion until the verification has been carried out. To be sure, one usually depends on past verifications, but this dependence only reflects our faith in future verifications. When we say, "Sugar is sweet," we think of all our experiences with sugar. But we certainly expect these experiences to be repeated if our faith in this assertion is to hold. We mean also, "The next time we taste sugar, we shall find it sweet."

Even statements about the past, if they are verifiable, implicitly contain predictions. The statement, "Napoleon entered Moscow in 1812," is verified by looking at records. To say that it is true is to say in effect, "Look at such and such records and you will find such and such accounts of Napoleon's sojourn in Moscow."

The truth of an assertion, then, is somehow contained in the predictions it implies. This leads to the following definitions.

An assertion is operationally true if all three of the following conditions are satisfied:

1. The assertion implies predictions to be tested by conceivable operations.

2. Operations have been carried out to test the predictions.

3. The predictions have been verified by the operations.

If Condition 3 fails, that is, if the suggested operations have failed to verify the predictions, we will say that the assertion is *false*. If Condition 2 fails, that is, operations have been suggested but not carried out, we will say that the assertion is *indeterminate*. If Condition 1 fails, that is, if no conceivable operations have been suggested, we will say that the assertion is operationally meaningless. Thus operational philosophy must recognize at least four different kinds of assertions (true, false, indeterminate, and meaningless), unlike traditional (Aristotelian) logic, which demands that an assertion be either true or false (the law of the excluded middle).

It may seem that the operational classification of meaningful assertions into three categories (true, false, and indeterminate) instead of two is unnecessarily fussy. Why, one might ask, if an assertion is in principle verifiable, should we not concede that it is true or false even if it has not been verified, since a verification can establish its truth or falsehood? The answer to this objection is that frequently we must deal with assertions, which although in principle verifiable, cannot be verified in a given situation. At other times, a single verification is not sufficient for our purpose.

To take an example, consider the assertion, "If a die is thrown, an ace will turn up." Is this assertion true or false? What does it mean to verify it? Will the result of a single throw constitute a verification? Perhaps, if the assertion refers to a particular throw. But if the assertion is about *any* throw, then obviously a single verification is not sufficient. These considerations lead to an extension of the notions of "true" and "false" to cover intermediate cases. We say, for example, "The probability of an ace turning up on a throw of a die is one sixth," that is, the assertion above is "one-sixth true."

A similar situation arises when even though we would be content with a single verification, we must act *before* we can verify the assertion (for example, place a bet on the result of a throw). The assignment of fractional truth values to indeterminate assertions leads to the theory of probability (or infinite-valued logic) about which more will be said in Chapter 14.

MEANINGFULNESS

Take the assertion, "Benares exists." Is it meaningful? According to our definition it is meaningful if it implies predictions. Does it then imply predictions? We cannot tell by just looking at the assertion. We must discover what the author means by the assertion, especially by the word "exists." If the author does translate the assertion into predictions, the assertion becomes meaningful. If the predictions are realized, the assertion becomes true. For example, this is what the author of the assertion "Benares exists" might mean:

"If you go in the vicinity of latitude 25°N. and longitude 83°E., you will find a city. If you ask its name, you will be told it is called Benares."

In this sense the assertion "Benares exists" is true. The assertion "Oz exists" can be treated the same way. If the author of that assertion means predictions about the latitude and longitude of Oz, the assertion is meaningful but false. If the verification of his predictions involves traveling to the moon, the assertion is indeterminate. If no predictions can be brought to light, the assertion is operationally meaningless.

The distinctions among the four types of assertions are not sharp. There is always the question of precision. For practical purposes a certain leeway of ambiguity must be granted; otherwise no quantitative assertions (except those about whole numbers) could ever be true. If I say, "My desk is five feet long," I mean approximately five feet and expect my assertion to be tested in that spirit. Again, the meaningfulness of an assertion is by no means easy to establish in each case. It depends on establishing an agreement on a procedure which is to serve as a verification of the assertion in question. (The ease with which the procedure can be carried out is not relevant.)

Difficulties in agreeing on verification procedures are not confined to esoteric assertions. They occur in the most common judgments of everyday speech as soon as attempts are made to establish a verification procedure. Assertions like "Tom is clever," "Dick is brave," and "The accident was due to Harry's carelessness" are typical examples. It is conceivable that the assertions about Tom's cleverness and Dick's bravery can be translated into predictions about how Tom and Dick will behave under certain circumstances. But until such translations are made, the assertions are *provisionally meaningless* operationally speaking. Their meaningfulness can be established only by an agreement about what should be observed to determine their truth. The meaningfulness of the assertion about the "cause" of Harry's accident is even more difficult to establish, but not impossible. It can be taken to mean, for example, that among people whose driving habits resemble Harry's there is more than the average incidence of accidents. However, a statement like "If Harry had been more careful, the accident would not have occurred" is meaningless as it stands, because the original situation cannot be reconstructed.

Assertions like "Truth is beauty," "Existence is God's thought," and "A Plutonian thinks with his blood" usually imply no predictions at all and hence are operationally meaningless. They may certainly be meaningful in another sense, being symptomatic of certain processes going on within the speakers, but this "meaning" can be got at only by examining the speakers and the influences impinging upon them, not the assertions or the things to which the assertions presumably refer.

Ludwig Wittgenstein, in particular (113), was severe in his treatment of traditional philosophy because of the lack of operational meaning in philosophical assertions. Such severity has perhaps served good purpose. However, once the shackles imposed on the human intellect by traditional philosophy and theology have been broken, there is no need to remain with Wittgenstein's rather uncharitable point of view. Just as it is often necessary to hold asser-

tions "provisionally meaningless" in order to secure further clarifi-
cation when we are already communicating with someone, so it is
often advisable to hold assertions "provisionally meaningful" when
we wish to *establish* communication and are careful not to scare our
would-be communicant away by too strict standards of meaningfulness. A friend told me how during his recent stay in India he was
suddenly addressed by a man sitting next to him in a Benares
streetcar.

"Do you believe man can see God?" the man asked.

If my friend had followed Wittgenstein's advice literally,[5] he
would have said nothing, which might have been interpreted by his
neighbor in a variety of ways. Believing, however, that the problem
at hand was one of establishing communication rather than of judging the operational meaningfulness of the question, my friend
allowed himself to be engaged in a conversation which, while it
cannot be said to have had much operationally meaningful content,
did serve to bring out an attempt at verbalizing very complicated
feelings.

We see, therefore, that it is not sufficient to define true, false,
indeterminate, and meaningless assertions in order to apply criteria
to the verbal output of the human race and separate truth from
falsehood and sense from non-sense. The operational meaning of
truth does not with one stroke solve all problems of philosophy by
declaring them to be meaningless, as Wittgenstein and other logical
positivists have implied. On the contrary, with the operational
definition of truth and meaning, the task of philosophy barely
begins. On this task a fresh start or a "reconstruction" (as Dewey
called it) can be based.

LOGICAL ANALYSIS

The first task of philosophy is essentially as the logical positivists
have defined it—logical analysis—that is, the determination of the
relations among assertions and between assertions and reality (between terms and the invariants for which they stand). What is
proposed here as an enlargement to this program is that logical
analysis probe deeper into "private" meanings, hidden meanings
behind the seemingly indiscriminate use of symbols by the human
race. When an assertion is made, one must "draw the author out,"
as it were. This process of drawing out someone's meaning can be
rewarding or frustrating, inspiring or irritating. It can lead to
understanding or hostility. Frustration, irritation, and hostility can

perhaps be avoided if in the process of logical analysis we are careful not to make a fool of our opponent. Socrates might have avoided trouble if instead of asking bluntly, "What do you mean?" and booby-trapping his questions, he asked instead questions which would have enabled his victims to save face, such as, "Do you possibly mean so and so?"

For example, the assertion "Benares exists" does not have an *intrinsic* meaning. The meaning, if any, is in the experience of the person making the assertion. To get at the meaning (*his* meaning) we must get at the experience. We can often do that by "sympathetic guessing." We must dig out the predictions implied.

"Do you mean that if you look in the *World Almanac*, you will find something there about Benares?"

"Do you mean that if you go to a certain place, you will find a city called Benares?"

"Do you mean that if you ask a sufficient number of people, some will tell you that they have been there?"

The totality of predictions implied by an assertion I shall call the *predictive content* of the assertion. Thus the predictive content of "Benares exists" may be a list of assertions, such as,

"If you look in the *Almanac*, you will read about it."

"If you look on a map of India, you will see it marked."

"If you meet enough people, you will eventually meet someone who has been there."

"If you go to $25°$ N. lat.; $83°$ E. long., you will see a city."

The truth, falsehood, and meaningfulness of an assertion is then with reference to a *particular predictive content*. It follows that we cannot expect to deal with "absolutely true" assertions. If *absolutely true* is to have any meaning, it should mean "characterized by the highest possible confirmed predictive content." But it is impossible to imagine the "highest" confirmed predictive content, that is, where no further predictions can be made. Moreover, one cannot expect that the predictions will be unambiguously and absolutely confirmed. In general, we must be satisfied with assertions with relatively high predictive content, especially in the case of assertions made in everyday life. Thus the predictive content of the assertion, "Green apples are sour" can be confined to the prediction,

"If you taste a green apple, you will have a sensation of sourness."

This is sufficient for practical purposes, even though the degree of confirmation of this assertion will not be impressive.

INDUCTION

The use of past experience to anticipate the future goes, in the theory of knowledge, under the name of *induction*. Awareness of this process goes under the name of inductive reasoning. Inductive reasoning supposedly enables us to conclude that all green apples are sour after we have tasted a sufficient number of them and have found them to be sour. It must be noted, however, to the credit of the philosophers, that they have been generally uneasy about just how we are able to make such "conclusions." By conclusions they often understood inescapable conclusions. For example, if it is admitted that John is taller than Peter, the conclusion that Peter is shorter than John is inescapable—you cannot deny it without denying what you have admitted (that John is taller than Peter).

No such necessity operates when we conclude that the fifty-first apple must be sour after we have tasted the first fifty and found them to be so. There is no contradiction in the assertion "Fifty green apples are sour, and one is sweet."

Nevertheless it was recognized by philosophers (at least by the empiricists) that we arrive at general truths by generalizing particular experiences. If, however, there is nothing which *compels* these generalizations, how can we be sure of those truths?

This difficulty reflected an insufficient realization on the part of the philosophers of the sharp difference between truth and validity, which was brought especially clearly into focus by the logical positivists (the founders of modern operational philosophy).[6] We shall see the implications of this difference in the two succeeding chapters.

Chapter 4. THE PROBLEM OF DEDUCTION:

"IS X VALID?"

To RESTATE the difference between truth and validity: The truth of an assertion is related to experience; the validity of an assertion is related only to its inner consistency or to its consistency with other assertions. More explicitly, an assertion is valid if it is analytic or if it can be deduced from other assertions admitted or assumed to be valid.

This definition seems to be circular, since the word it defines ("valid") itself appears in the definition. However, in all definitions one must start *somewhere*, assuming that one knows what one is talking about. Such a start is really an agreement to consider some things recognizable. So in defining valid assertions, one agrees to call certain fundamental assertions "valid" by listing them. The definition, then, is not so much a definition of validity as an agreement on how to determine whether *other* assertions are valid with respect to the fundamental ones. It is the same as defining "the rightful monarch." A "rightful monarch" has often been defined as the eldest son of a deceased "rightful monarch." The question whether the original rightful monarch was "rightful" never was raised.

It follows from the definition that there can be validity only with respect to certain assumptions and with respect to certain rules of deduction. Change your assumptions or change your rules, and what has been valid may become invalid with respect to the new system. Similarly, moves legal in checkers are illegal in chess; plays legal in pinochle are illegal in bridge.

A typical example of a logical deduction—that is, the deriving of a valid assertion from other assertions assumed to be valid—is a syllogism, such as

All X are Y.
All Y are Z.
Therefore all X are Z.

The first two assertions of the syllogism are called "premises," and the last is called the "conclusion." Here the conclusion "All X are Z" is valid *with respect to the premises.* The old-fashioned way of saying it was, "The conclusion is true if the premises are true." *But once the distinction between truth and validity is made, the notion "true" disappears from the theory of deduction.* One cannot conclude anything at all about the *truth* of "All X are Z" by deduction alone. Truth (as we defined it in Chapter 3) can be established only by testing the assertion by experience or by verifying the predictions inherent in it. Validity, on the other hand, has nothing to do with either experience or predictions but only with assertions from which the given assertion has been deduced. We have, then, still another way of stating the difference between truth and validity:

The truth of an assertion follows from its *consequences.*

The validity of an assertion follows from its *antecedents.*

How, then, does one establish the validity of the antecedents, say, the premises of a syllogism? One can agree that the premises are valid if they are deduced in accordance with certain rules from other premises, which are valid. Pushing the process back, we may ultimately trace the "ancestry" of our valid assertions to a set of assertions which themselves had not been deduced. *Their* validity is simply a matter of agreement. We may, for example, agree that those fundamental assertions derive their validity from being *true* (checked by observation). But this is not necessary. Fundamental assumptions may become valid by simply having validity conferred upon them by agreement. They need not be true, nor even determinate or meaningful, to serve as a basis of a *logical system,* that is, a collection of assertions deduced from the original ones in accordance with prescribed rules.

THE SYLLOGISM

Let us look again at our syllogism. Suppose the premises are chosen from among the fundamental assumptions of our system, and suppose the agreement is to call those fundamental assumptions "valid" because they are true in the ordinary sense. Then the validity of, say, the first premise, "All X are Y," depends on what X and Y stand for. For example, if X stands for chariots, and Y for vehicles, "All X are Y" is valid according to our agreement. But if X stands for chipmunks, and Y for bureaucrats, it is not valid. Since the validity of the conclusion depends on the validity of the premises, it too depends on the "values" of X, Y, and Z. Since the symbols X, Y, and Z can stand for many things, they are called variables. Therefore the validity of the conclusions depends on the values of the variables in the premises (that is, on the referents for which they stand).

However, the validity of the *entire syllogism* does not depend on the values of the variables.[7] No matter what X, Y, and Z stand for, the syllogism *as a whole* is valid. It is a stronger kind of validity. It is like the validity of *identities* in algebra as distinguished from the validity of *equations*. For example, the equation $x + 2 = 5$ is valid if and only if $x = 3$, but the identity $x + 2x = 3x$ is always valid, no matter what x may stand for. The validity of the whole syllogism and of identities depends not on the validity of assertions and on values assumed by the variables but on the *rules* of reasoning or reckoning only. In fact, the rules are *defined* in logic by stating which syllogisms are always valid, just as the rules of algebra are defined by stating which identities always hold (cf. p. 168).

Aristotelian logic is largely the art of deducing valid assertions by means of syllogisms. There are many kinds of syllogisms, but all of them are variations of the one just cited.[8] The variations are formed by substituting "some," or "no" for "all" and "are not" (or "is not") for "are" (or "is"). An example of such a variation is

Some X are Y.
No Y is Z.
Therefore some X are not Z.

The validity of Aristotelian syllogisms is so convincing that for more than two thousand years it seemed unthinkable to professional logicians that other kinds of correct reasoning could exist. This view was reinforced by the prevailing attitude toward logic as the "science of the laws of thought." Correct thinking was *equated* by professional philosophers with syllogistic thinking.[9]

Yet an examination of the concepts with which the syllogism operates shows that their *range* is certainly not great. It is not likely that "all X," "no X," and "some X" exhaust the subjects to form judgments about, and certainly "is" and "is not" do not exhaust the possible relations between any two things in the universe. In other words, there is more to say about the world than "something belongs or does not belong to some class." There are relations other

than the relation of class inclusion. Other subjects and other relations may require different rules of deduction than those used in
the Aristotelian syllogism. To see this point in the case of other relations, let us *generalize* the syllogism by writing it as follows:

All X R Y.
All Y R Z.
Therefore all X R Z.

If you read this "generalized syllogism" out loud, it will sound
exactly like the previous one. But we have replaced the special
relation "are" by an abstract symbol "R." Our new syllogism now
means, "All X are in certain relation (R) to Y; all Y are in the same
relation to Z; therefore all X are in the same relation (R) to Z."

Now the *particular* relation treated in the Aristotelian syllogism
is the relation "are" (or "is") which is used to express class inclusion (all X are to be found among the Y). Class inclusion is so
defined that the syllogism "All X are Y; all Y are Z; therefore all
X are Z" always holds. In other words, the linguistic rule for using
the word "are" is that it shall be used only in such a way as not to
disturb the validity of the Aristotelian syllogism.

But what about relations other than that of class inclusion? For
example, we can conceive of "greater than" as a relation between
two quantities, and this relation implies neither identity nor class
inclusion.* It is interesting whether the syllogistic rules or, perhaps,
some other rules can be applied in reasoning about such other
"non-Aristotelian" relations.

Let us, then, take this relation "greater than" and see whether
the syllogism still holds if we substitute it for R. For simplicity,
consider only a single X, a single Y, and a single Z. The syllogism
now reads

X is greater than Y.
Y is greater than Z.
Therefore X is greater than Z.

Referring to the rules of language we ordinarily use, we see that
the syllogism still satisfies these rules. Therefore we can say that the

---

*—Although one can twist language in such a way as to make it appear that it
does. One can say, for example, " 'A is greater than B' means that A belongs to the
class of things greater than B." But such a use of language is artificial. It buries
the relation "greater than" in the definition of the class to which A belongs and
sidesteps the problem of handling the relation logically.

abstract syllogism "X R Y; Y R Z; X R Z" holds in a logic more general (that is, with a greater range of relations) than Aristotelian logic. But the validity of this "syllogism" is certainly not universal for every conceivable relation. For consider the relation "is the son of" and try to substitute it for R. The syllogism now becomes

> X is the son of Y.
> Y is the son of Z.
> Therefore X is the son of Z.

We see that now the syllogism fails with respect to our linguistic rules.

If you are tempted to ask what linguistic rules have to do with it, seeing that the conclusion is *factually* false, please remember that the conclusion *is* valid in a language which uses the same word for both son and grandson. There may very well be such a language. Our own language, for example, is quite primitive when it comes to describing kinship. We use the same word (uncle) for mother's brother and father's brother and even mother's sister's husband and father's sister's husband and sometimes more loosely. There is no more "logic" in this usage than in using the same word for both son and grandson. In fact, we do have such a word, namely "descendant," which, as you can readily see, makes the syllogism come out right. We conclude, therefore, that the validity of syllogisms and other logical derivations depends entirely on linguistic rules and in no way on "facts."

Another important aspect of the validity of the syllogism is that it is independent of the truth of the premises or even of their meaningfulness. Take, for example,

> All thistles are firecrackers.
> All firecrackers are dowagers.
> Therefore all thistles are dowagers.

Nonsensical or absurd as the individual assertions seem with reference to "facts," the conclusion nevertheless *follows from the premises*, and the syllogism as a whole is valid.

This paradoxical independence of validity and truth does not seem so strange if one keeps in mind that the realm of validity is exclusively language, not the relation between language and experience (which is the realm of truth). There is always an element of arbitrariness about validity, because it depends on man-made rules.

Is Mathematics True?

One of the most dramatic events of the nineteenth century was the discovery that mathematics deals not with truth but with validity, and that therein lies its superlative reliability. The story has been often told, but I will repeat it here for the sake of continuity (besides, a good story is worth retelling).

For two thousand years classical (Euclidean) geometry has been held in highest esteem by philosophers, because it represented a triumph of man's reasoning powers. One could, by applying the principles of logical deduction to a discussion of the properties of space, arrive at profound truths *independently of experience*, that is, without working. (I suspect that the philosophers' veneration of geometry stemmed from an aversion to working with *things*. This aversion was most pronounced in Plato, whose contempt for the material world as unworthy of the attention of a thinker is well known. Plato was among the most ardent admirers of classical geometry and of its method.)

The method of classical geometry represented deduction in its purest and most powerful form. Euclid begins his exposition with "definitions" of the simplest geometrical concepts (point, line, plane, etc.) and a statement of "self-evident" truths about these elements, for example, that one and only one straight line can be drawn between two points; one and only one perpendicular can be erected in a plane to a given line at a given point, etc. He also states "self-evident" rules of reasoning (the axioms), such as that two things equal to the same thing are equal to each other; that if two equal magnitudes are added to two other equal magnitudes, the resulting magnitudes are again equal.

From these self-evident truths and rules, Euclid deduces a great number of most interesting "propositions" (theorems), using deductive methods *only*, that is, without relying on measurement or any other kind of experience to establish their "truth."

The truth of Euclid's theorems follows inexorably from the truth of the postulates (here, as in most conventional philosophy, no distinction is made between validity and truth—we are climbing into the shoes of the thinkers who got into trouble that way). But the tantalizing question remains—are the postulates true? Again and again the reassuring answer was given: they must be true since they are self-evident. But the tempting question kept forcing itself on the minds of the thinkers: are they?

One postulate in particular gave trouble, the fifth. Euclid stated it in an unnecessarily complicated way. I re-state it here in the way it is usually assumed, which is equivalent to Euclid's.

The Fifth Postulate of Euclid: Suppose we have a straight line and a point outside it, and suppose we draw all possible straight lines through that point, all in the same plane with the given line. Then there is *one and only one line* among them which fails to meet the given line no matter how far either line is produced.

Somehow this "self-evident" truth did not seem self-evident to many mathematicians and philosophers who followed Euclid. They sometimes asked, "How do we know there is such a line? What if *every* line *eventually* meets the given one? Or what if there are several lines which fail to meet it?"

There were many attempts to *prove* the fifth postulate, that is, to show that it could be deduced from the other postulates. All these attempts failed.

Then early in the nineteenth century two mathematicians with unprecedented boldness made a gigantic intellectual experiment.[10] They decided to replace the fifth postulate by another one (namely, that several lines can be drawn through a point which fail to meet the given line) and proceeded to derive the logical consequences of that postulate. Many of the consequences, of course, contradicted the theorems of Euclidean geometry, but they *did not contradict each other*. Some years later another mathematician,[11] replaced the fifth postulate by still another one, namely that *no* line through a point outside a given line fails to meet it, and constructed an equally self-consistent geometry on that basis. These were non-Euclidean geometries. One could not deny the validity of their theorems without denying the validity of their postulates, but there was no way of denying the validity of the non-Euclidean postulates. One could not do so by an appeal to observation, because observations are made not on mathematical objects but on physical ones, which are only "approximations" of mathematical objects.[12] One could not do so by appeal to logic, because the postulates were assumed, not logically deduced.

If one thinks in old-fashioned terms (that is, that the theorems of geometry are truths about the real world), one is, of course, tormented by the question, "Which geometry *is* the true one?" The question cannot be answered by measurements, as we have just pointed out, because the measurements are not sufficiently exact. Nor can one answer the question by "logic."

There is only one road out of this impasse, and progressive mathematicians took it. They recognized that the theorems of geometry should not be considered "true" but only "valid" with respect to the postulates. Euclidean geometry is valid with respect to its postulates, and the non-Euclidean geometries are valid with respect to theirs. There is no sense in asking which theorems are "true" any more than there is sense in asking whether a given act is legal or whether a given play in cards is allowed without specifying the laws of the land or the rules of the game. This recognition was perhaps the first clear-cut distinction between truth and validity.

Now similar considerations apply to logic. A logic is a set of rules for deriving assertions which are valid relative to other assertions. Aristotelian logic allows the derivation of assertions in which the relation is always class inclusion (or its special case, identity). For different relations, different rules of deduction may hold.

Arithmetic, for example, is a set of deductive rules and therefore a logic. Some of the relations in arithmetic are transitive, just as the class inclusion relation is, so that the syllogism "X R Y; Y R Z; therefore X R Z" holds. An example of such a relation is "divisible by." Other relations are not transitive; nevertheless one can reason with them just as stringently. For example,

> X is twice Y.
> Y is twice Z.
> Therefore X is *four times* Z.

This is not a syllogism, since the relation in the conclusion is not the same as that in the premises. Nevertheless it is a valid logical form with reference to the rules governing the relations "twice" and "four times."

Geometry too is a logic and has relations which do not fit the syllogism but fit into other logical forms. For example,

> Line AB is perpendicular to line MN.
> Line MN is perpendicular to line PQ.
> Therefore line AB is *parallel* to line PQ.

There are also non-Aristotelian logics in which more general rules of reasoning than Aristotle's postulates hold. There is, for example, the infinite-valued logic of probability (to be discussed in Chapter 14), of which the two-valued Boolean logic of classes is a special case; and Boolean logic itself is an extension of Aristotelian syllogistic logic. Thus the entire field of deductive reasoning, which includes logic (both Aristotelian and its extensions) and the whole vast realm of mathematics are seen to be a single kind of intellectual activity, namely the drawing of necessary conclusions according to rules agreed upon in advance.

The attractiveness of this activity is in the seeming certainty of the conclusions one arrives at. One has a feeling of discovering immutable truths. It is understandable why many philosophers (always in search of such truths) should have thought that the deductive method was the only really reliable key to such truths. So long as the truth of an assertion was felt to be in the assertion itself or in a feeling of satisfaction one had in contemplating it, no objection could be raised against the deductive method. One could make syllogisms with *any* words. Not guided by the need of relating words to experience, the scholasticists of the Middle Ages spun their deductions of pure verbiage, hoping thereby to find the way to salvation. So long as they arrived at conclusions which continued to give support to the intellectual hegemony of the Church, they had almost unlimited intellectual freedom: one could make syllogisms with any words, and so by selecting the words properly one could come to any conclusion. Only when the needs of practical men became vociferous during the Renaissance, when the need became sharp to have truth reflected in experience, did the pointlessness of unbridled deduction become apparent.[13]

Francis Bacon, a man of the Renaissance (or an "Elizabethan," as those men were called in England) led the rebellion against the deductive method. He recommended pure induction (that is, the accumulation of "facts") as the way to knowledge, which he defined not in terms of salvation as the men of the Middle Ages did, but in terms of power, as the men of the Renaissance did (5).

However, pure induction also proved sterile. There are just too many facts. It is hopeless to go after all of them. The inductive method says nothing about which facts are important and which are not. Practical needs are not a good guide in this matter either. For example, the amusing behavior of amber rubbed with fur (electricity) and of "lodestones" (magnetism) did not have any discernible relation to "practical needs."* How could a man in

---

*Magnets were known in Europe long before the compass was invented.

search for "useful facts" know that the facts about electricity and magnetism would prove of the utmost importance to man?

Fortunately pure induction, as recommended by Bacon, never became a method in the early development of physical science. From its birth, modern science became a synthesis of the two methods, induction and deduction. The one passed the ball, so to speak, to the other. What was lacking in one was found in the other. Induction was based on experience but could not reveal the relationships among the facts. Deduction did this. Deduction was divorced from experience and therefore could not establish new facts. But it could lead to hypotheses, whose verification would answer questions which could never even have been asked if one relied on "fact collection" alone.

The union of induction and deduction in modern science became the union of theory and practice, of thought and action, of the work of the philosopher and that of the craftsman and artist.*

The most famous and often cited success of the synthesis was the foundation of celestial mechanics by Isaac Newton. The induction was in the experiments of Galileo with falling bodies and in Kepler's description of planetary motions based on the observations of Tycho. The deduction was the mathematical derivation of these phenomena from *postulated* laws of motion and the famous inverse square law of gravitation.[14] It would have been impossible to arrive at the law of gravitation by induction alone, simply because the forces acting on the planets cannot be directly measured. Nor would it have been possible to arrive at it by deduction alone, because one could not possibly guess what to postulate, nor could one be convinced of the truth of the law without observing its effects. The synthesis of the two methods enabled Newton to use one in support of the other.

This double-barreled attack on nature's secrets constitutes what is generally known as "the" scientific method. Actually the "the" is misleading, since no scientist follows any cut-and-dried procedure. Intuition and idiosyncrasies probably play as important a part in the work of the scientist as they do in the work of the artist. Nevertheless a schema of scientific procedure can be made (43, 62). One can begin with the gathering of facts (for example recording the positions of the planets at different times, as Tycho did). One can then attempt to give a general description of the facts, noting es-

* That is why Leonardo da Vinci is sometimes named the first scientist of the modern era.

pecially the invariants and regularities describing in mathematical language the motions of planets, as Kepler did). Then one can formulate a *hypothesis* to account for the facts (as Newton did in postulating the laws of motion and the law of gravity). From this hypothesis the known facts can be deduced. But that is not enough. There are also other *sometimes still unknown* facts to be deduced from the same hypothesis—the "dividends" of deduction. In Newton's case this was the motion of the moon and the tides. These new facts are part of the predictive content of the hypothesis. If the new facts are verified, the hypothesis is accepted as (provisionally) true.

Another equally dramatic example is Einstein's theory of relativity. Here one can start with the fact revealed by the Michelson-Morley experiment that there is no evidence for the "ether drift." An inductive conclusion from this fact is that the velocity of light is an invariant for all observers moving with uniform velocities relative to each other. The hypothesis is Einstein's special theory of relativity, which is a set of mathematical rules for calculating a velocity of a body relative to one observer when it is given relative to another. The invariance of the speed of light can be deduced from these rules. But there is more. There is a "deductive dividend" in the form of an equation, which equates one gram of matter to 900,000,000,000,000,000,000 ergs of energy. The recent achievement of controlled nuclear fission is a verification of the "deductive dividend" of the theory of relativity.

SUMMARY OF CHAPTERS 3 AND 4

We have essentially two distinct ways of obtaining knowledge. One, called induction, applies to knowledge about the real world. Its primary cognitive act is direct experience. You look at the sun and see that it is bright. The way knowledge accumulates is by repeated associations of similar experiences. We taste green apples and find them sour. We verbalize these experiences in a conclusion leading from the particular to the general case: "This green apple is sour; that green apple is sour . . . all green apples are sour."

The other way of obtaining knowledge is deduction. Deduction is concerned not with experiences but with assertions. It is knowledge not about the world but about language or the use of symbols. The way knowledge accumulates is by arriving at new assertions by applying certain rules of reasoning (or reckoning) to assertions admitted or assumed to be valid.

Induction is grounded in the events of the real world but as a method of cognition it has two fundamental weaknesses. First, it is never completely reliable: no matter how many times some sequence of events has been observed, there is no guarantee that it will be observed again. Second, induction alone limits conclusions to the prediction of events similar to those already observed. Experience with green apples leads only to conclusions about green apples.

Deduction is reliable with respect to its *validity* (if one only follows the prescribed rules) but has no necessary connection with the real world. The results of deduction are, however, far more interesting than those of induction. The conclusions are often far removed from the assumptions with which the deductive process starts. The magnificence of mathematics bears witness to this.[15]

Science (or operational knowledge) is the synthesis of the two methods. The scientist can use deduction to predict events seemingly unrelated to his past experience, and he can use induction (experiment) to determine whether, in addition to being valid, his deductions are true. Since new deductions can always be made on the basis of what is known, it follows that the predictive content of scientific "truths" can always be enlarged. It also follows that we should not expect any scientific "truth" to remain a truth, because there is no assurance that the *enlarged* predictive content will be confirmed. Thus every scientific truth is a hypothesis. The search for truth is the search for better hypotheses, that is, for those with more predictive content.

Chapter 5. THE PROBLEM OF CAUSALITY:
"WHY IS X?"

T<small>HE</small> task of philosophy is sometimes contrasted with that of science as follows:

"Science confines itself to descriptions of how things happen and does not pursue the more fundamental question of *why* things happen as they do. It therefore remains for philosophy to investigate this more fundamental question."

It is not entirely true that science ignores the "why" questions. It gives answers to many such questions on the basis of its own criteria of what constitutes a suitable answer.

Examples:

Q. Why do planets move in ellipses around the sun?

A. Because an attractive force acts between each planet and the sun, and the magnitude of the force is inversely proportional to the square of the distance between them.

Q. Why are animals and plants adapted to the environment in which they live?

A. Because of differential survival rates between those more adapted and those less adapted.

Q. Why is the average age of the inhabitants of the United States becoming greater?

A. Because both the birth rate and the death rate are declining.

Now it is possible to raise serious objections to explanations of this sort. First, the connection between "cause" and "effect" is in some cases anything but apparent. One can, for example, say,

"Suppose there *is* an attractive force which varies inversely with the square of the distance. This still does not tell me why the planets move in ellipses. Why should they move at all? Why should the orbits not be squares? Or why should the planets not fall into the sun if the sun keeps attracting them?"

Second, the "why" can be applied to the answers. One can ask, "Why are the birth and death rates declining?"

Third, it is often pointed out that there are two kinds of cause, one implying a deterministic necessity, the other a purpose. Science, it is maintained, inasmuch as it is at all interested in causes, treats only the first kind of cause and ignores the second. It is felt that "purpose" is more important (if not supremely important) in human affairs and may be of importance even in large-scale natural phenomena, such as cosmological, organic, and historical evolution. Since scientists often explicitly decline to speculate about such "purposeful" causes, the philosopher must presumably turn his attention to them.

The difference between the two kinds of causes appears in the two answers to the following question.

Q. Why did General Z, upon seizing power in Plutonia, order the execution of all cross-eyed individuals?

A_1. (implying purpose): To prevent the disclosure of military secrets to Neptunia, whose agents in Plutonia are recruited among the cross-eyed.

A_2. (implying deterministic necessity): Because General Z's father, who was cross-eyed, beat him.

It seems to some people that the emphasis on deterministic factors in human affairs (as is the trend in modern psychology, and in some social science) divorces the study of man from ethical considerations. The seeming irrelevancy of moral questions in the scientific inquiry of human affairs appears to release man from moral responsibility and to degrade him to an automaton. It is assumed that man can keep his self-respect only if he considers himself a "free agent." Therefore, it is maintained, it is necessary to find answers to "why" questions without reference to deterministic necessity. This, it is thought, science is not equipped to do.

I will use the same approach to the question "Why is X?" that I have used with regard to the other standing questions of philosophy, those dealing with the nature of things, reality, and truth.

A question, I repeat, is a social act. It is a request for an answer in terms "understood" by the one who asks. Therefore it is a request for certain *kinds* of answers. To analyze a question is to inquire into the kinds of answers wanted.

In preceding chapters I have tried to show that the question "What is X?" may call for a name, so that it can be applied to future experiences of the kind one currently faces; or the question may call for an experience to match with a word one hears. The question "Is X real?" is a request for an assurance that something one experiences has a certain "stability" with regard to future experiences or the experiences of others. The question "Is X true?" is a challenge to make predictions verifiable by experience. The question "Is X valid?" reflects a need to check whether one has followed established rules of reasoning.

The question "Why is X?" seems to reflect a need to *order* experiences, to makes things *fit*. Now whether things fit or not depends on the framework into which one tries to fit them. By a framework I mean a set of preconceived notions. To be acceptable, explanations must always be in terms of those preconceived notions. Therefore if any explanation is rejected as inadequate, it must be either because it contradicts preconceived notions or because no such notions can be found on which to hang the explanation.

Examples:

"I've whipped him and whipped him," says an exasperated father of a fifteen-year-old delinquent, "and he still keeps going with that gang of hoodlums."

"Maybe he continues to do so *because* you whip him," suggests a social worker.

"Are you kidding? Does he *want* to get whipped?"

The explanation contradicts the father's preconceived notion of learning, according to which punishment invariably acts as a deterrent.

Physicist: Why do you think it thunders?

Peasant: The prophet Elijah is riding over the clouds in his chariot.

Physicist: No. I will tell you why it thunders. Thunder results from a detonation accompanying an electrical discharge.

Peasant:???

The explanation finds nothing to connect with in the experience of the peasant.

Social psychologist: Why has the birthrate of Neptunia fallen?

Physician: Because effective contraceptives have become available to the Neptunians.

Social psychologist: Yes, but why should people *want* to use contraceptives?

The physician views reproduction in terms of the mechanics of conception. The social psychologist, on the other hand, views it in terms of the *motivation* to reproduce. What fits as an explanation in the framework of one does not fit in the framework of the other.

We are again faced with the relativity of meaning. And again, if we wish to resolve the "contradictions" arising from a misunderstanding of this relativity, we must proceed as before: analyze the various meanings of the question "Why is X?" and try to find a common denominator for them.

It seems that in all cases, to answer the question "Why is X?" (that is, to "explain" something) is to show that something which seems strange is really only another instance of something familiar. To explain means to show that something which does not seem to "fit" really fits.

In the simplest possible case, the "fitness" may be nothing more than an association of two events in a certain sequence. Every time the sun went down, it became cooler. Every time there was a dry summer, the crops were bad. Every time there was a famine, there was an epidemic. A way of expressing these experiences is to say, "It is cooler, *because* the sun has gone down"; "The crops failed because there was not enough rain"; "Sickness came because there was not enough to eat."

Pavlov's work on the conditioned reflex has suggested that the awareness of cause and effect as a recurrent sequence of events may have a clearly discernible physiological basis. When a dog has repeatedly experienced the presence of food in his mouth following the sound of a bell, he "learns" to salivate following the sound of the bell even when no food is given. If we choose to describe the dog's behavior in terms of what we ourselves experience in similar situations, we can say, "The dog *expects* to be fed when the bell rings." We often rationalize our own feeling of expectation by saying that an earlier event has been the "cause" of the later.

A keen analysis of these subjective factors was undertaken by David Hume (39). Hume concluded that our notion of causality could not be divorced from our habitual association of events, which regularly follow each other. He even went so far as to suspect that this was all there was to causality, that it was only a reflection of our habits.[16]

If that were all there was to our notion of causality, if it depended only on habitual perceptions of sequences of events, we would be no better and no worse off than the other higher vertebrates.

I say "no better off," because the relations among events more subtle than a simple sequence relation would forever escape us. Conditioning, as we observe it in animals, depends strongly on a close association of the events to be linked by conditioning. If the unconditioned stimulus and the conditioned stimulus are separated by a sizable interval of time, or if other stimuli occur between them, ordinarily no conditioning results. If we were only passive observers of events among us, relying on habit to associate them into causes and effects, we could never conclude that mosquitoes are the "cause" of malaria or that the inclination of the earth's axis to its orbit is the cause of seasons. There just are too many things to observe, and they can be "paired off" into sequences in a hopelessly large variety of ways.

But I also say "no worse off" than the higher vertebrates because if we took no active part in seeking out causes, we could not promote to causal relations purely coincidental sequences or assume the existence of such sequences just because we have been told about them. We could never acquire notions that walking under ladders causes misfortunes or that social security measures cause communism. Such notions could be acquired through "habit" only if the "causes" were fairly immediately and consistently followed by the "effects." Since this is not the case in the instances cited, other factors besides habitual association must underlie our notions of causality. What are these other factors?

To begin with, our learning does not depend on the classic Pavlovian conditioning process nearly to the extent that the learning of other animals does. Pavlovian conditioning is a long, drawn-out affair. It usually takes scores or hundreds of associations of two events for the response to one to become conditioned to the stimulus of the other. In other words, an animal will "think of one event as the cause of another" (I am speaking anthropomorphically, of course) only if the one has frequently and consistently preceded the other. Not so with us. *One* association is often sufficient with us, especially when we are actively *looking* for a "cause." When we have a stomach ache, we look for a cause. If we remember having eaten a pickled tomato, we are likely to conclude that it was the cause of the stomach ache, regardless of whether we had ever eaten pickled tomatoes before.

Furthermore, once we have "established" a cause, we need no further experience to reinforce our conviction. Our memory is so good that we may avoid pickled tomatoes for the rest of our lives and yet nurse the conviction that "pickled tomatoes cause stomach aches."

Moreover, we pass our convictions to other people and to our children (which other animals cannot do). In other words, our notions as to what causes what do not depend on what we ourselves have experienced. Thus it is conceivable that one man's stomach ache following a feast of pickled tomatoes may be the origin of a taboo on pickling tomatoes (and by generalization all other vegetables) affecting a whole nation and lasting for thousands of years.

Finally, the facility with which we substitute words for experience gives us the impression that we are relating experiences when we are only relating words. The grammatical form of the "because clause" is so often associated with the explanation of causes that it tends to be taken *to be* an explanation regardless of the experiences (if any) to which it refers. Characteristically, small children often become so strongly conditioned to the word "because" as introducing an explanation that they will use it *alone* in answering the question "Why is X?"

The substitution of grammar for meaning leads to the so-called pseudo-explanation[17] which has been extremely prevalent in traditional philosophy and which pervades a great deal of everyday thinking about causes.

Example:
Q. Why does John hate to work?
A. Because he is lazy.

Here we have a pseudo-explanation. It seems to point to a causal relation between two conditions (hating work and being lazy), but it really only relates two *expressions*. For if we ask, "What does it mean to be lazy?" we find, if we recall what sort of people are called lazy, that to be lazy means to hate work. Therefore all that was said was,

"John hates to work, because John hates to work."

Traditional philosophy (including pre-scientific "natural philosophy") and especially theology are full of such pseudo-explanations.

"Opium puts you to sleep because of its dormitive properties."

"The darker races are less intelligent than the white race because they are inferior."

"God cannot commit a sin because he is perfect."

I have presented an unattractive view of the way human beings acquire notions about the causes of events. There is, of course, another side of the picture, an extremely attractive one. The remarkable thing about the power of human reason is that the very factors in it which are at the root of so many human misfortunes are also at the root of man's achievements.

I have described the dangers inherent in concluding a causal relation from a single experience. There are also obvious advantages in being able to do so, since it enables us to learn much more rapidly than other animals do.

I have described the dangers inherent in relying on the experiences of others. In this reliance is also man's ability to cooperate with his fellow men to his great advantage.

I have given examples to show how the manipulation of words substituted for the experience of events can lead us astray. However, in the ability to do so lies the secret of man's superlative position on this planet. For to manipulate words can mean to perform experiments in one's imagination—that is, to perform experiments more rapidly and more safely than they can be performed in reality. It is this ability to "experiment with ideas" which has extended man's learning capacity far beyond that of any other animal.

An awareness of this double-edged character of man's learning process determines the operational attitude toward explanations and so toward causality. Operational philosophy regards every statement about causality as a hypothesis to be tested. The operations performed in the test give meaning to the assertion that event A is the cause of the event B. When we look at those operations, we find that at least three distinct kinds of causality must be distinguished.

Observational Causality

Sometimes the assertion "A causes B" means simply "Watch for the occurrence of A, and you will observe the occurrence of B." In this situation nothing can be done about either A or B except watching for their occurrence. If A consistently precedes B, we can say that A is the (observational) cause of B. For instance, having observed that thunder always follows lightning, we can say that

lightning causes thunder. If A and B occur simultaneously or if
their sequence is sometimes interchanged, we can say that either
causes the other.

Example: The vertical position of the hands of the railroad clock
is always either immediately preceded or followed by the arrival
of train No. 384. We can say, "Either the vertical position of the
hands causes the arrival of the train or *vice versa.*"

This conclusion may look silly, but we must remember that it
looks silly only to someone who knows something about trains,
clocks, and timetables. On the basis of such knowledge, a more "rational" explanation can be offered: train No. 384 is due to arrive
at 5:55, and its arrival time varies from 5:55 to 6:05. It is wise,
however, to approach questions of causality naively, that is, without the compulsion to seek "rational explanations." To be sure,
rational explanations are in the long run to be preferred to naive
ones, but we must also remember that rational explanations are
often so firmly rooted in preconceived notions that they become an
obstacle in the attainment of new knowledge or deeper insight.
We shall see, for instance, that the naive conclusion about the
causal relation between the clock and the train, although "false,"
nevertheless contains an important idea—that cause and effect are
often interchangeable.

Manipulative Causality

The assertion, "Either the vertical position of the hands makes
the train come or *vice versa*" can be shown to be false, but only in
the light of another definition of causality, namely, of *manipulative*
causality. Here to assert, "A causes B" means "Make A occur, and
you will observe B" (in this case we can say that A is a sufficient
cause of B); or "Prevent A from occurring, and B will not occur"
(in this case, A is a necessary cause of B). In other words, if you
wish to test "A causes B" in the manipulative sense, do not just
wait for A to happen—make it happen or prevent it from happening.

Now we can see that the clock does not make the train come or
prevent it from coming, because we can set the clock at 6:00, and
the train will not thereby appear; or else we can stop the clock,
and the train will eventually come anyway. Or else we can delay
the train, and the clock will not wait for it.

The possibility of testing causality by means of manipulating events is at the basis of experimental science. In certain areas it is difficult or impossible to experiment. It is not allowed to perform certain experiments on human beings, and certain social situations cannot be brought about at will. Therefore, in many instances psychologists, social scientists, and other investigators must confine themselves to the discussion of observational causality. We have seen, in our example with the railroad clock, that it is a "weaker" sort of causality: it can be often refuted by an appropriate experiment. Therefore observational causality is in general less convincing than manipulative causality. To emphasize this difference, the name "correlation" is used for what I have called observational causality. If a causal relation in a correlation is unlikely, the name "spurious correlation" is used. If it is found, for example, that fluctuations in the kangaroo population of Australia follow closely the fluctuations of the market price of aluminum, one suspects a "spurious correlation" rather than causality.

The distinction is useful in reminding us how dangerous it may be to jump to conclusions about "causality." Indeed, such conclusions are at the root of many foolish notions. On the basis of correlation, it is possible to conclude that smoking causes divorce (since increase in smoking has gone hand in hand with the increase in divorce), that vitamin C causes tooth decay (because both the intake of vitamin C and tooth decay have increased in recent decades), and that going to bed is fatal (because so many people have died in bed).

Still it is well to keep in mind that the assertion, "It got dark because the sun has set" is based on no more than passive observation, that is, can be taken to be only as an instance of observational causality. We cannot make the sun set when we please or prevent it from setting to see whether it will get dark.

The test of manipulative causality also reveals sometimes that "cause" and "effect" are interchangeable. We find that often what one considers to be the "cause" is only what one happens to be manipulating at the time.

Example: Think of a small hand-driven dynamo, by means of which we can make a current pass through a wire. As we operate the dynamo it appears to us that the dynamo (that is, a coil of wire rotating in a magnetic field) is the "cause" and the current the "effect." However, if we connect two ends of the wire to a source of alternating current, the dynamo will be driven by the resulting current (that is, will behave like a motor). Now in our estimation, the current is the "cause" and the motion of the coil in the dynamo the "effect" instead of *vice versa*.

Objectively there is no difference between what happens in the first case and in the second. Only our attitudes (based on what *we* happen to manipulate) determine for us what is the "cause" and what the "effect."[18]

The discovery that what seems to be a "one-way" causality is often only a reflection of our point of view and turns out on closer inspection to be a "two-way" causality has led to extremely important results. For ages it was known that "work makes (causes) heat." In fact, this principle was utilized technologically in making fire by friction. The reverse relation, "heat makes (can be converted into) work," did not occur until the Industrial Revolution, and when it did, the resulting technology (based on the heat engine) changed the face of the earth.

For the physical scientist the concept of causality has lost much of its usefulness. The physicist does not say, "Gravity causes the planets to revolve around the sun," or "Friction is the cause of heat" except when he lapses into the loose talk of every-day speech (for instance, in answering questions so worded as to demand such answers). Instead, the physicist manipulates equations which enable him to calculate the motions of the planets in terms of the gravitational forces or the amount of heat in terms of the amount of work done. In most references to human activity, however, loose talk still prevails, and so the concept of causality must be subjected to logical analysis. At times such analysis when translated into action may be of great social significance. Of importance to us are questions such as these,

Does bad housing cause decline in ambition and productivity, or vice versa?

Do price increases result in wage increases, or vice versa?

Does the imminence of war result in armament races, or vice versa?

Operational philosophy, by emphasizing the operations required to establish manipulative causality, suggests that the important question is not "Which factor is the more fundamental?" but *"Which factor can be more easily manipulated?"* Operationally speaking, the contention of many social scientists that bad housing is the cause rather than the effect of the apathy of people is simply another way of saying that it is easier to improve housing directly than to influence people's attitudes directly.

In this light, the whole Marxist thesis that the economic structure of society determines the moral outlook of its members and not *vice versa* appears as a recommendation for a certain kind of action: change the economic structure, and the moral outlook will change accordingly. The assumption of Marxism is that it is possible to change the former directly but not the latter. The role of philosophy ends with the formulation of a thesis in terms of the operations which could conceivably verify or refute it. The impasse in the ideological struggle between the East and the West can be partly traced to a mistaken belief that philosophy is equipped to determine whether the thesis is "true."

POSTULATIONAL CAUSALITY

Event A is considered to be a (postulational) cause of B if the following happens: B appears to us surprising when we are ignorant of the occurrence of A, and it ceases to be surprising when we learn of the occurrence of A. Roughly speaking, we regard A as the cause of B if the explanation "B occurred because A occurred" makes us say "Oh!" Here the subjective aspect of causality is most clearly brought out. If we continue to see the question "Why is X?" as a social act, this aspect of causality is seen to underlie all others.

Example:
Q. Why are all those people running in the same direction?
A. There is a fire down the street.

Contained in the question is an observation of an *unusual* event. Ordinarily the people in a city street do not all run in the same direction. But we have observed that people tend to run toward a fire. The fire is taken to be a cause of the running. The unusual event (people running in the same direction) becomes through the explanation a usual one (people running toward a fire).

We are satisfied with the explanation only if what we consider unusual (that which led us to ask "why?") becomes usual (what we ordinarily would expect). Therefore the *subjective adequacy of any explanation depends on what we consider usual or unusual.*

Note that the test of postulational causality consists neither of observations nor of manipulations. We do not look at events outside of us to decide whether "A causes B." We look at our own expectations. If we are sophisticated, we may look at our reasoning. In view of what was said in Chapters 3 and 4 about truth and validity, assertions of postulational causality can be only *valid* (not true). They can *become* true if, in addition to the logical criteria for their validity, operational criteria for their truth are applied.

Example: I assert that water is intoxicating and support my assertion by the following reasoning. Mr. A drank a quantity of whiskey with water and became intoxicated; Mr. B drank a quantity of brandy with water and became intoxicated; Mr. C drank a quantity of gin and water and became intoxicated. Therefore water, being the constant ingredient in all three cases, must be the cause of the intoxication.[19]

This argument has a certain validity if one admits the principle that if several situations lead to the same effect, one looks to the invariant in the situations for the cause. The *truth* of the assertion, however, is in its predictive content, such as is implied in the statement, "If Mr. D drinks a quantity of pure water, he will become intoxicated." In view of this prediction, the assertion, "Water is intoxicating," is clearly false. However, the principle of the invariant ingredient still holds: the invariant is alcohol, not water.

Example: The assertion, "The laws of motion and gravity determine ('cause') the motions of the planets," is *valid* in the sense that the motions which were already observed can be logically (mathematically) deduced from the laws. It is *true* in the sense that *future* motions can be predicted on the same basis.

Any explanation can be made valid with respect to certain assumptions, that is, any explanation looks reasonable to one who accepts certain assumptions and rules of reasoning. Among certain tribes in Africa, the question "Why did A die?" means "Who was the cause of A's death, and what magic was used to bring it about?" To be valid with respect to the fundamental assumptions of that tribe (death is due to magical practices) an explanation must be made in those terms. The *truth* of the explanation, however, is an entirely different matter. To test the truth of the statement "B killed A by burning A's shirt," one would have to make some prediction, such as, "B can kill C by burning C's shirt," or "If no shirts are burned, no one will die." The truth of the first assertion stands or falls with the test of its predictive content.

Again, as in so many other cases, a great deal of confusion arises when the "validity" of explanations (as referred to certain assumptions) is mistaken for their truth, that is, postulational causality is mistaken for manipulative causality. The greater part of medical practice until recently was based on such confusions. The causes of diseases were carefully reasoned out according to an accepted schema of reasoning. "Cures" consisted of certain operations (administration of drugs, blood-letting, baths, etc.). But it did not occur to the physicians to employ the operations as experiments to test the truth of the supposed causes of disease.

The greater part of political thinking in our day is based on taking postulational causes of events as being true causes. During the 1930's the Russians were convinced that every industrial setback they suffered was due to sabotage. They asked, "Who is the cause of this failure, and what foreign power hired him to wreck our effort?" Answers had to be in those terms. In the early 1950's in the United States the question was frequently asked, "Who are the Communists in our State Department who are responsible for the failure of our foreign policy?" Answers to such questions must necessarily be postulational (since they are hardly ever based on systematic observation or experiment), but they are seldom recognized as such.[20]

The recognition of the difference between postulational and manipulative (or observational) causes is really an extension of the recognition of the difference between validity and truth. It too must be credited largely to operational philosophy.

One application of this recognition might be made to clarify an argument which has been raging for several years among social scientists. There are some social scientists, particularly in the United States, who maintain that there is no reason why the methods of social science should not eventually resemble those of physical science. That is, the goal of social science should be to discover "laws" (in the scientific, not judicial sense) which govern the behavior of man in society, the evolution of societies, etc. These laws should be subjected to the same rigorous tests that apply to the laws of the physical sciences. Their proof should be in the possibility of predicting events by means of them. These social scientists, therefore, look favorably on the application of mathematical techniques in constructing theories and in evaluating data, on the design of controlled experiments to study social behavior, etc. Their opponents maintain that this program is sterile. Some of them deny that it will ever be possible to predict events in the social sphere, that prediction is irrelevant to the understanding of man and of his social behavior.

The argument is about the meaning of the term "understand." To the first group, "to understand" means to state observational and (preferably) manipulative causes of events. To the second group, "to understand" means to state postulational causes. They feel they "understand" if events fall into a pattern, become ordered in some scheme.

From the operational point of view, there can be no quarrel about a definition. Each group chooses to understand the word "understand" in a different sense. It is well to keep in mind, however, that the word is used in two different senses, and to be aware of the possible consequences of one's commitment.

If one limits the meaning of "understanding" to subjective criteria, as the second group of social scientists tend to do, one must be prepared to abandon attempts to reconcile various kinds of "understanding." Society was "understood" also by Plato and by St. Augustine, and by Rousseau and by Hegel and by Marx. All of them had "systems," in which everything fit beautifully and which were generally irreconcilable with each other. Furthermore, every paranoiac has a "system" into which all his observations fit with uncanny accuracy.

It may be that the "nonpredictive" social scientists are prepared to admit that there is no such thing as objective criteria of understanding in their field. To this one can only say that physical science was once in the same fix. Before the advent of the experimental method every philosopher had a "system" in which the events could be "fit." The fitting was made possible by a judicious or, perhaps (to do justice to the sincerity of the philosophers), unconscious *selection* of events. The events observed were selected to fit the system instead of the system being modified or extended to encompass the greatest possible range of events.

One of the tasks of operational philosophy is to discover the frameworks into which philosophers (and scientists, for that matter) fit their systems of explanations. In other words, the operational philosopher must reveal to someone who seeks answers to the question "Why is X?" the sort of answers to which his search is limited because of the limitations of his framework. The hope is that by revealing the diversity of the conceptual systems in the history of thought, operational philosophy can develop a fruitful critique of the theory of knowledge.

In particular, the claim of traditional philosophy that it offers a more fundamental approach to the question "Why is X?" than is offered by science must be examined by analyzing the conceptual systems within which traditional philosophy has pursued its investigations and by noting how the conceptual systems of science are related to them and to each other.

Chapter 6. FRAMEWORKS OF THOUGHT

To EXPLAIN an event, we have seen, is to point out its connection with another event or with a class of events. The connection may be in repeated observations of the two events together or in our ability to affect one event by manipulating the other. Such connections are rooted in our experience. But there are other connections perceived among events which may or may not be rooted in experience. These are the connections of analogy. Two events are thought to be causally connected, because two other events which somehow resemble them have been observed or thought to be causally connected.

We experience a desire or need to push something. We push and observe the effects. We establish a causal connection between our desire and the final result. Next we see trees bending under a strong wind. This resembles the results of our own pushing. Consequently we think of "the wind pushing" the trees. We attribute our own pushing to our "will." Consequently, we conclude, the wind has a "will." Human wills can sometimes be influenced by requests, bribery, or threats. Consequently, the forces of nature (wind, sun, rain, etc.) can be so influenced. Heavy wagons on rough roads make a noise like thunder. Consequently, thunder must be caused by some heavy vehicle, possibly the prophet Elijah's chariot.

Such explanations underlie the metaphysics of *animism*. It is tacitly assumed in animism that natural and supernatural beings influence the course of events by their "wills." Acceptable explanations are analogies between desires observed within oneself and those attributed to agencies responsible for events. The desires of others, however, particularly those of the gods, are notoriously erratic. Accurate prediction, therefore, is impossible. One seeks to manipulate nature (for example, by magic), but successes are attributed to the special talents of the manipulator and failures to the special talents of someone who opposes him.

65

As the attention shifts to the regularities in nature, the criterion of predictability begins to underlie explanations. It is no longer sufficient to find an analogy between the observed event and some other event at random. It is no longer satisfying to attribute causes of events to the whims of the gods. The meaning of cause becomes more closely related to the *order* of things. The concept of the "law of nature" emerges.

A metaphysics which forms a transition between animism and science has been called by various writers *organismic*. This was the framework of thought which governed the philosophy of the Middle Ages. It was characterized by the so-called teleological view of causation. This view presents more than a historical interest, because it is still extremely prevalent outside of the physical sciences. Let us therefore look at it more closely.

TELEOLOGY

We have seen how "why" questions about human acts can be interpreted in two ways:

1. What was the genesis of the act (how did it come about)?
2. What was the purpose of the act (what goal determined it)?

When any event is explained in such a way as to make some goal appear the cause of the event, the explanation is teleological. The goal need not be in the intent of the actor. It may represent the fulfillment of a "fate" or a prophecy.

Example:

Then said Pilate unto them, Take ye him, and judge him according to your law. The Jews therefore said unto him, It is not lawful for us to put any man to death:

That the saying of Jesus might be fulfilled, which he spake, signifying what death he should die (John, 18: 31–32).

The explanation implies that the Jews declined to judge Jesus, because Jesus' prophecy (that he would die on the cross) had to be fulfilled.

Teleological explanations were the backbone of organismic metaphysics. Like animistic metaphysics, the organismic projects man's inner feelings of "desire," "drive," "intent," "will," etc., into physical objects. But unlike animism, organismic philosophy seeks regularities and "laws" in nature instead of attributing all happenings to the whims of the gods. According to organismic philosophy, everything seeks its "natural" place in the world. Heavy things fall toward the earth because that is where they belong, being "of" the earth. Ethereal things, like gases, smokes, and flames, rise because they belong in the heavens (witness the sun and the stars, which are fire). Each bird seeks its nest (therefore birds can fly, because the nests are up in the trees); each field creature its hole. Everything, living and nonliving, has an "essence," which it constantly strives to realize in a way proper to it.[21]

The beginning of experimental science dealt the first heavy blows to teleology. The theory of inner drives and goals was abandoned in the new method of investigation. The center of interest in the theory of motion became not the goal of the motion (a teleological idea) but the process of the motion itself. Not "where is the body trying to get to?" but "How does it move?" became the important question. Therefore more attention was paid to measurements, especially the measurements of velocity and hence to the *changes* in motion.

Causation (at least in the theory of motion) became *mechanical,* that is, was seen to reside in the action of forces, which act on material things in accordance with certain general laws. This change in the point of view marks the beginning of classical mechanics and the advent of *mechanistic* metaphysics. In mechanics, the important forces are *external* to the body, while in organismic philosophy the important "forces" (in the sense of being the causes of motion) were *within* the bodies.*

From the standpoint of teleology, the effects of forces on motion could never have been clarified. The vague notion of force that did exist mostly associated "force" with "a striving toward a goal." It would therefore have been impossible for an organismic philosopher to understand how an attractive force exerted by the sun on the planets could move the planets *around* the sun. To such a philosopher "that to which a force is directed" would mean "the goal to be reached." Therefore, in all likelihood, if he assumed an attractive force toward the sun, he would have to conclude that the planets must fall into the sun. Since this does not happen, his logic would tell him that the sun's attractive force is an absurdity.

From the standpoint of mechanistic metaphysics, however, forces have nothing to do with goals. A force merely *interferes* with the

---

*Strictly speaking, forces always come in pairs. For every force which the environment exerts on the body, there is a force which the body exerts on the environment. However, the emphasis in classical mechanics is on the forces *on* the body.

motion of a body, by changing its speed, its direction, or both. A force does not care where a body is bound for. It affects only the *here* and *now* of the body's motion, without regard for the body's "inner drives," which are supposedly (according to organismic assumptions) determined by its "essence." Nothing matters to force about a body on which it acts except the body's mass. The force has the more "respect" for the body, the more massive the body is. More precisely, the amount of change in the motion of a body produced by a given force varies inversely as the mass of the body. This places the "causes of motion" wholly outside the body and dispenses with "goals." It is a complete break with teleology.

Of biological science, however, teleology took much longer leave and, in fact, still lingers in many of biology's darker corners. Early theories of evolution were strongly teleological. Lamarck, for example, talked of a "vital force," "a will," which was supposedly responsible for the adaptation of animals to their environment. The idea is obviously an attractive one. It admits the possibility that "wishing makes it so." In the eighteenth century, the "will" idea fitted in especially nicely with the rising stock of individual initiative and responsibility. Where formerly "Providence" was credited with endowing her creatures with the means of survival, this achievement now turned out to be the result of diligence and perseverance. The giraffe kept stretching his neck to get at the succulent leaves, and the neck kept getting a little longer with each generation.

The theory of natural selection put an end to evolutionary teleology just as mechanics dispensed with the teleological theory of motion. The theory of natural selection placed the most important causes of evolution *outside* the organism. The more adapted individuals in each generation survive longer than the less adapted and thus have a chance to have more progeny (which resemble them). The whole population, therefore, shifts gradually toward the predominance of the more adapted types. There is no need to suppose any purpose for the modifications in the heredity of the organism. These modifications may well be simply accidental. A generation of giraffes may have some individuals just lucky enough to have somewhat longer than average necks. They will be the favored ones, since they will reach more leaves. Their more numerous progeny, inheriting their long neck bias, will have longer average necks than the average necks of the last generation. What has happened once can happen twice, etc., until giraffes become what they are (92).

Practically all the discoveries of genetics, physiology, and embryology have tended to substantiate the basic premise of natural selection: there is no need to postulate a "purpose" in evolution; no need to suppose that the future influences the present; no need to suppose anything but that the present (with its accumulated past) influences the future.

This change in thinking about evolution is perhaps the most important example of how a deeper understanding of a phenomenon permits us to discard previously entertained notions of purpose and goal which we took to be the "cause" of the phenomenon. The following example is much more limited but serves to illustrate the process rather sharply.

Along the sides of hills where there is strong erosion of the soil by water, formations are sometimes seen which resemble stalagmites found protruding from the floors of some caves. These formations, however, are formed not by deposited minerals, as stalagmites are, but on the contrary by erosion of the soil around them. There is usually a pebble sitting neatly on the top of each of these "stalagmites." The immediate impression is that someone has carefully placed a pebble on the top of each protrusion. A little reflection, however, reveals that in all likelihood the erosion responsible for the formation of the protrusions occurred precisely where the ground was the softest (that is, *not* protected by pebbles), in other words, in the spaces between the pebbles strewn randomly about. When the soft ground was eaten away, the portions protected by the pebbles remained as the "stalagmites" with the pebbles sitting on the top.

In a way, the progress of natural sciences tends to reveal "nature" as less "purposeful," less "wise" than she appeared to early observers. This "debunking" of nature can be taken as a sign of the growing maturity of her children. Still, as I have said, teleology is by no means dead in biological matters, that is, in matters of life and death. Although they are becoming rare in serious works, explanations such as the following appear plausible to a surprisingly large number of people.

Q. Why is the wall of the stomach elastic?

A. So that the stomach can expand when it is filled.

Q. Why do birds fly south?

A. Because it is warm there.

Q. Why are polar animals white?

A. So they can better escape their pursuers or better approach their quarry.

But the same people who do not regard these answers as in the least naive are likely to smile at someone who thinks that it rains so that the crops may grow or that steam expands in the locomotive cylinder so that the wheels may go around.

Teleological explanations tend to disappear when manipulative causes are discovered. Thus the expulsion of teleology from physics has gone hand in hand with the development of the experimental method, that is, the discovery of how to *make* things happen. Now one does not manipulate the "future." One manipulates the present and *then* observes the result. The mechanistic explanation, in contrast to the teleological, accordingly is associated with the sequence Cause-Effect, not the other way around.

Why do teleological notions persist? It is important to note that they have persisted most stubbornly in the explanations of actions of beings which resemble us most. They have persisted in biology longer than in physics and in behavioral sciences (psychology, sociology, etc.) longer than in general biology. It appears that our subjective experience of desire and intent is a crucial element in the genesis of a teleological explanation. Our projection of these subjective experiences on the outside world is at the root of teleological reasoning. The desire or intent is a sort of mental rehearsal of the act or of its result. Actually, the neural events associated with this anticipation of the result precede the act. But since we think of the result as being in the future, it seems to us that the "future" (that is, the purpose) is the "cause" of our actions.

It may be that spatial projection of vision is a similar psychological effect. The events which make up seeing are all inside of us—chemical reactions in the retina, propagation of impulses along nerve fibers, excitation of the occipital lobes of the brain, etc. But we are not conscious of all this. To us the object we see is *out there*. Similarly, the cause of our action seems to us to be "out there," in the future. But to someone able to observe our neural processes our acts would appear as simply the consequences of those processes. To him cause and effect would appear in their natural sequence. If, moreover, he could *manipulate* our neural processes, he could fully predict our actions, and all traces of purposefulness would disappear (in the opinion of this superhuman observer) from our behavior. Purposefulness thus appears to be not necessarily something inherent in a situation but rather something in the way the situation is evaluated. There will be more to say about this matter in Chapter 7.

THE AGE OF MECHANISM

As we have seen, teleological notions have practically disappeared from physical science. They have given place to mechanistic ones. Now "mechanism" as a framework of thought may be considered in a narrow sense and in a broad sense. In a narrow sense, it is a framework in which all acceptable explanations must be in terms of motions of material bodies determined by forces acting on them. In a broader sense, a mechanical framework is simply a deterministic one, that is, it is based on the assumption that if everything is known about the state of the world at a given moment, then, in principle, everything can be known about it for all time, because each "present state" determines the state immediately following it, etc. This outlook too can be called "mechanistic," because it assumes a certain "automatism" in nature (as if the universe were wound up and let go once for all, like a mechanism). If this broader interpretation of mechanism is taken, then all of classical physics is seen to fit into the mechanistic framework. Mechanics certainly fits into it. However, so does thermodynamics, electromagnetism, and optics. True, electromagnetism and optics were developed independently of the assumptions of mechanics; yet they gave an outlook on events as deterministic as mechanics did. Once one knew enough about the present, the future was supposed to be an open book, which one only had to learn to read.

By the middle of the nineteenth century, there were four distinct branches of physics, namely,

1. Mechanics, which dealt with the motions and stresses suffered by material bodies under the influence of forces;

2. Thermodynamics, which dealt with temperature and heat and with the conversion of heat into work and vice versa;

3. Electrodynamics, which dealt with electric and magnetic phenomena and the relations between them; and

4. Optics, which dealt with the propagation of light.

Each field was highly developed as a theoretical scheme. That is, each was woven into a logical system, as geometry had been two thousand years previously. The assertions made in mechanics, for example, were not only "true" in the sense that they could be verified experimentally. They were also *valid* with respect to a few fundamental postulates in the sense that they could be logically (mathematically) deduced from them. Thus there was an aura of certainty about mechanics (as there had been about geometry). But this certainty was not confined to space relationships. It was a certainty dealing with *events*. One could predict what was going to *happen* by means of mathematical deduction—a gratifying state of affairs.

Perhaps because mechanics was the earliest field of physics to develop, its theoretical framework enjoyed the highest prestige. There was a certain grandeur about it. The universe was thought to be Space, having three dimensions and stretching out to infinity in all directions. The universe had an "age" measured by the flow of a uniformly flowing "time." If one did not choose to believe in an Act of Creation and a Final Judgment, time too stretched infinitely in both directions. The universe was populated by matter. The chunks of matter and energy in the universe moved in accordance with strict laws. The total amount of matter and energy was conserved forever. That is all there was to know "factually." All the other knowledge could be deduced from these "facts."[22]

So attractive was this picture that many theoretical physicists entertained the ambition to reduce all physics to mechanics, that is, to discover a logical connection which would enable them to deduce all assertions of physics from the postulates of mechanics alone. Some such attempts were crowned with success. The theory of sound, for example, was shown to be deducible from purely mechanical principles.

Toward the end of the century, the "unification program" had partially succeeded. Electrodynamics and optics were shown to be derivable from the same set of postulates (a set of equations proposed by Clerk Maxwell), and a connection was discovered between thermodynamics and mechanics in the so-called kinetic theory of matter, in which temperature appeared to be an aspect of the kinetic energy (a mechanical concept) of the minute particles (atoms and molecules) of which matter was composed.

There remained, then, essentially two major fields—mechanics and electrodynamics—and it seemed that nothing remained but to find the link between them for all physics to fall into a single scheme. Such a link was attempted in postulating the "ether."

Someone once pointed out that the invention of the "ether" was a *linguistic* necessity. In response to the question, "What is light?" physicists of the nineteenth century had to answer "Light is waves." The next question, "Waves of what?" could not be answered unless something could be put after "Waves of. . . . "

But the notion of the ether did not last. Already at the start, when the mechanical properties of the ether were investigated theoretically, it was found that to behave as it apparently did (as a medium for light waves) the ether had to have a rigidity far exceeding that of steel, in spite of the fact that it had no "substance" of any kind!

Whatever was done about these conceptual difficulties, the notion of the ether became untenable after the Michelson-Morley experiment,[23] which was specifically designed to measure an effect which the ether had to produce on the transmission of light if it existed at all, namely, the effect due to the velocity of the earth relative to the ether. This velocity turned out to be zero—a result one could not accept unless one went back to the biblical doctrine of a motionless earth, and this was not possible for other reasons. The Michelson-Morley experiment was a serious blow to the attempt to unify physics under the leadership of mechanics.

There were other chinks in the philosophical armor of mechanism. The unification of thermodynamics and mechanics was brought about but only at a price of introducing mathematical methods which were not based on deterministic assumptions, namely the mathematics of probability, of which there will be more to say in Chapter 14. In statistical mechanics (the border field between mechanics and thermodynamics) the mathematics of probability was only an intellectual tool—it was used because it made possible without knowing in detail the behavior of each particle to obtain knowledge about the behavior of large masses of particles. However, later, when physicists began to study the structure of atoms, it was found that determinism had to be abandoned *as a conceptual framework*, that is, the basic assumptions, had to be formulated in probabilistic terms instead of in deterministic ones, as they had been in classical mechanics.

Thus the metaphysical certainties of mechanistic metaphysics, Absolute Space, Absolute Time, and Absolute Causality (determinism) all had to fall by the wayside in twentieth-century physics. However, long before their final demise, these metaphysical certainties had already come under critical scrutiny and were found to be not nearly so free of contradictions and ambiguity as had been imagined.

POSITIVISM

A leader in the early critique of classical mechanics was Ernst Mach (33, 81). His outlook is often referred to as "positivism."[24] It was the first serious challenge to the framework of mechanistic metaphysics which had reigned supreme from the time of Newton.

According to the positivist scheme, the ultimate job of the scientist is to *describe* what set of "sense data" regularly follow what other set. Positivism was an attempt to do away with metaphysics altogether, that is, to evade the question about the nature of reality. In the positivistic formulation (I suppose it would be facetious to call it the positivistic metaphysics), it is not necessary to talk of causes and effects; it is unreasonable to demand that all phenomena be analogous to the behavior of certain kinds of engines, or, in fact, that they fall into any kind of a prescribed scheme. It is even unnecessary to postulate "forces" or "matter" as having any kind of existence. The scientist is faced not with "facts" but with "sense data," that which he sees, hears, feels, smells, or reads on dials. His job is to describe one set of "sense data" in association with another. The more general are his descriptions (that is, the more phenomena he can describe with the fewer symbols) the better job he is doing. Thus if the laws of chemical reaction can be stated by chemical equations, there is no need to postulate the existence of "atoms." If the laws of electrodynamics can be stated as a set of partial differential equations, there is no need to invent an "ether" or any other metaphysical prop.

Positivism, then, is in a way a resurrection of Hume's sceptical attitude. It abandons the search for "ultimate realities" and "causes." It seeks to describe only what "obviously" is, what one can really be positive about, that is, sense data. A strict positivist, seeing a black sheep on a meadow could not say, "There is a black sheep." He could only say, "I see a sheep, one side of which is black." If asked whether he did not really believe it was a black sheep, he might say "My previous experiences with sheep whose one side was black lead me to expect that if that sheep turned around, I should receive similar sense data." If pressed still further to say whether he was not after all saying that the sheep was black, he might, perhaps admit, "Yes, you may say 'That is a black sheep,' but you must remember that it is just a short way of saying all those other things and nothing else."

In other words, the strict positivist denies that "The sheep is black" is a fundamental fact, from which all the observations flow. He takes the observations to be fundamental. The observations *add up* to saying (for short), "The sheep is black."

Mach was probably the first to be conscious of the need for operational definitions. Although he did not stress the predictability criterion of truth, he came close to defining the truth of assertions in terms of their predictive content. In a way, it can be said, therefore, that positivism was the direct forerunner of operationalism.

THE OPERATIONAL OUTLOOK ON KNOWLEDGE

Yet positivism and operationalism are not identical. Operationalism is less extreme than positivism in disavowing metaphysical concepts. The operationalist would call such notions as "phlogiston," "ether," and others, which the positivist unequivocally condemned, "conceptual models." The operationalist sees no harm in constructing such models provided they are not taken too seriously. Models have a *heuristic* value, like diagrams in a geometric proof: they stimulate thinking and the asking of fruitful questions (22). It does not matter from the operational point of view that the notion of the "ether" turned out to be untenable. *Talking* about the ether led to certain questions and certain experiments. The experiments led to negative results, but even negative results are often instructive and stimulating. The negative result of the Michelson-Morley experiment led to the theory of relativity.

Where the positivist would demand an operational definition for every concept in physics, the operationalist admits a less strict type of definition—the postulational.[25] To indicate the difference between the two, the "ether" is again a good example. All attempts to define the "ether" operationally failed, that is, no effects could be observed which could be attributed to the "ether." However, it is a simple matter to define the "ether" postulationally: "The ether is a hypothetical medium pervading all space, such that if you postulate it, you can explain the propagation of light and of electromagnetic waves on the basis of mechanical assumptions."

The postulational definition thus reflects the need to describe something *in certain terms*. If there were no need to describe electromagnetic phenomena in mechanical terms, there would have been no need to postulate the "ether."

It follows that everything can be postulationally defined, if you want certain kinds of explanations badly enough. For example:

Phlogiston is a substance, such that if you postulate it, you can explain certain facts about combustion.

The dormitive property is a quality, such that if you postulate it, you can explain why opium puts you to sleep.

Luck is a certain principle, such that if you postulate it, you can explain why some people are more fortunate than others.

The will of God is a causative agency, such that if you postulate it, you can explain everything.

Operational philosophy, in allowing postulational definitions, does not condone such orgies of "explanations." Postulational definitions are to be chosen with a certain aim—to explain something in terms of something else *already known*. Nothing is gained if a new term is invented which does all the work of "explaining," becomes a scapegoat of the explanation, so to say. This cautionary principle was already known to William of Occam (1300–1349), who stated it as the since famous principle of parsimony: *Essentia non sunt multiplicanda praeter necessitatem.* ("Concepts are not to be multiplied beyond necessity.") Medieval scholasticists in their shop talk referred to the principle wittily as "Occam's Razor."

The principle of parsimony in a stronger form, namely, "The reduction of fundamental concepts is the aim of science," is the guiding principle in operational philosophy in the choice of notions to be defined and explanations offered. The principle of parsimony was recognized already by the positivists, who, however, considered it as only a time-saving principle. Of two descriptions of events, the shorter one was to be preferred. For the operational philosopher, the principle of parsimony is more. It is not only a guide in making formulations as economical as possible but also a measure of one's state of knowledge. To know more means, operationally speaking, *to be able to explain (or predict) more by assuming less.*

The principle of parsimony is thus a guide for making postulational definitions (definitions not recognized by the strict positivist). Where a positivist would object to using concepts because they are difficult or impossible to define strictly operationally, the operationalist can sometimes justify their use on the basis of the principle of parsimony. Examples of such concepts are the highly abstract terms of modern physics, such as "electron," "quantum," "probability wave," etc. Thus, the "electron" can be defined as an entity, such that if you assume its existence, a great many *seemingly unrelated* facts become consequences of a few principles.

The reason the operationalist today will not accept the postulational definition of "phlogiston" is because it would now violate the principle of parsimony. A great many more facts can be organized more consistently on the basis of another theory of combustion. The definitions of the "dormitive property" and "the will of God" violate the principle of parsimony even more obviously.

They are strictly *ad hoc* postulates. Like the rules in the court of the Queen of Hearts, they were invented "on the spot" to fit a given situation without reference to other situations. They lead to pseudo-explanations like the one about hating work because one is lazy.

Things defined by an operational definition are considered by the operational philosopher to be "more real" than those defined by postulational definitions. Whenever conceptual difficulties arise, the operationalist seeks operational definitions of things previously defined postulationally or left undefined. It was the operational definition applied to "an interval of time" (whose "reality" was previously considered intuitively given, and which is still defined postulationally in the classical treatment of mechanics) that led to the theory of relativity. Operational definitions of "position of a particle" and "momentum of a particle" (also assumed obvious on the basis of mechanistic metaphysics) led to the self-consistent formulation of quantum mechanics, which is the core of our present knowledge of atomic structure.

The admission of the postulational definition allows the operationalist to assume an attitude of tolerance toward areas of investigation in which operational definitions cannot yet be applied, such as in certain areas of psychology. Those areas had been under bitter attack by the adherents of the behaviorist movement, which swept over the United States in the early decades of our century. The behaviorists (the positivists of psychology) demanded an operational definition for every concept used in psychology and refused to have anything to do with any other concepts. Lately a reaction set in against behaviorism, and in certain quarters the controversy between behaviorists and their opponents is still raging.

A similar situation exists in social science. Social science too has its positivist school, where no concept which cannot be "cashed in" for "measurable observables" is taken seriously.[26] And, of course, there are those who insist that positivism in social science is sterile.

The operationalist attitude is neither strictly positivistic nor anti-positivistic. The operationalist will admit concepts postulationally defined, provided the principle of parsimony is served. Whether it is or not can be determined only by examining the framework of thought underlying every formulation. Operational philosophy serves to bare these frameworks. It is a sort of psychoanalysis applied to past and current systems of rationalization and has an aim similar to that of psychoanalysis: to free human thought from compulsions. This can be done when it becomes clear how at various times human thought was confined to this or that framework, unable, as Whitehead put it (109), to break through the current abstractions of a particular culture.

To the scholastic philosopher, knowledge was "salvation." And by knowledge he meant knowledge of eternal principles coupled with unshakable faith.

To the classical scientist (1600-1900) knowledge was power. By knowledge he meant knowledge of "facts," and the ability to manipulate and control.

To the operational philosopher, knowledge is freedom. By knowledge he means, besides the knowledge of facts and principles, the knowledge of knowledge, that is, a knowledge of how the cognitive process operates in man.

Summary of Chapters 5 and 6

The old claim of philosophy that it is concerned with the question, "Why is X?" more profoundly than science must be re-examined in the light of the meaning of the question. One should first seek out the cases where science has failed to give a causal explanation of some phenomenon and where philosophy has given it. One should then see whether the explanation offered by philosophy was truly a correlation of two distinct kinds of events or observations, and whether such correlation is corroborated in many separate instances. If such a correlation is not evident, one can only conclude that the causal explanations of philosophy are only verbal ones: they give two names to the same event.

The operationalist's attitude toward causality is a pragmatic one. Any causal explanation is acceptable if it serves the principle of parsimony or indicates a manipulative situation. These are also the operationalist's criteria of "reality." Real is what can be operated upon. Operations can range from moving things about to using symbols in equations. There are many levels of reality depending on the operations involved. The reality of beer is in that you can drink it. The reality of π is that you can compute areas of circles and probability integrals with it. The reality of the causal relation between bad housing and delinquency is in the fact that if one improves housing, delinquency decreases. Thus "reality," "causality," and all the other metaphysical categories are defined by the operationalist in terms of situations in which certain regularities occur in which the usefulness of such concepts seems justified. Their usefulness is justified if the principle of parsimony is served or if the manipulability and predictability of the world is increased.

Attempts to define operationally some of the time-honored "fundamental" concepts of classical physics have led to the overthrow of those concepts. The expected invariants were shown not to be invariants. But even as the imperfection of the old invariants became apparent, new, more general invariants were discovered revealing the regularity and constancy of nature in all its splendor.

These invariants, however, can be won neither by symbol manipulation alone (as old philosophers thought) nor by observation of "sense data" alone (as the empiricists from Francis Bacon on thought). They are forged by the teamwork of experimenters and "philosophers," that is, philosophers in the modern sense who are experimenters with ideas. This teamwork has introduced into creative scientific thought a unique mixture of discipline and freedom. The discipline results from the imposition of severe tests on statements seeking promotion to meaningfulness and truth. The freedom is in the exercise of the imagination, in the creation of significant constructs, the kind of imagination that has led to the invention of "space curvature," "electron spins," and "probability waves." This is no longer the imagination that gave birth to naive metaphors and superficial analogies of animistic and organismic metaphysics. It is the disciplined imagination of the mature, creative, self-critical mind, the sort of mind that cannot feel free without a self-imposed discipline.

Part II. OPERATIONAL ETHICS

Chapter 7. IS THERE A CHOICE?

Eᴛʜɪᴄs, traditionally an important part of philosophy, is concerned with the question, "What is good?" In applying logical analysis to this question, we might proceed as before, that is,

1. Put the question into a more specific form: "Is X good?" (just as we replaced "What is truth?" by "Is assertion X true?");

2. Look for the commonly accepted criteria for "good" (just as we did for "true");

3. See how these criteria are applied, especially noting the confusions between the various meanings of "good" and the limitations imposed by particular frameworks of thought; and

4. Derive operationally sound criteria, that is, those which enable us to avoid pitfalls and contradictions.

Before I embark on this program, however, I would like right at the outset to make one obvious point. If one accepts the operational point of view (that thought needs to be related to action), there does not seem to be much sense in worrying whether X is good or whether X ought to be if nothing can be done about X. To be specific, it seems reasonable to ask, "What kind of a government ought we to have?" but silly to ask, "How many planets ought there to be?" This is so, because most of us believe that something can be done about governments but that nothing can be done about the number of planets.

Philosophers, however, are not always guided by such practical considerations. Hegel, for example, once offered an argument on why there "ought" to be exactly seven planets.[27] He also offered a proof that the ultimate form of government for humanity will inevitably be something closely resembling the Prussian state of his time. It is not likely that Hegel believed that one can do something about the planets. His "ought" (to give him the benefit of the doubt) was probably derived from a "logical" not an ethical compulsion. But the distinction is by no means clear. Nor is it clear whether he considers the inevitability of the "perfect state" as following from logical necessity or from ethical conviction.

Examples of how questions like "What is?" or "What will be?" are confused with "What ought to be?" are common in our own day. A few years ago, at a "scientific" conference some Soviet biologists and philosophers argued* in effect that characteristics acquired by an organism during its life ought to be transmissible to its offspring, because such a mechanism of heredity would be beneficial to Soviet agriculture and would embarrass Western biologists.[28] On the other hand, it is quite common to hear arguments that one side or another will win a conflict, because "right" is on that side.

I will try to keep the question of what is true or inevitable distinct from the question of what is desirable. In fact, I believe that the very nature of the term "desirable" implies an element of choice and therefore an indeterminacy of sorts. Questions of ethics are therefore relevant if and only if a choice exists. Of importance in ethics, then, is the question, "Is choice ever possible? If so, when?" People who take an extreme deterministic view and deny (or think that they deny) that choice is ever possible should never say what "ought" to be, because what they say will, according to their own view, make no difference. If there is no choice, one cannot make or influence choices. For people who take the other extreme and maintain that all human behavior is a result of choice, all activity becomes tinged with morality. They are unable to see how human behavior can be studied in terms of causes and effects.

Our own ethical and legal systems reflect a conviction that a man has a choice to steal or not to steal but that he has little or no choice in becoming or not becoming sick. Accordingly, we punish theft and sympathize with disease. Samuel Butler in his novel *Erewhon* (15) points up the arbitrariness of this attitude by describing a society in which the exact opposite occurs. People who commit "crimes" (in our sense of the word) are cared for and coddled, while those who become "sick" (again in our sense of the word) are censured and punished. Underlying this philosophy is simply an opinion opposite to ours as to what is and what is not a matter of choice.

Since there are so many conflicting ideas on the nature of choice, some sort of definition seems called for. Instead of defining choice,

*They won the argument.

however, I will define the absence of choice, what is commonly known as determinism. The meaning of choice or "free will" (as it is known in theology) will emerge from the meaning of determinism.

DETERMINISM AND "FREE WILL"

Determinism involves a relation among specific events and an invariance. An event Z will be said to be determined regardless of certain other events A, B, C, etc., if Z occurs regardless of whether A, B, C, etc., occur or do not occur.

Example: Event Z is the arrival of train No. 384. A, B, C, etc., are various events which can in no way affect the arrival of the train, such as the conversations in the waiting room, the dishes served in the restaurant, the behavior of the railroad clock, or the weather (within limits). We see at once that event Z is not determined regardless of *any* event. For instance, a heavy snowfall or a faulty switch can prevent the arrival of the train.

There are, however, events which seem to be determined regardless of what happens, such as astronomical events. The common saying, "It is certain as night follows day" is a reflection of our experience that the succession of day and night is a determined sequence regardless of all known events. That is to say, no one can name a situation in which the alteration of day and night can be disturbed. Let us call such events *apparently absolutely determined events.*

The notion of determinism comes from generalizing the experiences dealing with apparently absolutely determined events. An obvious apparently absolutely determined event of great importance to men is death. There are also other such relentless processes which occur no matter what men try to do to prevent them. By far-fetched generalization and extrapolation (activities peculiar to the human kind) men have in many instances inferred an absolute determinism in nature. In some philosophies, this appears as the irresistible will of a god (for example, in Judeo-Christian religion and in Greek mythology); in others, something to which even the gods must submit (for example, in the writings of Spinoza and of Richard Wagner). Whatever its mythological origin, the principle of determinism (be it called fate or *kismet* or predestination or historical materialism) emphasizes the helplessness of man and the relentlessness of the course of events unfolding to their predestined conclusion.

A. N. Whitehead (109) points out that one of the pillars of scientific philosophy has been (until recently) the principle of determinism, which, he says, is rooted in the ancient conception of fate. Whitehead even draws an analogy between scientific ritual and the stagecraft of Greek tragedy. He relates, for example, how at a meeting of the Royal Society the announcement was made that Einstein's prediction concerning the bending of light rays in a gravitational field was confirmed. The atmosphere of that meeting, says Whitehead, was reminiscent of the dramatic climax of a classical Greek tragedy where the fulfillment of the prophecy is announced by a messenger.*

Determinism, then, is the stuff of which both science and tragedy seem to be made. The tragic character of determinism is most clearly apparent when the future is *known and appalling,* but nothing can be done about it. A famous example is the tragedy of Oedipus (93). Horrified at the prospect that his son will kill him and marry the mother, Oedipus' father does everything he can to prevent it. But it so turns out that the very things he does insure the fulfillment of the prophecy.

Science, on the other hand, reveals the "happy" side of determinism. If nature is deterministic, it can be *relied* upon. If natural phenomena occur with regularity, they can be *predicted,* not only by gods or by oracles or by rarely inspired individuals with a gift of prophecy but by ordinary people using well-defined and teachable techniques.

There is another crucial difference between the ancient tragic conception of determinism and the modern scientific one. Tragic determinism is absolute. It presupposes events determined regardless of *all* other events, in particular regardless of human knowledge. The tragic character of this determinism is rooted in this irrelevance of human knowledge to the course of events. Peter denies his association with Jesus *in spite* of having been told that he would do so.† The determinism of science, on the other hand, is relative to certain events only. The predictions of science are usually stated in "If so, then so" terms, that is, a limitation is placed on those events regardless of which other events are determined. For example, the

*See also *Macbeth,* Act V, Scene 5:
　　　　Messenger: As I did stand my watch upon the hill,
　　　　　　　　　　I look'd towards Birnam, and anon, methought,
　　　　　　　　　　The Wood began to move.
(Macbeth had been told that he has nothing to fear "till Birnam Wood do come to Dunsinane.")
†Matt. 26:69-75.

statement, "If the water supply is polluted, an epidemic will occur," implies a limitation on the determinism of the epidemic, since the epidemic can be prevented if the pollution of the water supply is prevented.

Does the ability to control a situation, then, constitute the existence of choice? Can we not say that our apparent choices are themselves events which are determined? Yes, we can say so, but our say-so would have more weight if we could support it by evidence. When the astronomer says that an eclipse will certainly occur (is determined), he means that no matter what you choose to do, *that specific event* will occur *as predicted*. To say with equal assurance that a man's choice is determined should mean that the man will make a choice (as actually predicted) regardless of any event, regardless even of his knowledge that someone has predicted his choice. Now in some instances this can be shown to be the case. Choices of men can actually be predicted and occur as predicted under a great variety of conditions. The behavior of large masses of people can be predicted even more accurately and under a greater variety of conditions. In these cases, the determinism of choices can be established. But it should be borne in mind that this determinism can be established only with respect to certain conditions. Extrapolation of these cases to a universal principle is unwarranted.

Determinism, therefore, is bound up with the fulfillment of predictions. Paradoxically, what we usually call choice (or "free will") is also bound up with the fulfillment of predictions. If I am asked to demonstrate what I mean when I say that I have a choice to raise my arm or not to raise it, I can do so only by saying, "Now I will raise my arm" and raising it, or "Now I won't" and not raising it. If it is now pointed out that I had no choice but say "Now I will raise my arm," I can go a step further back and say, "Now I will say 'Now I will raise my arm' " and then say it. My opponent can, of course, carry the argument another step, but then so can I. The argument about the existence or nonexistence of choice reduces to a contest of endurance.

This, then, is not a fruitful way to analyze the meaning of "choice." Nor do deductive arguments serve any purpose. The most they can do is demonstrate that the existence of choice follows from certain assumptions. But it can be proven equally well that determinism follows from certain other assumptions, and we are nowhere.

The fruitful way to proceed is to examine the situations in which the presence or the absence of choice is usually assumed and thus get at the *usage* of the terms "choice" and "determinism." Further investigation can then show, perhaps, whether the usage is internally consistent and whether it bears some relation to facts. Let us take a few cases at random.

Case 1: Mr. A says, "I am going to fly to Montevideo next Tuesday," and does so. The prevalent opinion is that Mr. A had a choice of going or not going.

Case 2: Mr. B says, "I will get a terrible stage fright when I have to give my speech next Tuesday. My voice will shake, and I will barely struggle through it." And so it happens. The prevalent opinion is that Mr. B had no choice in this matter.

Case 3: Mr. C says, "I keep quarreling with Mrs. C. Neither of us wants to quarrel, but we do." Opinion of whether Mr. and Mrs. C have a choice of quarreling or not quarreling is divided.

Case 4: While Mr. D is under hypnosis, it is suggested to him that on waking up he will open the window, and he does. Asked why he opened the window, he replies, "It is stuffy here." Those who know that Mr. D was acting out a hypnotic suggestion think that Mr. D had no choice in this matter, while those who are ignorant of that fact (including Mr. D himself) may insist that he had.

In these and in similar examples, we can see that

1. We tend to consider a course of events determined if we can successfully predict it under a great variety of conditions.

2. We tend to exclude our own actions from the class of determined events though we can predict them, because of our "inner" feeling that we can change our minds at a moment's notice. By projecting this inner feeling to beings most like ourselves (usually other people) we attribute the same ability to them, especially in actions over which we have no control and over which they seem to exercise control.

3. If an act is performed "against the will" of the actor, we tend to conclude that the actor had no choice. What should be considered "against the will" is not usually specified clearly; hence the divided opinions about choice in matters involving "compulsive acts."

We see that with regard to the outside world, the connection between determinism and predictability is clear (the more we can predict, and the wider the range of events which are irrelevant to the prediction, the more "determined" is the event predicted). Not so with regard to our "inner" world. Here the question of "will," "intention," or "desire" enters as an extra component and complications arise. If we can predict our own actions and if they seem in accordance with our desires, we say we have choice. By projection, we extend this criterion to others: if someone else predicts his actions, which he declares to be in accordance with his desires, we usually concede to him the possession of choice. On the other hand, if we can predict someone's action, and he cannot, or if someone acts contrary to what we believe to be his desire, we conclude that he has no choice.

It follows that every predicted action would be an action of choice *if the desires themselves could be chosen at will*, because if we could predict our actions, we could choose desires to fit them, and so all our actions would harmonize with our desires. This is what Schopenhauer said cannot be done (87). "Man can do what he will, but he cannot will what he will." Implied in this opinion is the assumption that the desires themselves are determined, and that our feeling about possessing freedom of choice is an illusion which arises when our acts are in accordance with our desires. It is only an illusion, Schopenhauer declares, because we are not free in the choice of our desires.

That this judgment is at least to some degree not unfounded can be seen from the example of post-hypnotic suggestion. The man who opens the window thinks that he has choice, because he feels that he is acting in accordance with his "desire." Those who have seen him under hypnosis know where this desire came from, and to them it appears that he has no choice. But the hypnotic experiment reveals something else, namely, that it is sometimes possible to "plant" desires.

But if it is *known* that desires are planted, it may be possible to discover where they came from. It is conceivable that if the man immediately upon waking up were told that he was expected to act under the compulsion of the post-hypnotic suggestion, he would suddenly acquire the "freedom" of not yielding to it. In fact, the entire therapeutic procedure of psychoanalysis was designed to trace the genesis of "undesirable desires" and thus to impart greater freedom of choice to people.* The importance of recalling the experiences of early childhood in psychoanalytic theory is precisely in the opportunity this provides for learning how and when desires were "planted." It is assumed that just as the "victim" of post-hypnotic

---

*It is noteworthy that before Freud developed the technique of psychoanalysis, he had used hypnosis in psychotherapy.

suggestion can cast off the spell by discovering the origin of his desire, so can the patient undergoing psychotherapy be rid of compulsions when he realizes where they came from.

Of particular concern to us (as they were to the ancients) are the *tragic* consequences of determinism, that is, situations where absence of choice coincides with a course of events undesirable to us. There are innumerable situations where we have no choice or freedom, but we hardly worry. For example, the reader has no freedom to commit suicide. No matter how strongly he feels he could if only he wanted to, he cannot prove it. It can only be concluded, therefore, that he has no freedom in this matter (or, more accurately, he has no freedom to *want* to commit suicide). This, however, should normally be of no concern. Nor should we be worried about the determinism of astronomical events. We have got along well enough, even though we have no voice whatsoever in the management of the cosmic universe. In fact, we should be glad that these matters are outside our reach. It is different if we discover tendencies within us which we cannot help but whose consequences we deplore. The alcoholic, the delinquent, the compulsive neurotic, who realizes his predicament, finds himself in this painful position.

Of even greater importance are situations where desires are deliberately planted into large masses of people by ruthless individuals or groups to serve their own purposes. We are living in an age when the behavior of millions is manipulated by demagoguery, propaganda, and slick "public relations." It often appears to the victims of this manipulation that they are acting in accordance with their choices and therefore are "free." There is more to freedom, however, than a feeling of acting in accordance with one's desires, as we usually realize when the consequences of our "choices" reveal themselves.

Since ethics can have a meaning only to the extent that choice is possible, a central problem of ethics should be to determine what we are free to choose, under what conditions and to what extent. Are the limitations of choice as stringent as Schopenhauer maintained? For example, we might ask whether it is not possible to push our "freedom" another notch, as it were, in learning to choose our desires? To be sure, even if we learn to do this, there will surely appear another Schopenhauer among us who will point out, "Yes, you do choose your desires, but this *latter* choice is still governed by *desires of a higher order* (the desire to choose a particular kind of desire), and with respect to these you have no choice."

This we will concede and only point out that a step taken once may be taken again. If it is argued that there will always be a "basic" set of desires (or drives) which are "there," built into our very "natures" and about which we can do nothing, this too can be conceded. But it is nothing to worry about. Schopenhauer was worried because he assumed that we are inevitably *frustrated* in our basic desires, because they are either unfulfillable or mutually contradictory. The hopeful assumption of operational ethics is that these unfulfillable and mutually contradictory desires are not *basic*. They are derivative or secondary, the results of inadequate or unsane evaluative processes in man. It therefore becomes the task of operational ethics to uncover basic desires, about which (it is true) we can do nothing, since they are part of the business of being human, but about which we need not worry, since they need be neither frustrating nor mutually contradictory. Once such basic desires are uncovered, it is the task of operational philosophy to point the way toward a possibility of choosing nonfrustrating and mutually consistent courses of action.

SUMMARY OF CHAPTER 7, AND SOME CONCLUSIONS

Ethical questions apply only where choice exists. In fact, ethics is the problem of making good choices. Therefore one of the principal tasks of ethics is to determine what is and what is not a matter of choice. The task is not easy, since "being a matter of choice" is not an objective fact but a consequence of a point of view. Part of the task is therefore to find out what matters become "matters of choice" from what points of view. This clearly relates the operational theory of ethics to the operational theory of knowledge, which deals with the analysis of the various frameworks of thought.

Another part of the task is to exclude from ethics the matters which are not "matters of choice" and which therefore do not belong in ethics. If, for example, it becomes clear that a man had no choice in performing a certain act (that is, the act was predictable by others and could not be forestalled in spite of having been predicted), it also becomes clear that ethical considerations do not apply to such an act. To some extent even our legal system realizes this limitation in not holding "insane" individuals responsible for their actions. For example, if we learn that we can do nothing about having sexual desires, it becomes irrelevant to ask whether we "ought" to have them.

On the other hand, many acts which at first seem compulsory

become, in the light of analysis, matters of choice. It may be possible, for example, to point out to a husband of an "erring wife" that what seems to him an insuperable compulsion to kill her in order to clear his name is not a compulsion at all (again in the light of analysis) but a matter of choice.

Of great importance, therefore, is the task of finding the "irreducibles," that is, those "values" or "desires" or "drives" or "basic premises" which we cannot abandon without resigning from the human race.

Chapter 8. ENDS AND MEANS

THE question, "Is X good?" can be asked only if X is a matter of choice. For example, we cannot ask "Is death good?" if we have admitted that death is inevitable. The reason the question seems to have meaning (most people would answer, "Death is not good") is because death can sometimes be avoided at a specific time. Generally speaking, however, "Is life good?" or "Is death good?" ("To be or not to be") is a meaningful question only if we are contemplating suicide.

With these considerations in mind, let us go on with our analysis. Following the method established in Part I, let us put the question this way: "To what do people refer when they speak of the 'Good'?"

Some students of ethics may feel that we are not getting to the bottom of things when we put the question this way. In the opinion of some philosophers there exists a "Good" independently of what people think is good. If there does exist such a Good, then the question we have put seems superficial. It aims to reduce one of the most important investigations of all time to an opinion poll. This would be so if we were content to go no further than to record everyone's opinion on what is good. However, let us see what happens if we treat our "opinion poll" only as a point of departure and not as the end of our investigation.

An investigation which begins with a recording of observations is called an empirical investigation. Therefore a study of ethics which would begin with such an investigation could be called the foundation of an "empirical ethics." If ethics is to be operational, it must have a root in empirical ethics. But if ethics is to be something more than just a record of what people say is "good," one must find significant *invariants* in the record. The logical construction of an operational ethics will be based on such invariants. For example, it may be found that large groups of people with a common history and

93

common pursuits tend to give similar answers to what they mean by "good." The record may then be simplified. Instead of a huge compilation of hundreds of millions of answers, it can be reduced to a few sets of answers, each a digest of the views of a large group of people. Whenever such summaries have been compiled, it was found that there are among various groups conflicting notions about what is good. Such inconsistencies lead some people to maintain that there can be no such thing as a *general* ethics, that the most one can hope to establish is the various notions that various groups have about what is "good."

Scientific experience, however, suggests that we may go a step further beyond the seeming inconsistencies. The possibility of doing so appears from the following analogy. It appears at first sight that the needs of animals and plants are so different as to be incompatible. Most animals move about in search of food and mates, while most plants are content to be fixed in one place all their life, in fact may die if they are uprooted. Yet plants eat, drink, breathe, and procreate just like animals. They appear to lead an entirely different sort of life, because they use different mechanisms to perform these functions. But when we look closely at what these functions consist of, we are impressed with the similarities between what plants do and what animals do. Metabolism for both is chiefly a synthesis of certain substances (enzymes, proteins, nucleic acids, etc.) and a breakdown of others (especially the oxidation of sugars). Procreation for both is essentially the division of cells to form new cells. All the other aspects of this process, such as courtship, the shedding of seeds, germination, mating, and pollination, are simply different mechanisms accompanying the basic invariant one—the formation of new cells similar to old ones. No matter how endlessly varied are the processes by which life goes on, one finds certain fundamental invariants in all life.

Such observations suggest that, granted that the pursuits of various human groups are widely varied and often in conflict with each other, we may find some that are common to all groups. The first such pursuit is common not only to all human groups but to all living things, animal and vegetable, and that is a striving to survive.

POSSIBLE INVARIANT NEEDS

Where does the desire to survive come from? The answer is obvious if the question is related to such questions as "Why do we have eyes, ears, stomachs, pancreases?" Because if we did not have them, we would not be here to ask the question. The question is of the same sort as "Why are there pebbles on the tops of protrusions in eroded areas?" (cf. p. 69). Because where there were no pebbles, there could be no protrusions. The "desire to survive" (or, in behaviorist terms, the patterns of behavior insuring survival) is the result of natural selection. Organisms endowed with it survived and left progeny in which it was perpetuated by heredity (92).

However, there are other ways to insure the survival of a species than for each individual to insure his own survival. From the point of view of perpetuating the species, the survival of the individual is important only until progeny has been produced. It is natural, therefore, that among some organisms, at least, another behavior pattern should have been selected for, namely, a "desire" to insure the survival of the offspring, even sometimes at the cost of the loss of the desire to insure one's own survival. Such patterns are observed among birds and mammals and are popularly attributed to "parental instincts."

And there are still other ways to insure the survival of species and groups. That is the development of behavior patterns in which the survival of the *group* is protected even at the cost of individual lives. Such patterns are also observed, as, for example in the defensive mechanisms of the bee, who often loses her life in stinging an "enemy." In less extreme form, these mechanisms are reflected in the gregarious habits of many animals (the formation of flocks and herds).

Man, too, is gregarious and it is almost certain that his gregariousness is a result of natural selection, since the high degree of cooperation in human societies is of enormous survival value. The behavior patterns associated with gregariousness I will assume to be determined by the second "invariant need" of man—the *need to belong*.

The need to belong is the need to identify the "self" with something that transcends it. It is exemplified in the child's relation to the family group, then to the peer group, then in adulthood to the various "in-groups" of local, political, cultural, or national character, and finally in the frameworks of thought underlying the Great Religions, in which the identification of the self with the whole of humanity (or even with something larger) is affirmed.

A third invariant need I will call the *need for order*. It seems to underlie all intellectual activity of man, both artistic and scientific. Art is essentially an ordering, a placing of events into space and time sequences with discernible rhythms. The most elementary art ᴀorms are rhythmic patterns (dance, percussion music, abstract geometric designs on textiles and pottery). The more involved art forms can often be seen as superpositions of various rhythmic patterns on each other (for example, in music, melodic and harmonic patterns superimposed on stress patterns; in painting, the fitting of forms and colors into spatial patterns; in poetry, the fitting of word sounds and of recurrent meanings into stress patterns). Esthetic satisfaction can thus be interpreted as resulting from the successful ordering of a portion of the world.[29]

Under the same category one can include "pure science," meaning any attempts to explain the universe without reference to immediate utilitarian needs. Thus the most profound cosmologic theories derived in modern physics and the naive legendary cosmologies of pre-scientific peoples both come under the category of "pure science."[30]

The fourth invariant I will call the *need for security*—for some assurance that the gratifications of the other needs are not only present but can also be expected to continue in the future. (Sometimes the present is altogether devoid of gratification. The need for "security" is then simply the need for hope.)

The need for security stems from the perception of time, which is highly developed in humans. The word "tomorrow" is probably present in all human languages. The time sense makes possible the "mental rehearsals" of the future, which can bring pleasure and pain often keener than the actual situations they depict.

These, then, are the apparent invariant needs of man: the need for survival, the need for self-extension, the need for order, and the need for security. The list can be lengthened if it can be shown that there are other invariant needs, or it can be shortened if it is shown that one of the needs listed here is only a variation or a special instance of another. But that *some* invariant needs do exist cannot be doubted if only because man is biologically a single species and has wandered freely over the earth, so that roughly the same selective factors have operated on all men and have made men what they are.

The important point in my argument does not depend on just how the invariant needs are to be described. The important point is that they exist. If they exist, then the question, "Are they good?" cannot be applied to them, simply because nothing can be done about them. The question, "Is survival good?" has no sense like the question "Am I really experiencing what I am experiencing?" *Just*

*as the important questions concerning the reality of experience have
to do with relating some experiences to others, so the important
questions of ethics have to do with relating some needs to others.*

It is sensible to ask, "Is the pursuit of power good?" or "Is the
pursuit of knowledge good?" if these questions lead to an investigation of how the pursuit of knowledge or of power is related to the
invariant needs, such as those of survival or security. But it makes
no sense to ask, "Is the pursuit of security good?" if it is found that
the pursuit of security in one form or another is universal. In short,
it is sensible to evaluate the ethical implications of the means
used in the pursuit of the goals, but not of the goals themselves.

Ethical Relativism

The recognition that the question "Is X good?" has sense only
if X is related to some need has led many thinkers (particularly
among anthropologists) to a position known as ethical relativism.
Ethical relativism has a certain formal similarity to operationalism
in the sense that a relativist refuses to judge the ethical value of an
action except by its fitness in a given value system, just as the
operationalist refuses to judge the truth of an assertion except by
its fitness in a certain scheme of prediction.

There is, however, an important difference between the two
attitudes. The operationalist assumes a common basis of human experience: the sun is bright and the snow white for all men. He extends this assumption to postulate a common basis of human need:
all men seek health and company of other men. The operationalist
therefore believes that it is possible to construct a general system
of values based on the ways and means of satisfying general needs.

The relativist, on the other hand, either does not recognize the
existence of invariant needs, believing that needs are largely determined by specific cultural patterns and therefore are as varied as
those patterns; or he does recognize the existence of invariant needs
but believes that each cultural pattern is an equally "justifiable"
way to seek the satisfaction of those needs. Since the value systems
associated with the different patterns often clash, it is impossible,
according to the relativist, to find a common value system for man.
In either case, the relativist insists that any ethical evaluation of an
act must be with reference to a particular ethical system.

The relativist's job in presenting a systematic approach to ethics
is the easier one. Culturally conditioned values are usually apparent.
They are declared or can be inferred from the religions, legal sys-

tems, literatures, or mythologies of the various cultures. The relativist does not undertake the job of evaluating a whole culture from an ethical point of view, because he has no supra-cultural point of view from which to make such an evaluation.

The operationalist, on the other hand, must undertake the ethical analysis of cultures, because he believes he does possess a supra-cultural point of view, at least with regard to the current notions of "culture." If these definitions are examined, it will be found that the term "culture" refers to a framework of "means" within which certain "ends" are pursued. If the existence of invariant needs is granted (and some relativists do grant it),* then every culture is characterized by the means of pursuing those ends. And so it is. Every culture has certain characteristic methods of insuring survival (hunting, agriculture, industry, mixed economies, etc.). It has characteristic patterns of self-extension and association (family organization, communities, various forms and conceptions of the state, religious ideas). It has a characteristic system of philosophy and "science," according to which the universe is explained, events are ordered, and accepted channels of artistic expression are developed. Finally, every culture has a system of security, such as a military organization or a legal system or a system of reassuring beliefs about the possibility of influencing events by science or magic or a faith in "salvation."

DIFFERENTIATION OF THE MEANS

How did the various cultural patterns and their associated value systems originate? It is reasonable to suppose that they became what they are by "transforming means into ends." The fact that man is able to retain his experience enables him to pursue his goals by indirect routes. This characteristic is in marked contrast to the ways of other animals. A grazing animal, for example, spends most of its life eating. Eating bears a simple and direct relation to survival. But man, relying on technological methods to insure survival, spends his working time in activities which only after a chain of intermediate ends insure survival. He tills the soil, sows seeds, harvests, builds shelters for himself and his cattle, etc. His attention is characteristically turned to these intermediate tasks, and it is the

---

*Other relativists do not grant it, but to those I have nothing to say. If *basic* needs of different groups of people are irreconcilable, then clearly any attempt to develop a general ethics is futile, just as it would be futile to arrive at any definition of truth if there were no common experiences among men.

problems developing from these tasks that tax his ingenuity and guide his aspirations. Thus the end, "survival," may be *identified* with a particular set of means on which a particular group may have concentrated to insure survival.

For example, one group may have noticed that more fish can be caught with more efficient fishing equipment. Consequently ship building, net making, etc., became important for that group. Abilities and circumstances which favor these activities became "values." Another group may have noticed that its increase of population outstrips available soil, but that more land would be available if the people inhabiting it were driven off. Consequently this group may develop a war technology, and for this group military skill, bravery in battle, etc., may become supreme values.

Until some general concepts of "ends," "means," "causality," etc., arise in the language of a culture, this fixation of attention on particular means for the achievement of a fundamental goal takes place without awareness. Such awareness can come only when the experience of the people has become so rich that they can *pose* their problems and consider alternatives for solving them. The history of mankind, although full of problem solving, has not been marked by a widespread consciousness of such general problems. The chieftains did not call the tribe together to say, "We are getting crowded. What shall we do? We can (1) make war on our neighbors; (2) develop more intensive methods of farming; (3) develop skills to produce goods for exchange; (4) practice birth control; (5) emigrate; etc. . . ."

In our detachment, we see impending starvation as a "problem" with alternative solutions. But our ancestors felt it in terms of fear and despair. Some form of action seemed *obviously* called for. If the action was successful, the pattern for further such actions was assured.

And so at various times at various places various ways of insuring survival developed. If one lived by war, one needed weapons and leadership. Therefore, one needed weapon-makers and leaders. Leaders were most effective if they possessed certain character traits. Leaders also had to be respected. Therefore certain character traits had to be held in reverence, etc. If one lived by agriculture, a strongly developed sense of property was useful. Slaves were also useful. Moreover, the notion "slave" and the notion "property" are easily harmonized with each other, etc.

The same sort of "piling up" process may have determined the other characteristics of a culture—its patterns of self-extension, its systems of ordering experience, and its security measures.

Take self-extension: In the growing child it seems to start with the identification of the self, perhaps with the sense of control over one's own body, which does not extend to other objects. "I can move my fingers and toes if I want to, but I can't make the ball come to me." The world is roughly divided into "me" and "not-me."

But the boundary is not a sharp one. The child can manipulate other things besides his hands and feet. There are objects to grasp and examine, and even persons to be manipulated, in particular one special person who can usually be made to appear by using one's vocal chords. The socialization process has started. The feeling is established that needs can be satisfied if they are communicated, at first by arbitrary vocalizations, later by the use of articulate language.

One can "extend one's self" by manipulating the world. But there is also an opposite process. One becomes aware of one's dependence on others. One becomes aware that the strength of the "greater self" (family, tribe, etc.) is far greater than one's own. This strength appears both as a limitation to one's own desires and as a bulwark of defense against the hostile "outside." One therefore extends one's self by denying the self as an independent entity, by dissolving it into the generalized self of the group.

I must forgo, of course, an exposition of a theory of personality development, since I would only be repeating what others with more right to say so have said.[31] Significant for my purposes are only the broadest conclusions of such theories, namely, that the development of a personality involves an established pattern of manipulating the world and of coming to terms with it. To the extent that the one or the other process brings greater gratifications of the need for self-extension, the means used will be promoted to "ends" and will develop the "ethos" of the personality.

The tyrant or the tycoon who thinks exclusively in terms of manipulating others, the mystic who strives to extinguish in himself all traces of "desire," or the docile conformist who guides his desires exclusively by imitating the apparent desires of those around him are all extreme products of this process. The actual distribution of personality types in a given culture will usually be determined by the values established in that culture and will, in turn, help perpetuate those same values.

Take now the need to order experience: We have already seen how the ordering of direct experience (explanations) proceeds by fitting the evaluation of experience into a framework of thought in which certain criteria of consistency are met. These frameworks constitute the various types of metaphysics in various cultures and so determine the state of science and philosophy that can be attained within its limits.

Similar frameworks determine the organization of esthetic experience. They constitute the *language* of esthetic experience. In Chapter 1, I called attention to the difficulties which beset a jazz enthusiast who wants to communicate his feelings about jazz to an addict of nineteenth-century musical taste. I said they did not speak the same "language," because they had no overlapping area of musical experience. I must now amplify this statement. Matters usually do not improve much even if the jazz enthusiast listens to a lot of Schubert, and the "square" visits a lot of jam sessions (although sometimes some improvement of communication does occur). The lack of understanding is deeper than in the lack of overt experience (listening to certain kinds of music). The lack of understanding stems rather in attempts to relate experience to a frame of reference into which it does not fit. The question of how various esthetic frameworks developed in various cultures is one of extreme difficulty. It has not yet been successfully attacked.

Take finally the need for security: This need is obviously related to the others. In fact, it has been defined as the need to feel that the other needs will continue to be satisfied. Now the learning process is such that successful patterns of behavior tend to be entrenched. What has seemed to satisfy our needs in the past will be relied upon to satisfy them in the future. Thus a sedentary culture will relate its security to the possession of land, while a nomadic culture will relate it to freedom of movement. A tradition-oriented civilization will see security in the perpetuation of its own social structure (where everyone knows and, perhaps, loves his place), while an expanding civilization will value the assurance that initiative is rewarded by a promotion in status (equal opportunity to all). In still other cases, where the present state of affairs is unbearable and there is no opportunity to speak of (as with enslaved or exploited populations), the need for security may give birth to ideas about an idealized state of affairs beyond the grave. Impressive examples of this sort are the outlooks of the early Christians and of the Negroes in American plantation life.

It appears therefore that a wide variety of behavior can be accounted for in terms of attempts to fulfill a few fundamental needs. The hoodlum, who identifies himself with his gang, the patriot, who identifies himself with his nation, and the saint, who identifies himself with all mankind, are all motivated by the same need, the need of self-extension. Elizabeth Tudor in having Mary Stuart beheaded, the Chinese philosopher in glorifying the ways of the ancestors, John Doe, in buying insurance, and the editors of *Pravda* in castigating the decadence of Western culture are all motivated by the same need, the need for security.

This is as far as the operationalist goes hand in hand with the relativist, who points out that various value systems are various ways of pursuing the same goals. Or rather, this is as far as the ethical relativist goes. The operationalist must go further. He must evaluate the value systems themselves.

The operationalist is convinced that some value systems are better equipped than others to facilitate the pursuit of fundamental goals. He challenges the argument sometimes offered by the relativist that *because* a certain culture with its associated value system has remained stable for a long time, it must be well fitted to serve the needs of its members. Such an argument may account for the survival of biological species, whose evolution extends over tremendous periods of time, so that natural selection has billions of variations to choose from. The "evolution" of human cultures, however, took place only in the last few millennia. There were not billions of subtly varying cultures with differential birth rates to choose from to insure the survival of the fittest. Therefore it was possible even for most "inefficient" cultures to survive, at least during the time under archeological and historical scrutiny.

To be sure, a counterargument may be offered. Even though the time of cultural evolution is much shorter than that of biological evolution, cultural evolution is also much faster, because it depends not on random mutations but on the much more rapid learning process (time-binding), in which useful patterns of behavior may be rapidly accumulated, since successful patterns tend to entrench themselves (like useful mutations). This argument is not conclusive. In the human learning process, not only do the successful patterns tend to entrench themselves, but so also do the unsuccessful ones. This happens because of the way "means" tend to be promoted to "ends," often long after they have ceased to be effective means. This is seen in the various taboos and compulsions which persist long after they have ceased to be of value and even when they become definitely harmful from the point of view of serving the invariant needs. *Fixation on nonadaptive forms of behavior is as characteristic of cultures as it is of neurotics.*

The operationalist, therefore, insists on putting the various culture patterns and especially their associated ethical systems under scrutiny. To facilitate a broad outlook some system of classification is needed. Various classifications of cultures have been attempted by anthropologists. The early attempts placed all cultures on a one-dimensional scale ranging from the "savage" state through "barbarism" to "civilization." A moral development was supposed to go hand in hand with the technological, so that the possessors of the most efficient machines and weapons (usually the countrymen of the anthropologists) were automatically the most virtuous characters. The rise of the "functionalist" school in anthropology was a reaction against these views. The functionalists showed that a "unilinear" evolutionary path could not be traced in human cultures and that it was naive to consider the Indonesians and the West Africans as retarded Englishmen, who, if only given enough time will inevitably embrace cricket, cravats, and Christianity. The notion of "universal progress" was discarded and with it went the notion that morality could be gauged on a scale.

Modern anthropology, therefore, adopts a different classification system for cultures. It can, perhaps, be called a "professional" system of classification, in which things go together which belong together from the professional anthropologist's point of view. It is much like the classification system applied by linguists to language, admirably adapted to the study of language as an isolated entity with its own laws of development. Such a classification of cultures, however, does not serve the purposes of a general ethics any more than the linguist's classification of languages serves the purposes of a general theory of communication.

For a general ethics, we need a classification of ethical systems independent of the cultures in which they arise. Such a classification will be attempted in the next chapter.

Chapter 9. TYPES OF VALUE SYSTEMS

In the construction of a general ethical theory, existing ethical systems should be viewed not as by-products of the various cultures (even though they may appear as such) but as orientations for certain kinds of action. When they are so viewed, certain types of action which arise in widely different cultures (different anthropologically speaking) appear strikingly similar. On the other hand, we may find different action orientations (as represented by different personality types) in the "same" culture. This discrepancy between action-oriented and culture-oriented classifications of value systems seems to me to be evidence for the existence of a supra-cultural point of view in ethics.*

Many cultural anthropologists deny the existence of such a supra-cultural point of view.

I was once made keenly aware of this denial in a discussion on ethics I had with a group of anthropologists. I outlined what I assumed to be the fundamental goals of man and argued that an ethical system derived from the practice of science and scientific method should be best suited to pursue these goals most effectively.

During the discussion I was asked what my attitude was toward witch burning. I said I disapproved of it. A professor of anthropology asked me why. I said I judged actions by their effects and that I saw no good that could possibly come of witch burning, only pain and loss of life to the woman involved.

"You feel that way because you do not see the purpose of the act," said the professor. "They burn a witch when it doesn't rain. The act is a social act. They are thinking of the crops, on which the life of the community depends."

*This is not to deny that each culture may be *dominated* by a particular value system and its concomitant personality type. What is recommended here is merely a change of emphasis from the dominant to those marginal value systems which can be integrated into types transcending cultural barriers (63).

"Does the burning of the 'witch' make the rains come?" I asked.
"Sometimes the rains come, and sometimes they don't," said the
professor. "But the rains themselves are not important. The important thing is that something is *done* about the rain. Those
people would feel frustrated if you didn't let them *do* something
about it."

"Does the witch like being burned?"

"Possibly not. But on what basis do you attribute more importance to her feelings than to the feelings of the tribe? Suppose you
were the governor of the island, and you put a stop to this practice.
You would save the life of some women, but you might also impose
serious suffering on a great many more people. What would you
be guided by if not by your culturally determined prejudices about
what is more important?"

The strength of my opponent's position is that it cannot be
demolished by a "moralistic" argument, if one has undertaken the
task of *analyzing* morality. I have undertaken the analysis in an
attempt to explain the origin of "morality" in the evolution of
patterns of behavior for satisfying basic needs. The only way I
can assail the anthropologist's position is by attacking his basic
premises, namely that "to do something" about an unfortunate
situation can fulfill a basic need. But how can I prove that it
cannot? Whether it can or not depends on the feelings of the
people who feel the need. Thus, the only "proof" would be in the
recognition on the part of the people who burn witches that there
are better ways to insure an adequate food supply. My remarks
should therefore be addressed to *them*.

Because of the difficulties in communication (cf. Chapter 1), I
cannot address the witch-burners effectively. I can, however, address
those to whom what I have said so far makes some sense. This does
not mean that in the last analysis I can reach those and only those
who are already "culturally conditioned" to lend a sympathetic
ear. Cultural conditioning and ethical orientation are not co-
extensive. From the standpoint of ethical orientation, the so-called
Western culture, in which my remarks are supposed to make sense,
is by no means a homogeneous entity. Three distinct ethical patterns
are discernible in Western culture, and counterparts of these patterns are found in other widely different cultures. It is for this
reason that the present analysis can make some claim to a generality
which transcends cultural barriers.

The Ethics of Retribution

It is possible to discuss such acts as burning "witches" to make it rain in a general context, because it is possible to trace such behavior to a pattern of events ranging from trivial to apocalyptic and pervading most cultures.

Case 1: Chicago, 1949: A man smashes a headlight of his car (a symbolic "punch in the eye") because it will not start.

Case 2: Paris, 1837: A man challenges another to a duel to "erase" the disgrace to his name.

Case 3: Kentucky, 1850: A man waylays another, because there is a "feud" between their respective families, and kills him.

Case 4: Anywhere in the "civilized world": A man is sentenced to twenty years in the penitentiary "to pay a debt to society."

Case 5: Rhodesia, 1900; Czechoslovakia, 1943; Indo-China, 1949; Kenya, 1952: A punitive expedition burns a village.

Case 6: Austria, 1914: A war is waged to avenge "national honor."

Case 7: Loyola University, Chicago, 1952: The existence of hell is proved on the assumption that God is "just." The argument: "It is observed that many evil-doers do not suffer for their sins during their lifetime. This contradicts the principle of justice, according to which God rules the world. Therefore one must assume that the evil-doers suffer somewhere after death."

Places, times, cultures, and degrees of sophistication differ, but the underlying idea is the same. Let us call the ethics from which this idea stems the "ethics of retribution." The argument about the existence of hell demonstrates this ethical principle and its implied definition of justice. Where does this notion of justice come from? Why is it considered necessary to punish offensive acts, objects, individuals, and populations?

It is futile to confront the revenge principle of justice with some rival principle. No rational choice can be made between them without an insight into the psychological origins of each. To make a comparison on a basis other than *a priori* emotional commitment, one must understand the "logic"* of different kinds of justice.

The ethical relativist will also recognize the necessity of con-

*Here logic is used in the psychological sense (cf. Note 9).

sidering the "logic" inherent in various kinds of justice, but he considers this "logic" clarified when the cultural compulsions have been discovered. The duelists duel, because this is the way "honor is defended" by the people among whom they live. The criminal is sentenced, because the judge must follow the prescripts of the legal code. The argument about hell sounds convincing to people who entertain certain notions about the nature of justice. But these are only the *forms* which the principle of retribution assumes in various cultural contexts. In the case of the man punching the car in the "eye," the form of the retribution passes the boundaries prescribed by the culture and seems foolish or insane even to people who see nothing foolish or insane in imprisoning a man for twenty years to make him "pay a debt to society" or in waging a war to "avenge national honor." We suspect that there may be other factors, more basic than the cultural code, underlying the origin of ethical patterns. Let us try to get at them.

The logic of retribution (revenge, punishment) comes, I think, from a rationalization of our attempts to neutralize frustrating experience. One source of frustration is in the attempts we make to extend ourselves to include the surrounding world. I have suggested that such early attempts at self-extension are attempts to manipulate objects. Some such attempts necessarily meet with failure. If the projection of one's will to the object endows (in the mind of a child or a naive person) the object with a will of its own, it appears that its "will" can be broken if the object is injured or destroyed. The destruction of the object may also be an attempt to convince oneself that the object *never* existed, to erase the very memory of frustration.[32] The repetition of such experience may be at the source of "retroactive" defense behavior. It is the logic of locking the garage after the car is stolen.

When the logic of retribution entrenches itself in the projections which underlie primitive religious ideas, an identification of retribution with "justice" occurs. The early form of Hebrew religion with its jealous God of Vengeance is an excellent example. In the same religion one can also see how a variation of the ethics of retribution arises, the so called ethics of *redemption*. Once it appears self-evident that every transgression must be punished, it becomes apparent that *my* transgression must be punished. The feelings of guilt and the concept of "sin" with the derived psychological abstraction "conscience" come to the foreground in man's preoccupation with himself. It seems impossible to avoid sin, because the web of taboos extends itself to every aspect of living and usually affects those areas of behavior most where there is a most pressing need to transgress. Hence it is inevitable that I sin. I am therefore naturally corrupt. This state of affairs is unbearable without an appropriate rationalization. It must be shown that I cannot *help* being corrupt, that is, that my corruption is not a matter of choice but of some sort of determinism, and some way must be found for me to escape the dreadful punishment. The first rationalization is exemplified by the legend of the Original Sin of Christian theology which is passed on from generation to generation like a defective gene. The second rationalization is seen in the concept of redemption.

Redemption justice is in a way a generalization of retribution justice. Retribution justice requires that the evil-doer be punished. Retribution justice views punishment as a "payment" for the privilege of committing the crime. Redemption justice abandons the principle that the evil-doer must pay and demands only that *someone* must pay. The most profound development of redemption justice is seen in the mystical aspect of Christianity. Jesus Christ, the embodiment of innocence (as indicated by the symbol of the lamb) suffers and thereby takes upon himself the sins of humanity. Redemption justice is found also in many European legends, for example in the story of the Flying Dutchman, whose curse is canceled by an innocent girl's sacrifice.

Once the ethics of retribution (or redemption) has become the framework of a value system, it determines to a great extent the development of the cultural matrix (religion, legal system, etc.). However, the value system is in turn reinforced by specific cultural practices. For example, commercial practice is an important source of reinforcement for the ethics of retribution. The books must balance. This aspect is most clearly seen in the early legal codes of the Mesopotamian cultures with their price lists for injuries (one pays so much for breaking a man's leg, so much for putting an eye out, so much for the life of a slave, etc.).[33]

In our own legal system, the same scale appears in the imposition of fines, jail sentences, etc. Originally, this "making good" of injury was taken literally: the injured party was also the beneficiary. But with us the compensation of the injured party has remained only in civil suits (torts), while in most law-breaking, the "injured party" is assumed to be the State or "Society," which supposedly benefits when the transgressor suffers punishment.

The notion that evil can be "washed away" by the punishment

of the evil-doer (or some other victim) has led to another rationalization of the ethics of retribution in our own day. It is thought that the evil-doer becomes "rehabilitated" in the process of punishment. In this light, punishment is viewed not as a "debt to society" but something which is administered to the transgressor "for his own good." So prevalent is this notion in some sectors of the "Christian" civilization, that transgressors sometimes actively seek punishment. Dostoyevsky's novels are full of that sort of thing. In *Crime and Punishment*, the murderer Raskolnikov subconsciously longs for redemption through punishment, while his conscious ("rational") self fights against this longing. The subconscious is pictured as the stronger force, so that Raskolnikov gradually, step by step, gives himself away to the inspector, who is aware of Raskolnikov's longing and relies on it in conducting his investigation. In *Brothers Karamazov*, Dimitri feels guilty for having *desired* his father's death and longs for redemption. This longing leads him to behave as if he were guilty and to be convicted for the murder which he did not commit.

The ethics of retribution (or redemption) stems from a notion that when things go wrong, they have to be "set right." A balance of some sort has to be restored. Such a notion would naturally be reinforced in a culture where security is identified with the *status quo*.[34]

The Ethics of Activism

A different sort of ethics is one which may be called "activist." Here the principal motivation is not the desire to restore things to their original state but to reach some *other* state, some pre-set goal. The goal itself may be motivated by various considerations, but inasmuch as an individual or a group is guided in the pursuit of this goal only by the relevance or irrelevance of the means for attaining it, they may be said to be motivated by activist ethics.

Good examples are Shakespeare's *Macbeth* and Becky Sharp in Thackeray's *Vanity Fair*. Macbeth commits and instigates his murders without hatred and without thought of revenge. He simply removes the people who stand in his way. For a moment, when he is told that "no man of woman born will harm Macbeth," he even seems to be relieved at the thought that it is not necessary to kill any longer:
"Then live Macduff! What need I fear thee?"
To be sure, he changes his mind in the next moment, not, how-

ever, because of a compulsion to "set things right" but to make double sure that there is no foul play.

Becky Sharp does not want to harm anyone. She is, in fact, pictured by Thackeray as "good natured." She just wants to make things easy for herself and does not shirk from any means available to her to achieve her goal.

Often the goal itself may be determined by the ethics of retribution as in the case of the forty-one retainers in the classical Japanese tragedy. In the *pursuit* of the goal (revenge), however, this ethics is discarded. Insults are swallowed, wrongs remain unavenged, everything is subordinated to the single goal—to avenge the original wrong.

The slogan, "The end justifies the means," a great favorite of revolutionists and opportunists, is an affirmation of activist ethics. It sounds like a realistic, down-to-earth principle and is often cited to counter ethical arguments based on "abstract" moral considerations or on sentiment. It is especially effective when the moral argument of the opponent can be shown to be insincere. Thus when the Jacobins of the French Revolution were accused of bestiality by the aristocrats, they could justifiably reply, "Look who is talking." The morality of one side being amply matched by the morality of the other, the "moral" argument could be discounted. There remained the "rational" argument—the end justifies the means. What are a few hundred drops at the guillotine weighed against the ends—Liberty, Equality, Fraternity, which obviously cannot be established without the liquidation of the class inherently opposed to them—the aristocracy?

Multiply the number of victims by a few thousand, substitute the Bolsheviks for the Jacobins, the "bourgeoisie" for the aristocracy, socialism for liberty, equality, and fraternity, and you have the ethics of the Russian Revolution. Again "morality" was invoked against this type of ethics, and again the moralists were quite justifiably rebuked for hypocrisy.

Nor has the liquidation of random population samples been confined to the activities of fanatics and commissars. The massacres of Hiroshima and Nagasaki were also "means" to achieve perfectly worthy ends, namely, a quick finish of the war and the saving of thousands of lives of American (and even of Japanese) soldiers. Again the moralistic arguments were weak in the face of "realistic" necessities.

THE ETHICS OF RESIGNATION

Diametrically opposed to activist ethics is the ethics of resignation. Here the primary value is not the manipulation of the world to bring about desired ends but the manipulation of oneself to bring one's desires in harmony with the world. One would guess that the source of this outlook is the view that only the self is truly manipulable. Attempts to manipulate the world lead only to frustration, immediate or delayed. The ethics of resignation is found in many Oriental philosophies.

In Western culture, the clearest exposition of the ethics of resignation is contained in the writings of Leo Tolstoy (1828-1910). In the novel of his middle age, *War and Peace* (102), Tolstoy pictures history in strict deterministic terms. The role of leadership is "debunked." The most "active" leaders (especially Napoleon) are shown to be the puppets of historical forces, over which no individual has any control. The wisest leader (Kutuzov) is one who simply does nothing and allows those forces to operate.

In his later years, Tolstoy talked of the ethics of resignation explicitly, especially in his folk tales such as *The Godson, The Tale of Ivan the Fool*, etc. (101). He believed this ethics to be the correct interpretation of the teachings of Jesus Christ. According to Tolstoy, evil can be conquered only if it is not resisted. Tolstoy's nonresistance goes even further than Gandhi's ethics of nonviolent resistance. A case in point is Tolstoy's folk tale, *The Candle* (101), in which a cruel landlord forces a devout peasant to work on Easter Sunday. A nonviolent resister of the Gandhi school would have simply refused to work. Tolstoy's peasant obeys but shows his defiance of the landlord by fixing a burning candle to his plow so that he can sing hymns while he works.

Needless to say, Tolstoy rejects completely both the ethics of retribution and activism, which are obviously incompatible with the ethics of resignation. The ethics of redemption, on the other hand, is accepted in part (consistently with the extreme individualism of resignation). That is to say, the only one who can redeem my sins is myself, and the only way I can redeem my sins is by changing myself.

Another example of the ethics of resignation is Christian Science, where health is equated to "belief in health." This assumption is, of course, incontrovertible by any evidence, because all evidence which could possibly refute it is automatically ruled out as stemming from a lack of faith, that is, from "illusion."

The ethics of resignation provides two extreme forms of "gratification" for the need of self-extension. In one form, the self is extended to include the whole universe (this is commonly encountered in some Indian philosophies, in Tolstoyan Christianity, etc.) No action can be brought to bear on the world, because all action is destructive. The world and I are one. Hence in attempting to manipulate the world I am hurting myself. At the other extreme, the individual withdraws entirely within himself and becomes indifferent to the world. This attitude is exemplified in the cynicism of Diogenes and in the utter scepticism of Timocles in Anatole France's novel *Thais*.

CONFLICTING IDEALS

To someone who has internalized one kind of ethics, actions motivated by another kind may seem immoral or amoral. Thus the ethics upon which our legal system is based is largely the ethics of retribution. "Justice" means the punishment of crime and the protection of the innocent, and much is made of the safeguards which guarantee the latter. Imbued with our own ideas of justice with its emphasis on a careful weighing of evidence to insure punishment of the guilty and vindication of the innocent, we view other notions of justice as bizarre.

Soviet justice, which is guided by different considerations, is considered by most people in the West as a "mockery," because the yardstick of "carefully measured retribution" does not apply to it. The Communists are guided by activist ethics to a greater extent than by the ethics of retribution. The latter is by no means negligible, of course, in the Communist countries. The Communists did not spring full-grown out of the foam of the Russian Revolution. They are people who have inherited the fundamental values of Russian culture, in which retribution and especially redemption played a vital role. Still, characteristics of activist ethics are clearly seen in the Communist notions of justice, especially in the years immediately following the revolution. Questions of "guilt" and "innocence" with regard to *particular* overt acts became relatively unimportant. The important criteria of "guilt" centered around the relation of certain *attitudes* (as evaluated by the Communists, of course) to the pre-set goals of the revolution. Significantly, the treatment of the "ordinary" criminal (the burglar, the passion killer, etc.) became milder (at least in the early years). Serious thought was given to establishing a penal system which would "restore the transgressor to a useful life," and the program was to some extent carried out in experimental work farms, homes for delinquent adolescents, etc. The "disloyal person," on the other hand, whether or not he committed overt acts against the State, was exceptionally harshly treated, more so than his counterpart in the old czarist regime and out of all "proportion" to his overt offense.

Another trivial but instructive example of the difference between two different notions of justice appears in the policies of city transportation systems. In Vienna (and many other European cities) the passenger holds on to his ticket on a streetcar or a subway, because a control officer periodically passes through the car asking everyone to show his ticket. The idea is that *no one shall ride without having paid his fare*. In a way, this is a form of "justice." On the New York subway, there are no tickets. If one slips past the turnstiles, one can ride free. Free rides could no doubt be practically eradicated if a sufficient number of guards were placed at the turnstiles or if a ticket system were introduced. Without doubt it would cost the City of New York more money to do this than would be saved. Possibly the control system in Vienna costs more than it saves. But Vienna seems to be motivated in such matters by a notion of "justice," while New York is motivated by pragmatic considerations. Hence the difference in custom.

The differences in ethical outlooks are reflected not only in the various notions of justice but also in the various conceptions of the "good life" or "the ideal personality."[35] Here the cultural anthropologists have made significant contributions in relating culture types to their associated dominant personality types. In some of this work, one feels a departure from "professional" (that is, largely descriptive, positivistic) anthropology, dealing primarily with directly observable data, toward an attempt to "psychologize" the anthropological approach to the study of man.

An example from an interesting study of American personality types bears a direct relation to the discussion of value systems.

David Riesman in his book *The Lonely Crowd* (83) describes three types of personality in terms of their internalized value systems. The so-called tradition-oriented person (characteristic of pre-industrial society) follows essentially a tradition-oriented value system. His loyalty is to the "established way of doing things." He neither strives to change nor criticizes the *status quo*. The second type, the "inner-directed" person, follows the compulsions of goal-seeking. He is characteristic of the expanding industrial age with its opportunities and its idealization of the future. The third type, which Riesman calls the "other-directed," seems to be motivated by the need of making an immediate adjustment to influences impinging on him from others, particularly his peers. He is now emerging, according to Riesman, in the American upper and upper middle class, where values arising from sensitivity to mass demand (the virtues of the advertising and public relations professions) are becoming increasingly internalized.

The resemblances of the tradition-oriented and the inner-oriented value systems to the ethics of retribution and of activism respectively is apparent. It is tempting to assign to other-directedness the ethics of resignation as the appropriate ethics, because both emphasize the virtue of adjusting to a situation *as it is,* neither anticipating nor resisting impending changes. It would be more accurate, however, to see in the modern other-directed personality a caricature of a genuinely resigned person (such as the Christian, the Stoic or the mystic), with whom he has in common only the lack of well-defined goals to be reached by action. One who has internalized the ethics of resignation often succeeds in making peace with himself and with the world, whereas the anxiety-ridden efforts of the other-directed person to "adjust", described by Riesman, are constantly frustrated.

There is, however, a way to characterize the three types of value systems I have described in this chapter, so as to associate the other-directed personality with the third type. This characterization will be useful in the critique which follows, and so will be given now.

The ethics of retribution and redemption is associated with a predominant preoccupation with the *past*. Things that have gone wrong must be atoned for; the *original* state of affairs must be restored.

The ethics of activism is oriented toward the *future*. The here and now must be so handled as to insure a better state of affairs to come, even to the extent of making enormous sacrifices or of injuring people in the present.

The ethics of resignation is associated with the emphasis on the *present*. This is the attitude shared by the Tolstoyan and the Epicurean, by the Oriental mystic and the American other-directed junior executive.

Each of the ethical frameworks described is a guide for certain types of action. Each has its uses in the pursuit of the invariant goals and each has its drawbacks. Each gives rise to a personality type relatively adjusted to a society where "his" type of ethical system prevails and maladjusted with respect to other ethical systems. In a world of disappearing boundaries, it is inevitable that the various value systems clash and compete with each other. The philosophy of "live and let live" (the ideal of ethical relativists) cannot be applied in those instances when action which seems imperative in the light of one value system interferes with action which seems imperative in the light of another. Even where the value systems of two cultures are the same (say embodied in the ethics of activism), the goals pursued may be incompatible with each other.

Therefore, if human conflicts are ever to be resolved or, at least, to be guided into less destructive channels, our analysis of value systems cannot stop with the recognition that they are different and often incompatible. A common denominator must be found. This is the task of operational ethics.

Chapter 10. OPERATIONAL ETHICS

Operational ethics rests on a single premise, namely, that rules of conduct and goals should not be stated *a priori* but should emerge as a result of the best method of inquiry at one's disposal.[36] Therefore the goals (the "good," the "ultimate ends," etc.) of this ethics cannot be explicitly stated (as they are in activist ethical systems), because there is always a possibility that improved methods of inquiry will reveal more desirable goals. Nor can specific rules of conduct be indicated (such as "an eye for an eye; a tooth for a tooth" in the ethics of retribution). Nor is the pursuit of specific goals necessarily discouraged (as in the ethics of resignation), because in the light of available knowledge these goals may appear to be desirable.

Just as there is no absolutely final fact in science, so there is no absolutely supreme good in operational ethics. Values may be *postulated* as one postulates scientific hypotheses. And just as some scientific hypotheses are supported by overwhelming evidence, so some of the postulated values may be supported by the success of their application. For example, the four invariant needs described in Chapter 8 seem to me to be a summary of what is known about man's basic strivings today. It seems to me, therefore, that ethics should be an inquiry into what sort of conduct can satisfy those needs most effectively. It is not inconceivable, however, that in the course of that inquiry it may appear that there are other invariant needs, or that some of those I have listed are not invariant, or that they contradict each other.

Of course the method of operational ethics resembles that of scientific inquiry. And it should, if it is described as based on the best (that is, the most successful) method of inquiry available today.[37]

Some thinkers, especially among the scientists, feel strongly this affinity between scientific method of inquiry and ethics. Why not bring to bear, they ask, these phenomenally successful methods of inquiry on the questions of how the goals of man may be achieved? To this the relativists reply either that the goals of man are not universal or that the belief in scientific method is in itself a special "value system," which cannot be imposed on the whole humanity.

George Lundberg, (55), Stuart Dodd (27), and others (81) get around the argument of the relativist by granting that goals cannot be *chosen* by scientific method. Goals, they say, must be *given* before scientific inquiry can be applied to the search for the means to satisfy them. This position is essentially that of activism. The goals are *set*, whether they are assumed or determined empirically by a public opinion poll or imposed by government decree. Ethics consists of evaluating the means with regard to their effectiveness in the pursuit of the given goals. To be sure, Lundberg does say that the practice of scientific inquiry may actually change the goals, but in my opinion he does not sufficiently emphasize this point.

Operational ethics, as, for example, formulated by Dewey, does emphasize the point that the methods of inquiry used in the pursuit of goals do change the goals originally postulated or altogether determine the *emergence* of goals. In Chapter 8, I described this process in connection with the conversion of means into ends in the development of a value system. Operational ethics seeks to reverse this conversion. It seeks to *reduce* the number of ends, so as to minimize the possibility of contradiction among them. In this way, operational ethics introduces the principle of parsimony into ethics.

Adherence to the principle of parsimony in ethical matters is another way of recognizing freedom as a value. The fewer "ends" there are, the more varied can be the means by which to pursue them, and so the more freedom there is in choosing a particular path.

Tolerance goes hand in hand with freedom. Thus the old "live and let live" principle is a fair expression of operational ethics. But the impasse of relativism is avoided—the impasse which arises out of a denial of the possibility of choosing among mutually exclusive value systems. If people in one culture want to hunt heads among their neighbors, and their neighbors object to having their heads viewed as collectors' items, the pure relativist has nothing to say about the situation. The operationalist also has nothing to say *a priori*. But he will try to bring some inquiry to bear on the matter.

Why do head hunters want to hunt heads (aside from wanting to adhere to custom)? Why do their neighbors object? Can the two be brought together to talk things over, to pursue the inquiry further *together*? Is it possible that out of such a common enterprise new goals may emerge which will allow the head hunters to satisfy the urge which had been responsible for their addiction and at the same time allow their neighbors to keep their heads? The old Russian saying, "To have the wolves fed and the sheep safe" is a good description of the aims of operational ethics in this case.

To sum up: the operationalist advocates a certain approach to ethical problems. This approach is characterized by (1) the principle of parsimony; (2) a freedom of choice among means in the pursuit of ends; (3) a knowledge of consequences of one's choices; and (4) a knowledge of one's motivations in making the choices one makes.

A Critique of Existing Value Systems

Out of the operationalist's approach to ethics emerges a critique of the existing ethical systems. The most fundamental criticism can, of course, be leveled at the "compulsive" value systems, those which characterize tradition-oriented societies, where rigid codes of conduct prevail. The most frequent rationalizations of such codes are statements of pseudo-purposes. When the question "Why is X?" is applied to the ethical prescripts of these value systems, the answers are usually tautologies. For example,

Q. Why must wrongs be avenged?

A. Because justice demands it. (But justice is *defined* in terms of avenging wrongs.)

Q. Why must women be chaste?

A. Because virtue demands it. (But virtue in women is *defined* in terms of chastity, etc.)[38]

These are make-believe explanations. All they do is give two names to the same thing and offer one of the names as the explanation of the other. It is like saying, "It is raining, because water is falling from the sky."

The next level of criticism is leveled at the "pragmatic" rationalization of actions. No value system rests on a "pure" ethics of a type described in Chapter 9. Our own penal code seems to stem from an ethics of retribution. But it is often justified by pragmatic rationalizations, for example, "Criminals are punished to deter others from committing similar crimes."

For an operationalist, such an assertion is a hypothesis to be tested. He would ask, "Does the threat of punishment in effect act as a deterrent? Under any conditions or only under some? What are those conditions? Is it conceivable that in some cases threat of punishment acts as a stimulant to commit crimes?"

In other words, wherever a "pragmatic" rationalization occurs, the operationalist would bring to bear the techniques of experimental science to test the hypotheses implied in the rationalization. Other examples immediately suggest themselves.

Is it true that if Soviet citizens are allowed access to certain information about what life is like in Western countries, the socialist program of the U.S.S.R. will be wrecked?

Is it true that if the United States liberalizes its immigration laws, wholesale unemployment and a subversion of American ideals will follow?

Is it true that if the East reduces its military appropriations, the West will immediately attack it?

Is it true that if the West reduces its military appropriations, the East will immediately attack it?

Is it true that if bathing suits are discarded on public beaches, wholesale sexual promiscuity will follow?

Is it true that if the formal teaching of English grammar in the schools is abandoned, the ability of people to communicate with each other will be impaired?

Experiments to test the truths of the assumptions involved in broad public policies are not easy to design, and even if they were, their execution might involve risks. It is not recommended, however, that one start immediately with far-reaching programs of experimentation. One could start with very modest experiments. For example, one could design an experiment to determine an "optimum" punishment (with respect to its deterring potential) for traffic violations. Then, armed with some experience, one could proceed to determine the optimum punishment for more serious offenses.

In foreign relations, one could also start with modestly designed experiments, for example, with attempts to reach agreement with the potential "enemy" by making concessions in matters which are not crucial for "security" (as it is conventionally understood). One could then see whether the slightly enlarged area of agreement and mutual trust could be further enlarged. The important thing in these experiments would be not the actual results achieved but the process of experimentation itself, which has hardly ever been applied in areas where actions are invariably labeled "right" and "wrong."

Next, operational critique concerns the relation between means and ends. Granted that certain "ends" can be reached by certain means, may not these means lead to *other* results, not foreseen or bargained for? Drugs of proven efficacy in the treatment of certain diseases are often withheld from the market for years, while responsible research workers try to ascertain whether the drugs have undesirable "side effects." National policies and standards of virtue are not often examined for their implications in areas other than where they are applied.

The foolishness of applying the "end justifies the means" principle blindly has been realized for ages and is reflected in folk wisdom, for example, in the fable about the fool who killed a fly on his friend's nose by smashing it with a rock. The ethics of activism, especially, often encourages the emergence of a personality type pathologically unaware of the costs involved in the direct unswerving pursuit of pre-set goals. Such personalities are common among our so-called "men of action," strong political leaders, revolutionists, practising visionaries, etc. One sees the results of their activities in the recurring demoralization following revolutions of the "seizure of power" type and in the final collapse of empires which commit themselves to programs of unlimited conquest.

Besides applying the "count the cost" principle to specific goals, the operationalist would apply it also to general notions characteristic of the various value systems. As an example, let us take a familiar notion in our own value system, that of "progress." In America, the popular definitions of progress are still made in terms of unlimited mechanization of all human activity. One could ask, "Granted that as a result of extensive mechanization, we eat better than did our grandfathers, do we also sleep better? What is the relative importance of good diet and good sleep? Granted that in developing mass channels of communication, each citizen has the opportunity of being better informed than was his grandfather, is he *actually* better informed? Judging by what standards?"

With regard to our unquestioned acceptance of "progress" in combatting ruthless exploitation of the weak by the strong, one could ask, "Granted that physical exploitation of children, so prevalent in industrial England of one hundred fifty years ago does not exist in industrial America of today, what do we know about the emotional exploitation of children which results from viewing children as a market for certain kinds of entertainment? What is the relative extent of harm resulting from each kind of exploitation?"

Note that the questioning of values does not go deep. At this stage of criticism, the operationalist does not question the roots of the values ("How do you know that progress is good *at all?*"). There must be something on which to "hang" a criticism. Therefore, the operationalist will always start with something to agree upon: "Progress is generally desirable, but have we stopped to consider how an unqualified support of 'progress' in one direction affects us with respect to our chances to progress in other possible directions?" Needless to say, the operationalist is not unqualifiedly opposed to all current values. But there is no value which he would not place under scrutiny and for which he would not suggest some operationally meaningful procedure to test its validity in terms of the rationalizations involved. The only "immutable" value is the one just implied: the possibility of questioning all values.

Most of this outlook is derived, of course, directly from the practice of the scientific method, particularly the rigorous method of the natural sciences. Yet operational ethics is more than a formal application of the methods of natural science to human problems. To begin with, an analysis of motivations has no exact counterpart in natural science. In natural science, the motivation is always assumed to be a search for truth as measured by the consequences of assertions. Already Marx and other theoreticians of the sociology of knowledge (57) have shown that motivation plays a much more crucial role in what will be considered "truth" in investigations dealing with human behavior. Freud utilized this idea (or applied it independently) in his theory of personality.

Operational ethics recognizes the importance of analyzing motivations in any ethical investigation. It goes even further, however, in distinguishing the methods of natural science from its own. In natural science, especially in classical physics, neither the observations one makes on an object, nor the assumptions one makes about a phenomenon usually affect the object or the phenomenon itself. Thus, my looking at a planet does not affect its mass, and the assumptions which I make about the shape of its orbit do not affect the orbit. This independence of facts from observations one performs on them and the assumptions one makes about them is a basic characteristic of natural science.

This is not nearly so true in human affairs. The observations we make of human beings and the assumptions we make about their conduct often do affect human behavior.

SELF-FULFILLING ASSUMPTIONS AND DISTURBING OBSERVATIONS

Assumptions which influence the course of events so that they become realized have been called "self-fulfilling assumptions."[39] As we shall see, they can operate both subjectively and objectively. An ancient Chinese story illustrates both of these modes of operation.

A farmer missed a sum of money and started to suspect his neighbor's son. He began to observe the boy closely and was soon convinced that he was the thief. The boy's eyes were furtive and his manner stealthy. Sometime afterward, the farmer found his money where he had mislaid it. When he saw the neighbor's son again, the boy looked him straight in the eye. His manner was open, honest, and friendly.

One explanation suggests itself immediately. The farmer saw in the boy's behavior what he wanted to see in it or what he was afraid he would see. This illustrates the working of the subjectively self-realizing assumption. That preconceived notions and prejudices distort the world for us is, of course, not startling. It is these distortions that science with its objective techniques of observation is supposed to correct. It is conceivable, therefore, that self-realizing assumptions of the subjective type can be eliminated by the application of objective criteria. For example, to show that the farmer's evaluation of his neighbor's son's manner did not correspond to fact, one could take a number of photographs of the boy before and after the farmer found his money and ask the farmer to separate the "befores" from the "afters." If the number of his correct guesses is not greater than is warranted by chance, we can say that the changes in the boy's manner were all in the farmer's "mind."

However, there is also an objective side to self-realizing assumptions, which can be illustrated by another interpretation of the Chinese story. It is possible that the farmer's assumptions about his neighbor's son brought about *actual* changes in the boy's behavior. He might actually have avoided the farmer's eyes under the latter's suspicious scrutiny. Possibly also after the money was found, he felt that the farmer's gaze changed to a friendly one, and accordingly his manner changed again. It is possible that people under constant suspicion do finally commit the acts they are suspected of. The proverb, "Give the dog a bad name and hang him" may thus be interpreted as referring both to the subjective and the objective aspects of self-realizing assumptions: a bad name will spoil a man's reputation, and it may spoil the man himself. Verbalizations *can* influence the course of events.

The effects of what we think about events on the actual course of events have important implications for social science and therefore for operational ethics, which, being based on available methods of inquiry, must be based on contemporary social science, such as it is. For we cannot simply choose hypotheses at will in the hope of coming through a series of experiments and modifications of the hypotheses (as the natural scientists do) nearer and nearer to "truth." The hypotheses we choose may determine the course of history, and so the "truth" which we are seeking. To take account of this circumstance means to bring ethical considerations into the *choice of hypotheses* (a problem almost nonexistent for the contemporary natural scientist) .[40]

To take an example, suppose A wishes to know whether his neighbor B is a "friend" or an "enemy." To proceed scientifically, A can choose either hypothesis and then put it to a test. But A's choice of hypothesis will be reflected in his behavior toward B. Suppose A assumes that B is an enemy. This assumption in itself gives rise to a hostile attitude in A, which may be (perhaps subconsciously) known to B. B may then react in such a way as to reinforce A's original hypothesis, and, as a result, A will become even more hostile. But then A's behavior may reinforce B's and B will become still more hostile, etc., until A and B do, in fact, become enemies.

The same procedure may, of course, operate in the opposite direction, starting with A's assumption that B is his friend.

To take an example from international affairs, suppose Neptunia wishes to obtain information about Plutonia's intentions. Such information is usually obtained by means of spies. But the very presence of Neptunian spies in Plutonia determines to a certain extent Plutonia's attitudes toward Neptunia and therefore her intentions.

The importance of the effects of observation on the results of social experiment has been recently dramatically demonstrated in studies on the productivity of factory workers (60). The object was to decide the effects of lighting on the output in a certain shop. Accordingly, the intensity of light was increased in the shop while in another "control" shop it was kept constant. The output in the experimental shop rose. This was a hopeful result. It seemed to indicate that within the limits of the experiment, brighter lights were responsible for greater productivity. To make sure of the result, the lighting in the experimental shop was diminished *below* that of the control shop. It was expected that this would result in a fall of productivity. Surprisingly, it was found that the output of the experimental shop was still higher than that of the control shop! It was now pretty clear that it was not the lighting that made the difference *but the experimental situation itself*. The workers knew that some test was being applied to them, and this knowledge somehow was reflected in greater output.

It is sometimes pointed out by social scientists that the importance of self-realizing assumptions in human affairs makes "scientific method" (which is usually equated to the methods of the natural sciences) *totally* inapplicable to social science, and therefore certainly not to ethics. An interesting example of this attitude is found in Popper's critique of Marxism (73). Marxism, as is well known, rests on an assumption that there exist "laws" of social science, not unlike the Newtonian laws of motion, which in Marx's time were thought to have been discovered by the physicists once for all as a part of "objective reality." Contemporary Marxists believe even more than that. They believe that the "laws of motion" of society are not only an objective reality but that they have, like the laws of physics, also been discovered, namely by Marx, and that it only remains to invent "engineering techniques" based on those laws in order to guide history into the proper revolutionary channel—the dictatorship of the proletariat, the classless society, and communism.

The Marxists also ascribe to Marx the discovery of the "nature" of the various social institutions, such as property, parliamentary democracy, and the state. Since, according to Marx, the law underlying all history is the "class struggle," all contemporary social institutions are also simply reflections of that struggle. Thus the state, *by its very nature*, is an instrument by means of which one class is kept in subjugation to another. Since the state cannot change its "nature" without ceasing to be the state, it follows from Marxian theory that after the (inevitable) overthrow of the capitalist system by the proletariat, the state must for a while retain its function as an instrument of class domination (with the roles of the classes, however, reversed) until the establishment of a "classless society" makes the state superfluous, since there will then be no classes to oppress or suppress.

Popper categorically denies both the determinism implied in the Marxist theory of history (which Popper calls "historicism") and the immutable character of social institutions (which Popper calls "essentialism" and which he traces to the outmoded physical theories of Plato and Aristotle).

The state, says Popper, has no "nature." It is what we make it. We can use it to oppress or to protect, to keep the rich in luxury or to assure equitable distribution of wealth. Nor is the course of history necessarily subject to determinist laws. We can choose our course by the proper application of "social engineering."

Popper's arguments emphasize the importance of self-realizing assumptions. The state becomes what we assume it to be. Our destiny depends on what we assume our destiny to be.

The truth is probably somewhere between the position of Popper and that of Marx. Both men in their study of history and of institutions abstract the features which lend strongest support for their respective theses, determinism for one, free will for the other. However, as was pointed out in Chapter 7, determinism and free will are not objective aspects of a situation. The amount of determinism we see in a situation depends on the amount of knowledge we have about it. It makes no sense to ask how much determinism there "really" is in it, because any answer we give must be in terms of available knowledge. Likewise the amount of freedom we have depends on how much we know. Therefore the whole question of historical determinism is senseless if no reference is made to our state of knowledge.

It is possible that something resembling the "laws of motion" of social forces will be discovered. But it is also conceivable that their discovery will give us more freedom, not less. Paradoxically, the Marxists give lip service to the principle that knowledge is freedom. "Freedom is a recognition of necessity" is a Marxist slogan coined, I believe, by Engels. It has since been interpreted as meaning that freedom is in falling in line with the "inevitable" course of history as interpreted by Marxists.* A more promising interpretation is in considering freedom to be in the possibility of choice which arises when a *potential* determinism is discovered. A potential determinism is expressed in the form "If so, then so." Freedom means the freedom to choose the "if" part. Freedom is meaningless, however, unless the "then" part is known. Thus freedom and re-

*Cf. the definition of freedom in Catholic doctrine: "Freedom means the freedom to obey the will of God."

sponsibility are forever linked. Freedom in the choice of "if" means responsibility for the "then."

We may be free to make our institutions what we want them to be, but only if we understand how institutions become what they are. We may be free in choosing the course of history, but only if we know where history would take us if we did not know how to steer. We may be masters of our individual destinies, but only if we know the motivations which often guide our actions independently of what we want.

The recognition of this relation between choice and necessity, between freedom and responsibility, is an essential feature of operational ethics.

SUMMARY OF CHAPTERS 8, 9, AND 10

The usual process in the development of an ethical system consists of means being stratified into ends. The result is a multiplication and differentiation of ends which often become incompatible in different cultures and even in the same culture. Conflicts and frustrations can be traced to this circumstance. Operational ethics, based on an operational analysis of means and ends, seeks to show that so-called ends are often the results of an inadequate evaluation of the means available in the pursuit of *basic* ends. It is also assumed in operational ethics that the basic ends are invariant for all mankind and are consistent with each other.

The chronic question, "Can science be applied to ethics?" is answered as follows from the operational point of view. The basic, invariant ends of man are not subject to ethical discussion, because *we have no choice* but to pursue them. They can, however, be determined by a scientific investigation (just as physiological needs are so determined). The proper subject matter of ethics is the *choice* of means to pursue the ends. Such choice is determined by one's action-orientation. At the center of operational ethics, therefore, is the scientific (objective) study of such orientations. This study, however, *itself* influences the action-orientation in that it frees man from compulsions which are at the root of out-dated orientations (the ethics of retribution, the ethics of compulsive activism, etc.). The important result of applying science to ethics, then, is not that science enables us to decide which ethics we should choose but that the practice of science already leads us toward the operational ethical system.

Chapter 11. INDIVIDUAL AND SOCIETY

Every ethical system involves a social philosophy, and so must operational ethics. However, as we have seen, operational ethics is not equipped to prescribe specific codes of conduct or to recommend specific social structures. Its only premise is that choice of action should be based on results of effective inquiry.

Effective inquiry is one which is not hampered by factors extraneous to the inquiry. It is free inquiry, where no restrictions are put on the sort of questions that can be raised. Some of these restrictions may be of a philosophical nature: they are imposed by the framework of thought within which questions must be asked. So in social matters, as Popper put it (73), if one keeps thinking in certain patterns, one asks questions which call for answers to assure the continuation of the patterns.

One asks, for example, "Who shall rule?" Depending on one's social philosophy, one answers, "philosopher kings," or "gentlemen of quality," or "the wise, the rich, and the good," or "the people," or "the working class." But the question is a trap. It implies that someone must rule. If one cannot accept this premise, one cannot answer the question. If one does try to answer the question, one has "swallowed" the premise and its limitations. Within the limitations of that premise, other questions are not likely to occur, such as, for example, "How can rulers be prevented from abusing their power?"

Here we see how certain questions can fail to be brought up simply because they do not occur as long as one stays within a certain framework of assumptions. There is, however, another restriction on questions, particularly those dealing with social philosophy—the restriction of fear. The asking of certain questions which *do* occur, sometimes persistently, is barred in most existing societies because they touch upon the supposedly immutable foundations on which those societies rest. These critical questions are barred by surrounding the whole area around which they revolve with an aura of sanctity. This is an exceptionally effective way of barring questions because it operates not only through specific threats of punishment but, more significantly, through making unhampered inquiry psychologically impossible. One usually does not ask searching questions when one is afraid. It follows, therefore, that if free inquiry is desirable, fear is not.

Fear operates under the conditions of threat. A threat is a danger foreseen (or imagined), but not every danger foreseen is a threat. A good driver, for example, constantly foresees dangers, but all through his awareness of danger he is aware also of his ability to avoid it. Therefore a good driver is not afraid. We can give this feeling of danger awareness coupled with self-confidence the name "apprehension" to distinguish it from fear. The foresight of danger (real or imagined) without the assurance of being able to avoid it constitutes a threat and evokes fear.

Not nearly enough is known about the physiology of fear. It is fairly well established that certain glandular activity accompanies it, notably the secretion of adrenalin into the blood stream and the flow of blood away from the brain and the viscera into the skeletal muscles. These changes prepare the organism for physical exertion and are useful in averting certain kinds of physical danger, such as repelling an attack or escaping by flight. For human beings, this mechanism of mobilizing physical resources is largely anachronistic. The fears we experience are most often generalized fears, involving not threats of immediate destruction of our physical selves but usually *symbolic* threats of *symbolic* injury to our *symbolic* selves.

For example, the changes going on in Mr. B (p. 88), who gets "stage fright," may be similar to those that went on in his ancestor when he was confronted by a bear. These changes helped the ancestor to fight the bear or to run away from him. But they do not help Mr. B make his speech. Even the physical dangers that we sometimes face are not often of the kind that can be averted by physical exertion (for example, the hazards of driving).

Why do we undergo those changes then? Why does Mr. B undergo them when he has to make a speech? There are no bears in the audience. No one will kill him if he makes a poor speech. Mr. B, with whom we may reason, knows this, but another Mr. B (who cannot reason at all) does not know it. To this primitive vestigial Mr. B, the threat of "failure" is a threat to the generalized "self" and operates just like the threat of physical danger, except that the reactions it elicits in Mr. B's glands are of no earthly use to Mr. B.

If we were still roaming the jungle, that is, if we were still competing in the struggle for existence on a par with the other animals, depending largely on our physiological equipment, these "useless" reactions (of being afraid when no physical danger threatens) would be eliminated by natural selection. But we do not compete on a par with the other animals. We rely less and less on our physiology and more and more on our "extracorporeal" equipment, the cultural and physical wealth accumulated in the time-binding process. As a result some of our physiological equipment (such as the fear reaction) has become useless or even harmful.

The most serious problems facing modern man are not occasions for acute fear (resulting from immediate threat) but for chronic long-term fears. The most unfortunate human communities are threatened not so much by immediate destruction but by drawn-out misery: disease, starvation, bondage. In more fortunate communities, where these physical threats are not serious, there are others, perhaps equally tormenting: the threat of loss of status. Whether these diffuse, vague fears (more properly anxieties) are accompanied by glandular and visceral activity similar to those operating in acute fear is not certain. But the handicaps to the pursuit of inquiry resulting from anxieties are quite apparent. The evidence revealed by some experimental work in education strongly indicates that the incentive to inquiry is seriously impeded by anxiety.

Of great concern, therefore, from the standpoint of operational ethics is the elimination of these anxieties. The elimination of anxieties regarding physical threats is largely a matter of technology. Technology has been so successful in the past century and a half in eliminating these well-defined threats in some areas that it seems more than likely that those results can be extended much further.[41]

However, the elimination of other kinds of anxiety are not matters which can be dealt with by technology. In fact, in the two dominant civilizations of our day, both based on a successful all-out technological development, fear in the form of a diffuse anxiety has become chronic.

The United States and the Union of Socialist Soviet Republics represent two opposite poles of social philosophy. Yet their ethos are similar in many respects. The social philosophies of both are based on activist ethics: their goals were *explicitly stated* in solemn documents and in holy books. Both social philosophies aimed at the elimination of fear through an egalitarian system. And both civilizations have succumbed to fears which were largely the products of their respective social philosophies.*

INDIVIDUALISM

Let us take the United States, the older civilization, first. It was born in the throes of a revolution led by intellectuals who were committed to the social philosophy of Rousseau, which was also the social philosophy behind the French Revolution.

The philosophy of Rousseau, an outgrowth of the ideas of the French Enlightenment, placed the *individual* at the center of attention. The rights of the individual were considered given and immutable. Societies and governments existed only for the purpose of insuring these rights for the individual. A social organization was based on *a social contract* among individuals, who in their "natural state" were thought to be free agents. Social organizations, therefore, were judged by the extent to which they abridged these "natural rights."

This social philosophy served as a framework in which to rationalize the revolutionary acts of the eighteenth century in America and in France. The acts were performed by a class of people who were becoming increasingly numerous and who were extremely eager to go places and do things. They were merchants, professional men, incipient industrialists, pioneers, all organizers of human activity. Individualistic philosophy gave them a conviction that they were *right* in doing what they did—breaking the colonial power of Britain in America and the feudal power of the aristocracy in France. Individualistic philosophy was therefore an effective means of implementing a specific social end—to put the organizers of productive activity, the middle class, in the saddle.

However, individualism did not appear to the victors as a rationalization of their struggle for power. It appeared as the most desirable and just social end. It had served to eliminate fear in giving to the new ruling class courage to break traditions and ties. Now it appeared as the ideal philosophy of courage. Each man his own

*For vividness of contrast and comparison, I will describe the extreme forms of these philosophies as represented, say, in the editorials of *Pravda* and the *Chicago Tribune*.

master. Each man given unlimited opportunities to "better himself." Each man stimulated by competition to do his best and taking full responsibility for his own success or failure. Thus individualism became a *value,* an immutable principle of social ethics.

The very assets of individualism become liabilities in a different social context. Freedom of contract between employer and employee (the sale of labor power in an open market) may have assured equitable compensation in a limited labor market, but it becomes an instrument of intimidation of the employee in a flooded labor market. The courage which accompanies the feeling of freedom in being able to choose one's job gives way to the fear of losing a job. In a rural economy of self-sufficient households, the feeling of responsibility for one's own welfare may be conducive to courage. But in an urban industrial economy, the feeling of being an anonymous unit in a modern metropolis is more akin to fear. When "success" meant simply reasonable prosperity and freedom from debt, competition might have acted as a stimulus for courage. But where success has come to mean "going to the top" with everything else labeled "failure," courage gives way to anxiety and the occupational diseases of executives.

Moreover, the world situation has changed. When we were young, individualism was a revolutionary idea. Our friends among the nations of the world were young up-and-coming countries destined to grow stronger because of the great vitality of the new social ideas they embraced. Our enemies were decrepit aristocracies on their way out. The future, therefore, was full of promise.

In our day, however, individualism in its *laissez-faire* form is an *old* idea. In fact, it is a *dead* idea, which is hardly taken seriously outside of the United States. It cannot even be said that the regimes we support today are dedicated to laissez-faire individualism. They are simply dedicated (or rather they say they are) to an unconditional hatred of the rival idea (collectivism). And so we support them, openly or shamefacedly, and stake our future on that support. It is the realization that there is no future in the social philosophy we are dedicated to and our failure to face this realization that gives rise to the diffuse fear which is now gripping us.

COMMUNISM

The analogous transformation of courage into fear in the U.S.S.R. is even more striking, perhaps because it took place so rapidly as to fall within the memory of a single generation.

The U.S.S.R. was born in the throes of a revolution led by intellectuals who were committed to the social philosophy of Karl Marx. Marx came a century after Rousseau, and his philosophy is more sophisticated. In fact, it contains a penetrating critique of Rousseau's individualistic philosophy. Marx pointed out that the free individuals in a "natural state," who supposedly signed the first "social contract," never existed. Man is man, said Marx, by reason of his participation in a *social* productive process. Therefore the origin of social relations is to be sought in that process.

Marx then went on to show that throughout recorded history human societies had a distinct structure consisting of two main classes—the exploited (slaves, then serfs, then industrial wage workers) who did most of the work, and the exploiters (masters, then feudal lords, then proprietors of tools of production), who appropriated most of the product. The course of history, Marx thought, was determined by the struggles of the succeeding exploited classes against the exploiters. Great historical changes occurred when one ruling class disappeared and another appeared in its place. Such changes brought with them new orientations, new vistas, and new ethical systems.

Marx's prognosis of future history was an optimistic one. Whereas the previous social changes had taken place through the operation of blind historical forces (the "laws of motion" of society), the next great change, the Communist Revolution, would be accomplished by a class (the industrial working class—the proletariat) *cognizant* of those forces. This class, having learned in the course of its struggle the lesson of history, would see to it that the tragic story (the emergence of a new class of exploiters) would not be repeated and that a classless (and therefore struggle-free) human society would be established. Marx characterized this last shift of power as a jump from the kingdom of necessity into the kingdom of freedom.

On the face of it, the social philosophy of Marx was no less egalitarian and libertarian than that of Rousseau had been. The degradation of Marxist social philosophy in the U.S.S.R. can be traced to the same kind of causes which were responsible for the transformation of the *laissez-faire* philosophy in the West from a philosophy of social progress to one of social stagnation.

In the U.S.S.R., Marxist philosophy began as a rationalization enabling the seizure of power. After power was seized by a minority group, the philosophy of class struggle was turned into a rationalization for holding on to power. The importance of the individual had been de-emphasized in the struggle for power, because without wholehearted unity of purpose and without strong military discipline the struggle could not have been won. But what had been a means was transformed into an end, into a *value*. Unanimity and conformity became social virtues in the "classless" society.

Since the old rationalization for keeping everyone in line was no longer tenable, new ones had to be invented (they were invented in abundance and with abandon, and without much regard for consistency). For example, it is sometimes argued by Communists that there is no need for freedom of political differences in a class-less society such as the U.S.S.R. because these differences are only a reflection of a class struggle, which is now nonexistent in the U.S.S.R. It is also argued with equal conviction that the dictatorship of the Communist Party cannot be relaxed, because new enemies are constantly lurking waiting for an opportunity of internal dissension to seize power. The second argument is given more weight, being more in line with the petrified dogma of social conflict as the basic social reality. Hence new enemies of the state kept emerging—the dissenting socialist parties, the intellectuals, the rich peasants, the deviationists within the Communist Party, the saboteurs and foreign agents, the un-Soviet cosmopolitans, etc., etc.

Anxiety is the constant by-product of a persistent necessity to invent rationalizations for values which have become untenable. Therein, in my opinion, is the basis of chronic fear in both the United States and in the Soviet Union. The most unfortunate thing about anxiety is that it is not only the by-product of holding on to useless values but it also precludes a state of mind wherein values can be re-examined. To examine something, you have to disengage yourself for a while; you have to hold it off at some distance and look at it. And this is precisely what you cannot do in a state of anxiety. You hold on for dear life like a fear-paralyzed driver who cannot take his foot off the brake of his skidding car.

THE DE-EMPHASIS OF CONFLICT

Since an operational approach to a social philosophy depends on freedom from anxiety, the first steps in this approach should be to allay the existing anxieties associated with social problems. One way of doing it is to avoid the either-or form in which such problems are usually cast. In a way, the either-or form is a result of anxiety. In an atmosphere of fear and threat, one tries to occupy a position as incompatible with that of the opponent as possible. As in conflicts between individuals, so in ideological conflicts, it is the fear and hatred of the opponent (who constitutes a threat) which leads one to contradict him as much as possible instead of as much as is warranted by one's convictions. The aim in conflict is to destroy. In an ideological conflict, one seeks to destroy the rationalizations of the opponent, hence the *raison d'être* of the opposing ideology, hence the ideology itself.

The present ideological conflict between East and West is verbalized in terms of an either-or question. The Western version of the question, loaded to favor the Western position, is "Does the individual exist for the state or the state for the individual?" The Eastern version, loaded in favor of the Eastern position, is "Is the welfare of (a few) individuals to be prior to the welfare of the entire society?" Even if the loaded versions of the question are avoided, so as to put it in a form to which both sides might agree, the question still remains a dichotomy: individualism *vs.* collectivism.

One is reminded of similar dichotomies around which bitter ideological conflicts have raged: materialism vs. idealism in philosophy; heredity vs. environment in social science; teaching the student vs. teaching the subject in education; form vs. content in esthetics. All these dichotomies are misstatements of the associated problems. For example, the real problem in bio-sociology is "How do hereditary factors interact with environment?" When the question is put this way, one is encouraged to *seek* the relation between heredity and environment, instead of regarding this relation as one of mutual exclusion or, in a more sophisticated version, regarding the relation to be additive (so much heredity *and* so much environment).

So in social philosophy, the real problem concerning the relation of the individual to society is, "What is this relation?" One might ask, more explicitly, "How can the needs of individuals be realized by social organization? How are those needs *influenced* by particular forms of social organization? How shall individuals be trained to insure the integrity of social organizations? How can we avoid unresolvable contradictions between the needs of the individuals and the conditions for the integrity of the social organization?"

With the problem so posed, the dichotomy disappears. If the relation between individual and society is assumed at all, it is assumed to be a symbiosis rather than conflict. The assumption may have to be modified, but it is a good one to start with, because it serves to de-emphasize conflict, allay anxieties, and thus to enhance an atmosphere conducive to effective inquiry.

The de-emphasis of conflict does not mean, of course, that the problem of social conflict is to be side-stepped or denied, as is often done in the pronouncements of the anti-Communist politicians, whose principal aim is to contradict Communist pronouncements. Wherever social conflict is a fact (can be described in extensional terms), it must, of course, be recognized. It is a mistake, however, to consider it a prime mover of society. Its prime mover role can never be conclusively proved, simply because history cannot be repeated. The fundamental role of social conflict can, of course, be *assumed* in an attempt to explain history. In Marx's theory of history, it has proved to be a rather plausible assumption. However, we must also remember that when the assumption is made not only in the privacy of a scholar's study but in the limelight of political leadership, it often becomes a self-realizing assumption.

The assumption of conflict becomes self-realizing in the subjective sense because if you assume conflict, you see conflict where it is and where it is not. It also becomes self-realizing in the objective sense: if you constantly call attention to conflict, you *get* conflict. To illustrate this, I offer a few examples from Soviet life, which also corroborate the point about the "enemies" which seem to be constantly plaguing the toiling masses.

The interpretation of all human activity as conflict has often driven the Communists to ridiculous positions. In the early twenties, for example, when the "class struggle" inside Russia was still officially going on, the national life was pictured as a series of fronts where bitter battles were raging. There was the economic front, the cultural front, the health front, etc. Each front had sectors; for example, the cultural front had a literary sector, a musical sector, etc. This metaphor was probably not a bad one in itself. It might have served as a stimulus for all-out effort and as an effective dramatization of constructive cooperative activity in terms of experiences still fresh in the memory of the people (the bitter civil war of 1918–1921). The metaphor, however, was carried further than that. On every front and sector there was, besides the obvious metaphorical enemy (illiteracy, disease, technological disorganization, etc.), also a *class enemy*, personified by real people, for example, by people of bourgeois parentage, people with an "intellectual" outlook (a term of derision in the twenties, now replaced by the "cosmopolitan" outlook), people with a wrong kind of sense of humor, etc. These people often enough instead of being drawn into the cooperative effort were pushed into really hostile attitudes because of the outcast role they had to play.

Furthermore, every situation had to be fitted into the metaphor of conflict. I remember reading about a conference on folk music (a battle on the musical sector of the cultural front) in which the merits of musical instruments and of musical scales were discussed in terms of class allegiance! A heated argument arose on whether a certain type of zither was really a folk instrument or only masqueraded as such, being really a relic of feudal domination. Another fierce argument concerned the class allegiance of major and minor modes.

This pattern of discussion among Communists goes back to 1907[42] and has not changed. The recent diatribes against Western art and science are consequences of casting all interpretations of human activity in terms of social conflict.

On our side, similar patterns prevail. The form of conflict we assume is less crass than the Soviet version but more pervasive. That is, the conflict is less sharp (not aiming at destruction), but there are many more conflicting units. We assume that the prime mover of progress is the striving on the part of each individual to "get ahead."* Social morality is defined as abiding by certain rules of the game, within which practically anything goes. The ability of an individual to "take care of himself" is a fundamental social virtue. Cooperative efforts not aimed at money-making are automatically suspect. The proponents of individualism are driven to take stands no less extreme than those of the Communists—to oppose measures aimed at improving housing, agriculture, and public health; to oppose appropriations for encouraging the development of social science; to oppose policies designed for making friends abroad. Inroads on the philosophy of *laissez-faire* made during the Great Depression have driven the die-hards to even more passionate defenses of individualism which, ironically, have culminated in a demand for orthodoxy and conformity as stringent as that demanded by the Communists.

The tensions and anxieties in both Soviet society and in ours stem from attempts to hold on to values which have become untenable. These values were stated *a priori* in the fundamental rationalizations of both systems: the principle of total self-reliance in one and the principle of total loyalty in the other. Neither of these principles can be lived up to by human beings as they are today.

*Note that in our legal system corporations are defined as "individuals."

Social Hygiene

Operational ethics views the relation of the individual to society not in terms of self-evident truths but as a question to be investigated. The question, "What sort of individuals function best in what sort of society?" is a difficult one and cannot be answered in terms of postulated principles of social justice. One must define the concepts of good functioning, both for the individual and for society. One cannot do so from either point of view to the exclusion of the other as, for example, in stating that "the good functioning of the individual is measured by his contribution to the welfare of the society," or "the good functioning of a society is measured by its contribution to the welfare of its members," because in both statements one tacitly assumes the primacy of the one or the other and thus cannot hope for a generally acceptable solution of the problem.

An approach possibly acceptable to both philosophies is in postulating that both individuals and societies are organisms in symbiotic relation to each other. This is not a new idea, in fact it is common in biology. The boundary between a collection of unicellular organisms and a multicellular one is not strictly defined: one can almost trace the transition from one to the other. The work of W. C. Allee, A. E. Emerson (1), and others has shown the fruitfulness of the biological approach to social science in terms of developing a physiology of "epi-organisms."* Such a physiology would be applicable to the "life" of societies, that is, their growth, maintenance, and even reproduction.

One must be careful, however, not to jump to conclusions about the "nature of society" on the basis of biological analogies. Such attempts were common in antiquity and in the Middle Ages, when states were compared to a human body, with the king corresponding to the head, the priesthood the heart, the army the arms, etc. Societies can be considered as organisms, but their "anatomy" and physiology" cannot be inferred from a figure of speech. They can be discovered only through a systematic investigation. Once the "physiology" of a society is understood, its needs become apparent. From these needs the principles of "social hygiene" can then be deduced.

The difference between "social justice" and "social hygiene" is analogous to the difference between individual virtue and individual (physical and mental) hygiene. The principles of virtue are

*The term "epi-organism" to refer to an organism composed of organisms was coined, I think, by R. W. Gerard.

usually stated *a priori* as parts of religious and philosophical systems, and so are the principles of social justice as parts of social and political philosophies. Principles of hygiene, on the other hand, emerge as a result of our knowledge of the human organism. To take an example, cleanliness is recommended by hygiene not because it is "next to godliness," but because it minimizes the danger of infection. As a matter of fact, cleanliness, if carried too far, may become hygienically undesirable. A baby brought up in a sterile environment would probably succumb to infection immediately upon leaving it. Principles of mental hygiene are also being established. It appears that "love," for example, is a good thing because it contributes to a wholesome personality.

On the other hand, there are "virtues" approved on religious and moralistic grounds which violate hygienic principles. Similar considerations apply to social justice and social hygiene. The "right of property" may be considered inviolable in one system of social justice and "equivalent to theft" in another, but from the point of view of social hygiene, its desirability or undesirability can be considered only in a given social context and with reference to its role in the "life process" of the society.

The operationalist, therefore, sees the relation of the individual to society in terms of the needs of the individual and also those of society. These needs can be ascertained only in the course of study and analysis, in particular of how given personalities function in a given social structure and, in turn, determine the functioning of that structure.

Chapter 12. COMMUNICATION, POWER, AND REVOLUTIONS

If A society is a quasi-biological organism, what are its needs? We do not know. We cannot talk to this organism as we do to individuals when we try to ascertain their needs. But to a certain extent we can guess the needs of a society. If it is like an organism at all, "it" strives to survive and to maintain its integrity. We may even suppose that it tries to grow, to learn by experience, to develop, and to become more complex, since we can observe these things happening to social organisms fairly consistently.

How does a social organism survive? Not through the survival of its members, necessarily, because all the members may die, as they do in each generation; but the social organism, say a city or a church, may maintain itself. On the other hand, the members may survive, but the organism may die, as, for example, when a corporation is dissolved or a political party "dies." To a certain extent, the distinction between the life of an organism and the life of its parts applies also to biological organisms. It is known that many tissues can be kept "alive" outside the body. Conceivably, all the parts of a body might be kept alive in artificial media. The "body" itself, however, considered as an organism, would be dead. The life of the body is more than the totality of its living parts. This additional entity, on which the life of the greater organism can be said to depend, is its *organization*, the totality of the functional relations among its parts.

Therefore to say that a society tends to survive means that it tends to preserve the functional relation among its parts—its organization. How does it do it?*

*In this discussion the terms "society" or "social organization" will be used to denote any group where any sort of systematic interaction occurs. Thus a prison is also a "social organization," because the prisoners have to obey the guards. The prisoners themselves may or may not constitute a social organization, depending on whether any systematic interaction occurs among them.

The first answer to this question is that it does not always do it. In fact, in the life of every organism, whether biological or social, there comes a time when it no longer is able to maintain its organization. We say, then, that the organism dies. Let us, then, modify the question and ask, "How does a society maintain its integrity when it does maintain it?"

Sometimes a society is held together because it fulfills the real needs of its members. Sometimes it survives because the members are deluded into believing that their needs are fulfilled. Sometimes a social organization is preserved by force.

The "use of force" in human affairs is largely a figurative expression. We say a man is "forced" to do something against his will, but we do not mean it literally because any action involves, among other things, a coordinated motion of muscles, and the muscles of another cannot be manipulated in a coordinated manner against his will. To take a few examples, we say:

The gunman forced his victim to surrender his watch.

The businessman was forced to sell his business.

The candidate was forced to withdraw his statement.

The soldiers were forced to fight.

The nation was forced to re-arm.

If we gave an operational definition of the word "forced" in each case, we would find that in each instance a *choice* was involved. The gunman's victim weighed his desire to retain his watch against the probability of being beaten up or shot. The businessman was torn between his desire to continue in business and the probability of going bankrupt, etc.

Freedom of choice is insignificant if the consequences of the "alternative" are so bad that the choice is a foregone conclusion. Such "freedom of choice" is usually called intimidation. A few individuals can be intimidated by a realizable threat. But large populations are intimidated in some other way, because the measures they are threatened with can be seldom carried out on the whole population.

Example: A group of one hundred prisoners of war is escorted by five armed guards to a camp where conditions are known to be so deplorable that a man has one chance in ten to survive a year. On the other hand, a sudden attack on the guards may provide an opportunity to escape. The chances of surviving and escaping are better than one in two, since the guards can kill only a few prisoners before they themselves are overpowered. Suppose that every man knows this. Yet no one acts. How does this "social organization" maintain itself on the march? Why does it not break up? It is assumed that the prisoners are intimidated into following the guards by the threat of being shot. However, we have assumed that every man knows that he has a greater chance to survive an attempt to escape than a sojourn in the camp. Why, then, does no one do anything about it?

To be successful, the action must be coordinated and sudden. There is no *organization* among the prisoners to make this possible, and so the group (prisoners and guards) preserves its own organization. The prisoners accept the leadership of the guards and go to their almost certain doom.

Example: Most people are aware that if every man refused to be inducted into the army, war would be impossible. Even a sizable percentage of refusals might make the organization of armies so difficult as to make war impossible. Furthermore, a vast majority of people probably feel that they would refuse to fight "if every one else did." But there is no machinery to enable all these people to say this at the same time. Thus the leadership of the military remains intact, and armies keep fighting wars.

Thus, the intimidation of large populations depends on a lack of organization among their members, and this is the situation which is usually called the preservation of order (or allegiance) "by force."

Organization can be effected by a flow of information (communication) among the members of a population. True, sometimes amorphous mobs are capable of short-term organized action, usually a simple act of violence. This probably happens as a consequence of a simple item of information suddenly passing through a crowd, say a signal. If such a stimulus elicits a response in a sufficiently large fraction of the mob, it will spread by direct imitation through the crowd (79).

On the whole, however, extensive organization is essential for any kind of organized action, and this can be accomplished only if communications can flow through the population. It follows that intimidation of populations is possible if the flow of information through them is curbed or strictly controlled. The slogan, "divide and rule" is a recognition of this fact. The most effective "division" is one which cuts communication lines in the population to be ruled.

Monopoly of Communication Channels

Autocratic and totalitarian states are examples of rule by intimidation. The important difference between them is that autocratic
regimes try to minimize the flow of communication in the population: they try to keep the channels silent. Therefore autocracies are
indifferent or hostile to mass education, frown on all forms of
popular organizations, and discourage any attempt on the part of
the population to participate in political life. Totalitarian regimes,
on the contrary, utilize the communication channels to the utmost:
they try to keep the channels *clogged* with their own brand of information, keeping all other brands out. Totalitarian regimes often
encourage mass education and mass organizations, provided that
their control remains in proper hands, and promote mass participation in politics (with the same provision).

A case in point is the article of the Soviet Constitution which
guarantees "freedom of speech, press, and assembly," and "puts
teeth" into this guarantee by placing at the disposal of the "toiling
masses" printing presses, streets for demonstrations, etc. The same
Constitution guarantees universal suffrage with secret ballot (106).

When the Constitution was adopted (1936), Trotzky is said to
have remarked, "The right to vote for Stalin has been finally
granted." Indeed, Soviet election ballots carry only one set of
candidates. The right of free speech, assembly, etc., must also be
understood in the same way: only opinions favorable to the regime
may be openly uttered; the only demonstrations which are allowed
are those where the "demands" are in strict harmony with current
government policy. Yet the Constitution of 1936 is not just a bad
joke. It demonstrates the very important difference between autocracy and totalitarianism. The old Russian autocracy did not allow
the people to demonstrate *even in favor* of a government policy.
Such a demonstration would have been considered presumptuous
and would have aroused strong suspicion. In short, an autocracy
demands a silent submissive loyalty. The totalitarian regime demands a noisy, enthusiastic loyalty, with full participation of the
population in politics. On this basis, totalitarian regimes often
claim the status of democracies.

Somewhat more subtle are the restrictions on the flow of information in the other great mass nation, the United States. Although
not at all evident as they are in the Communist countries, the
restrictions are hardly less effective. In the United States, the mass

channels of communication are also clogged predominantly with one brand of information, which glorifies individualism and the consumption of goods. Rival points of view are usually not excluded. They are simply shouted down.

The monopoly of communication channels (which is effected by keeping the channels "empty" or "clogged") enables social organizations based on *undelegated* power to maintain themselves.

DELEGATED AND UNDELEGATED POWER

A power in an organization which does not stem from the explicit consent of its members and therefore performs no function in serving the needs of the member may be termed an undelegated power. Such a power may, however, serve the needs of the *organization*, at least temporarily, by enabling the organization to maintain itself.

No sharp lines can be drawn between delegated and undelegated power, but extreme cases are clearly recognizable. For example, the power of the guards over the prisoners is clearly not delegated by the prisoners to the guards. The power of most governments is a mixture of delegated and undelegated power, ranging from one extreme to the other. The power of the chief engineer of a construction project or of a conductor of an orchestra is delegated power. The fact that these positions are not "elective" is not essential. The authority of the engineer and that of the conductor are essential in the performance of the task at hand. Thus if the need of the workers or the musicians is to perform these tasks, they *consent* to submit to the authority of the leaders. The last examples show that delegated power may be absolute.

The characteristic thing about delegated power is that its range is limited to specific areas of activity and usually to specific times. The engineer has no power over his subordinates off the job; the conductor has no power off the stage; the democratically elected official has no power when the term of his office expires. On the other hand, the characteristic thing about undelegated power is that its area is usually not clearly defined; in fact it is often not recognized as power. Such is the power of a political boss. Such is economic power.

Traditional democratic doctrine maintains that the only legitimate power is delegated power, that is, power by consent of the governed. A democratic revolution occurs when undelegated power is overthrown and delegated power, usually duly recognized in a constitution, is put in its place. The characteristic tragedy of democratic revolutions has been their failure to recognize new sources of undelegated power. For example, the American revolution of 1776 was a revolution against the undelegated power of the British Crown. Accordingly, the makers of the Constitution were careful to define the extent of the delegated power of the new government. We read, for example, in the Bill of Rights that soldiers shall not be billeted in time of peace in anyone's house without the consent of the owner. When this provision was made, the memory of King George's abuses was still fresh.

No one today would think the matter of billeting soldiers of such importance as to include it in the Constitution. On the other hand, powers which were unknown or unimportant in the early days of this nation have assumed an immense importance, but it so happens that those are not the powers of the state, and there is nothing about them in the Constitution. Those are the powers of the large economic units: the power to hire and fire, to produce and to stop producing or to move the production plants; the power to flood the market with a product or to withdraw a product from the market; the power to develop a technological process or to shelve it; the power to create by means of high-pressure propaganda a desire in millions of people to dress in a certain way or to acquire certain habits or to spend a certain portion of one's income in a certain way; the power to exploit and even to deplete natural resources, to influence legislation by lobbies, to invest or not to invest capital at home or abroad. All these powers have not been delegated in any formal way to the organs which exercise them any more than the privileges of the old aristocracy were formally and consciously delegated when the feudal system came into being.

The Communist Revolution of 1917 was also conducted in the democratic tradition in the sense that the undelegated powers of the large proprietors and of the officialdom were broken, and the delegated power of the "workers', peasants', and soldiers' councils" (the Soviets) was put in its place.* It was naively assumed by the intellectual leaders that since Marx had foretold that the proletarian revolution would be the last, no new undelegated power would arise. It did arise, however, in the structure of the party bureaucracy and remains today the more strongly entrenched the more categorically it is denied.

*The mixture of democracy and totalitarianism in the Russian Revolution was apparent from the start: together with the undelegated powers of the old regime the strictly delegated power of the Constituent Assembly was also overthrown.

The bitter feud between the liberals and the revolutionists today is rooted in the fact that each faction sees the dangers of undelegated power in the method of the other. The revolutionist scoffs at the legalistic reforms of the liberal because he believes that they do not touch the undelegated power of the ruling class. The revolutionist believes in breaking that power by "direct action," that is, by physical capture of the current instruments of power, blanket imposition of new laws to reflect the new power structure, and proscription of the leaders of the opposition, etc. The liberal deplores such methods, points out that the excesses of revolutionary struggle are often worse than the evils fought, warns against the usurpation of power by ruthless persons, etc. The revolutionist then accuses the liberal of hypocrisy. He points out that a great deal of bloodshed can be prevented by a little blood shed in the right places. He argues that if the Spanish Republican government had executed a few hundred military leaders in time, two million Spaniards would not have been killed in the civil war. He points out that the Russian Revolution was "successful" only because the Bolsheviks did not flinch from administering violence. The liberal points out that such arguments are wholly inconclusive, that it is a moot question whether any violent revolution can be called "successful." He points out that only slow revolutionary changes "take," etc.

The Nonviolent Revolution

The struggle between the liberal-reformist and the direct-action revolutionist is another instance of a "polarized" conflict, where the opponents have been driven by mutual distrust and fear to the opposite poles of a dichotomy. The basic problem has been lost sight of: "How can undelegated power in a social organization be prevented from arising?"

A third approach to the problem of social reorganization is offered in the principle of "nonviolent" revolution. This principle combines the "direct action" of the revolutionist with the non-violence of the reformer. The nonviolent revolution comes closer to an operational approach to social problems because it attacks the very basis of undelegated power by dissipating the illusions which hold it together. Hence this approach has no use for the moralistic invectives of the revolutionist (largely based on the ethics of retribution) nor for the legalistic niceties of the traditional reformer. Examples of nonviolent revolutionary action are the strike, the boycott, the renunciation of loyalty to established leadership, and civil disobedience.* In its purest form, the disruptive action of nonviolent revolution is directed at the power structure only and not at the persons comprising the ruling group. These are simply disregarded.

Long-term results of the nonviolent approach to social problems which circumvents the channels of legalistic reform are seen in the growth of the industrial labor unions, the growth of cooperative enterprises, and most clearly in the recent achievement of independence by India. In each case, action was guided by a conscious disavowal of existing power structures.†

A labor union is a challenge of the power of the employer to dictate conditions of employment. This power is undelegated, being bestowed on the employer not by the employees, nor even by legislative action, but simply by the economic structure of society (the conditions of the labor market, the accumulation of capital, the technological potential, etc.) which cannot be discerned by the population at large, since it takes a rather penetrating analysis to uncover it. Once the sources of this power *are* discerned, however, the freedom to challenge it appears, since weapons to combat it are suggested. Similar considerations apply to the growth of the cooperative movement in Europe and in America (the challenging of the economic power of cartels and trusts) and of the civil disobedience movement in India (the challenging of Britain's political and economic power).

Thus the nonviolent revolutionary approach to social change emphasizes the dissolution of the organizational structure based on undelegated power instead of the supplementing of one power structure by another (as with the revolutionist) or the use of delegated power to curb the undelegated powers (as with the reformist). Toynbee's theory of revolution (103) also stresses this point of view. In Toynbee's estimation, a significant revolution occurs when the "proletariat" (which Toynbee defines as the sector of the population which is *in* the society but not *of* the society, that is, with

---

*It is recognized, of course, that none of the actual instances of the actions cited are conducted in an ideally nonviolent way. There is often violence in strikes as well as plenty of moralistic invective and hate-mongering. Still, the actions cited on the whole come closer to the ideal of nonviolent revolution than the political revolutions of the conventional "seizure of power" type.

†Legal reform may, of course, accompany "direct action," but such reforms characteristically *follow* a *fait accompli*. The Wagner Labor Relations Act is an example.

no sense of membership in it) loses faith in the values of the ruling classes (in other words, becomes aware of the undelegated nature of their power).

THE OPEN SOCIETY

A society in which the principal social values consist in keeping the free flow of information through its channels has been called by Popper and others an "open society" (73, 63). It would appear at first glance that Popper's open society is an idealization of the existing parliamentary democracies. If, however, one takes the "free flow of information" seriously, one sees that in many respects the existing democracies (especially the largest ones) are almost as far from being open societies as the dictatorships. For freedom of information must be defined not formally in terms of statutory laws but operationally in terms of the actual flow of information through the communication channels. One must consider not only the *possibility* of a given item of information spreading through the population but also the *probability*.[43] One must also consider the capability and the inclination of those entrusted with making far-reaching decisions to seek, absorb, and utilize information. One must evaluate the commitment of the leaders to set ways of doing things. One must examine the educational system and the habits of evaluation instilled by it in the young. One must measure the amount of information flowing into the society from the outside. Above all, society can be called an open society only if its structure is such that it *continues* to remain open, that is, undelegated power cannot be consolidated within it.

The cliché, "Eternal vigilance is the price of liberty" applies to the open society. There is a danger in the attitude of "vigilance," however, in that it tends to be focused on specific dangers, which may become irrelevant. For example, the vigilance of American democratic leadership has long been concentrated on the danger of the emergence of undelegated power in one of the branches of the federal government, especially in the executive. The admirable system of "checks and balances" prevented this from happening. But formidable undelegated powers sprang up elsewhere. The vigilance of the Russian revolutionary leaders was concentrated on the danger of counterrevolution, and counterrevolution was effectively crushed. But undelegated power emerged within the revolutionary leadership itself and was maintained by the very apparatus (the secret police) originally designed to protect the delegated power of the councils. Vigilance has meaning only if the nature of power is understood. It can be understood only by systematic, open-minded investigation, not by a verbal definition, by philosophical insight, or by political dogma.

Coming back to the question, "How can a social organization maintain itself?" it appears that, *in the long run*, it can maintain itself as long as it serves the self-extension needs of its members. This it can do only by preventing the accumulation of pressures which make for its dissolution. An open society seems to possess this safety device. It appears at this stage of knowledge that an open society must be egalitarian, that is, power within it must be delegated power only, entrusted to a leadership only for specific purposes in strictly delineated areas of activity and for limited periods. In other words, the power of decision-making must be based on functional not on status relations. This appears so because, given a free flow of information, it seems that any undelegated power will be ultimately challenged. Hierarchical social structures seem to maintain themselves only by denying the free flow of information, especially by excluding the possibility of asking why a hierarchy must be maintained. There is some evidence for this in that whenever information barriers crumble, hierarchical structures (paternalistic, autocratic, etc.) are generally undermined. Conversely, the maintenance of such structures is always accompanied by the restriction of information.

Egalitarianism, therefore, in operational social philosophy appears not as a postulated principle but as a conclusion, flowing out of the only premise of that philosophy—ethical principles must be arrived at as a result of free inquiry.

SUMMARY OF CHAPTERS 11 AND 12 AND SOME CONCLUSIONS

1. Barriers to information are concomitant to a concentration of undelegated powers. The barriers serve to hide the origins of those powers from the population or to mask their nature. The maintenance of fear through direct intimidation or of diffuse anxiety by more subtle means helps maintain the information barriers.

2. An attack on the undelegated powers is equivalent to an attack on the information barriers. The end result of a successful attack is the disruption of the fears (and the loyalties based on fear) and the anxieties through which the holders of undelegated powers operate.

3. The aim of eliminating fear precludes the use of hatred and invective in revolutionary activity, no matter how useful hatred and moralistic invective seem for the purpose of disrupting existing loyalty structures. Hatred and fear are psychologically related and sometimes indistinguishable. If the purpose of a revolution is a long-term elimination of undelegated power, the mastery of non-violent techniques by revolutionists is indispensable.

4. The revolutionist's critique of the liberal's legalistic reform methods and the liberal's critique of the revolutionist's seizure of power methods are both valid. It is not likely that legal (delegated) power can essentially disrupt the framework of undelegated power. On the other hand, new undelegated power has been seen to arise inevitably on the heels of conventional revolutions. The nonviolent revolution concentrates on building new cooperative frameworks in the population *outside* the existing power structures, which it prepares to challenge.

5. Although a stable hierarchical structure without fear and hatred is conceivable (where everyone knows *and loves* his place), it appears that such structures can be preserved only behind effective information barriers. Egalitarian ideas, once penetrating a hierarchically structured society (even presumably a "stable" one) seem to become inevitable disrupting influences. On the contrary, egalitarian structures seem to be impenetrable to aristocratic ideas from the outside. Therefore under conditions of free information flow, egalitarian structures seem to be the only stable ones and capable of being the embodiment of a universal ethics.

6. For the purposes of coordinated action in the accomplishment of specific tasks, temporary power structures must arise in an egalitarian society. The power involved is, however, always delegated power, strictly circumscribed for a specific task. Such power may even be absolute, such as the power of a ship captain on a voyage, a traffic policeman at a busy intersection, or the military dictator in the early Roman republic. The test of egalitarianism is the nonpersistence of these powers. The ship captain must not carry his authority ashore nor the traffic policeman into a tavern. The military dictator of the early Roman republic used to go back to his normal occupation after the "duration." When he failed to do so, the republic fell.

7. The formal equality of all persons (as legalized in democratic and even in totalitarian countries) becomes *actual* in the egalitarian society in the sense that no undelegated power is tolerated. This

can come about only if constant vigilance is maintained against the concentration of hidden undelegated powers and against the concomitant establishment of information barriers.

8. Questions pertaining to the technique of revolution cannot be fully answered on the basis of any existing theory because not enough is known about social dynamics. Such questions can be answered only on the basis of experience and a critical analysis of experience. Some such experience already exists. On a small scale, it can be found in case histories of democratic organizations and organizations which have become democratized through local victories of democratic processes over usurpations of power. On a large scale, the recent growth of the labor union movement in the United States and the nonviolent revolution in India should provide valuable material for study. Even the violent revolutions conducted on doctrinaire principles (Russia) and the conventional long-term programs of social reform (Sweden) contain within themselves aspects of nonviolent revolution which can be studied with profit.

9. The only general principle of an operational social philosophy is that it is operational. Like operational knowledge, it is guided by the analysis of experience. Based on operational ethics, it is guided by freedom of choice, knowledge of consequences, and self-insight.

Part III. THE FRONTIERS

INTRODUCTION

I F I WERE to fix a date for the birth of operational philosophy, I would choose sometime at the beginning of this century when scientists became acutely critical of linguistic means at their disposal. That was the time when the foundations of mathematics were being overhauled by Russell and Peano, when the conceptual framework of space and time was being rebuilt by Einstein and Minkowski, and when the foundations of metalinguistics were being laid by Malinowski and Sapir.

Operationalism involves a sharp awareness of the communication problem in its broadest sense, that is, the problem of mapping experience upon language and of evaluating language in terms of experience. An awareness of a problem affords opportunities for exploration, and as long as these opportunities are pursued, there exists a "frontier" and with it a challenge to man's creative abilities. Operational philosophy has such a frontier today. The expansion of this frontier consists in expanding and refining the linguistic means at man's disposal with a view of improving the communicating and the evaluating processes.

There are two "fronts" on this frontier which seem to be facing in opposite directions. One is the "analytic" front. The tasks here are to analyze experience in terms of the simplest possible components. Practically everything said so far in this book revolved about this task. The "meaning" of the persistent questions of philosophy was analyzed by showing how these questions evolved from simple experiences, complicated by "evaluations" piled up on each other. Once this meaning of the questions is perceived, one can proceed to answer them by the development of appropriate analytic and empirical tools. All the "exact" sciences have proceeded in this way. The other front could be called the "synthetic." The task there is to see great areas of experience all at once.

It is maintained by some philosophers (I am referring in particular to some thinkers in the social sciences who are concerned with methodology) that the analytic method is not sufficient for the understanding of some phenomena. They frequently illustrate their position by the "pile of bricks" analogy. "A house," they point out, "is more than a pile of bricks. You cannot understand the house no matter how thoroughly you examine each of the bricks that compose it." This criticism of the analytic method is not quite fair, because the analytic sciences do not confine themselves to the study of "bricks." On the contrary, the triumphs of the physical sciences (which are entirely analytic) are marked by the emergence of the understanding of "totalities." Thus, the understanding of the solar system emerges out of understanding how the elementary laws of motion act on each of its components. The understanding of the gross behavior of substances emerges from the understanding of the atoms. The analytic sciences *do* succeed in putting the elements together into wholes.

Yet there may be something to be said for the opposite approach. Perhaps it is not a good idea to start with the chemistry of clay if one's object is to study the history of architecture. Perhaps more can be gained in the understanding of human behavior if one starts with a description of "culture profiles" instead of with the study of neural physiology. Perhaps, on the other hand, the two approaches can be shown to be complementary to each other, so that the "analytic-synthetic" dichotomy will find a natural resolution along with the other dichotomies of yesterday (materialism-idealism, heredity-environment, etc.).

In particular, I will try to convince the proponents of the synthetic approach that the power of quantification (the stock-in-trade of the analytic scientist) is today much greater than it was even a couple of generations ago; and I will try to make the hard-boiled exact scientist see the point of the synthetic (holistic, organismic, intuitive, gestaltist) approach to certain areas of knowledge.

In a way, this attempt at a reconciliation may be viewed as a retreat from the positions of *strict* operationalism (as defined, say, by the radical logical positivists). I view it, however, as an extension of operationalism, since it stems from an awareness of a communication problem and constitutes an attempt to establish meaningful communication between two schools of thought, which have so far been thinking in different languages.

Chapter 13. QUANTIFICATION

The simplest known quantification is counting. Counting provides also the simplest and the most universal common basis of experience. Numbers are the simplest and the most universal linguistic invariants. What one may estimate as many, another estimates as few, but the meaning of "fourteen" is unambiguous, both in its formal sense and with reference to aggregates of objects. That is, twice seven sheep are fourteen sheep wherever there are sheep and numbers.

Somewhat more complex than counting is *measurement*. Measurement involves the recognition of a *unit*, hence the recognition of a physical invariant and an agreement to speak in terms of that invariant. Early units of length indicate the recognition of the rough invariance of the sizes of human hands, feet, etc. Later attempts to fix standards for these units indicate the awareness of the problem involved.

The next step is measurement combined with calculation. It was found long ago by people concerned with agriculture that one need not cover a rectangular field with unit squares to measure its area: the measurement of two of its sides will do, if one knows how to multiply. The introduction of calculation in combination with measurement opens the mind to a host of new quantities defined by *combinations* of units. For example:

velocity: units of length traveled divided by the number of units of time spent in traveling;

income: units of money per unit time;

interest: units of money per unit of money per unit time;

density: units of weight per unit of volume (which is itself a unit of length cubed, etc.).

Note that to someone unfamiliar with these complex units of measurement, the quantities they measure appear as "qualities." An example of historical importance is the quantification of "density" by Archimedes. Faced with the problem of determining the composition of the alloy used in making a crown, Archimedes must have pondered on the difference between the *quantity* of metal and its *quality*. The quantity was there: every ounce was accounted for. But the quality was in question: did the goldsmith substitute a cheaper metal for part of the gold? The famous exclamation "Eureka!" marked Archimedes' insight into the relation between quantity and quality. He saw *density* as a quantity, namely the ratio of weight to volume. It was, therefore, subject to measurement, and the whole question of "quality" could be answered in terms of this measurement.

The more general philosophical question is whether we can translate everything which we experience as "quality" into quantitative (and therefore objective) terms.

The number of qualities is, of course, enormous. Besides being long and short, heavy and light, enduring and transient (categories early recognized as quantities), things appear also cold and hot, smooth and rough, red and green, sweet and sour, loud and soft, high pitched and low pitched, reedy and fluty, wet and dry. One feels that some speech is "guttural," some "lisping," some "liquid." All this tremendous range of sensual experience seems to defy quantification.

Nor is this all. Beyond the world of sensual experience is another world of evaluative experience. Substances are fragrant and fetid, foods delicious and insipid, persons are kind and vicious, courageous and cowardly, intelligent and stupid; nations are civilized and barbarous; religions true and false.

Can this universe of sensations, judgments, and evaluations be incorporated into a quantitative language? The prevalent opinion is, I believe, that it cannot. This opinion (that it cannot) stems from many considerations. To begin with, some people are honestly at a loss to imagine how quantitative measurements can be applied to "qualities." They will admit that one shade can be "redder" than another, and perhaps, one country "more democratic" than another, but they cannot imagine what can possibly be meant by "twice as red," or "twice as democratic."[44]

Other people believe that quantification is somehow degrading as a measure of human experience, especially if applied to moral qualities and sentiments. Still others, although convinced of both the necessity and the possibility of an objective language for all areas of experience, maintain that the language of quantity is not sufficiently general to provide such a medium. Finally there are those who are concerned with the role of philosophy in a progressively "scientized" world. They declare that there are areas of "truth" which cannot be described in quantitative language. The more extreme among them (those inclined toward mysticism) go further and declare that there are things which cannot be described in any kind of language, let alone objective or quantitative.

I shall take up these objections in order.

QUANTIFICATION OF "QUALITIES"

We have seen how the qualitative notion of "density" was quantified by Archimedes by the introduction of a unit of measure which was a *ratio* of weight units and volume units. Another successful quantification of a quality dates even further back, namely to Pythagoras (about 500 b.c.), who performed this feat for musical pitch.

Pythagoras is said to have invented the "monochord," probably the first full-fledged piece of experimental apparatus. The monochord is simply a taut string mounted on a board with a movable peg, so that when the string is plucked, the length of the vibrating part of the string can be varied. Pythagoras showed that what we subjectively conceive as the "octave" can be objectively described as the ratio 1:2 of the lengths of string producing a tone and its octave respectively. Furthermore, he showed that the ratio 2:3 corresponds to the "fifth," 3:4 to the "fourth," etc. The Pythagorean scale consists of tones which are octave equivalents of successive perfect fifths, placed in a sequence within a single octave. That is, if one starts with, say, F and proceeds by perfect fifths to C, G, D, A, E, and B, and then places these tones within a single octave, starting with C, one gets what we call the major scale.[45]

It was discovered later that the invariant involved in pitch perception was the frequency of the sound waves associated with it. Thus each pitch is associated with a certain number. For example, the middle C on the piano is the pitch associated with the frequency of 256 vibrations per second. The mathematical theory of sound has gone even further. Not only pitch but also "timbre" was found to be completely quantifiable. The difference between the violin tone drawn by Heifetz and that produced by little Willie practicing can be precisely described by analyzing the tones for their constituent frequencies.[46]

The quantification of sound characteristics is only one instance.

The entire history of physics is essentially a history of quantified "qualities." Temperature, elasticity, viscosity, luminosity, color, energy are all examples. The history of chemistry is not too different. The backbone of chemistry is the atomic theory, which is essentially a quantification of quality based on the discovery that innumerable "qualitatively different" substances can be described as combinations in strict quantitative proportions of comparatively few (less than 100) basic substances, the elements.

It appears, therefore, that in a great many instances, the gulf between quality and quantity is only a chimera, an indication of our ignorance of how the two can be related.

The Human Element

The crux of the objection against quantifying psychological and social events is the so-called "human element," which supposedly cannot be quantified. The argument involving the "human element" is often difficult to deal with, because it is likely to have emotional roots. It is an attitude which stems from a disinclination to analyze, which in turn may be a reflection of a fear that one's prejudices may be argued away.

Still, with some people the objection is "honest," that is, it comes from a genuine bewilderment concerning the "human element," by which presumably is meant the great variability of human behavior. This great variability seems to defy quantitative description.

I will try to meet the "honest" part of the objection first. It is an objection against the oversimplification inherent in the attempts to quantify complicated events. Any quantification is, of course, a simplification. Quantitative science describes ideal, not actual, situations. In those areas where reality approaches the ideal description (for example, in astronomy), the inadequacy of the idealization is not felt. But where the discrepancy is great (for example, in human affairs) the inadequacy of the simplification is apparent.

A critique which points out this inadequacy is the more constructive the more specifically it brings out the limits within which the quantification is useful. A case in point is the I.Q. test. To the extent that an individual will make consistent scores on the I.Q. test, the test measures *something*. To the extent that I.Q. test performance can be used to predict other performances of the individual, the measurement is *useful*. But it is foolhardy to jump to the conclusion that at last such an intangible quality as "intelligence" has been reduced to a number. There may be many kinds of behavior which usage associates with "intelligence" but which are not consistently correlated with the I.Q. score. The reasonable conclusion to draw, however, is not the defeatist one that "there is always a human element which defies measurement," but that the quantification techniques of the I.Q. score have not been sufficiently developed.

What applies to I.Q. applies with equal force to aptitude tests, personality tests, psychiatric diagnosis, etc. Experience shows that mass classification of individuals on the basis of quantitative measurements is useful in many situations. To the extent that such measurements are useful, it must be admitted that quantitative determination of human "qualities" is possible. In areas where existing measurements are not useful, others can conceivably be devised. Moreover the very language of quantification is undergoing extensive modification so that it can be applied in areas which had been thought to be impermeable to quantitative language. How this is being brought about will be described below.

The emotionally rooted objections to the quantitative approach are of a different nature. Here we are dealing with an aversion to "cold, de-humanized science" applied to areas which, it is felt, are the proper domain of empathy, sentiment, and intuitive understanding. Such objections are at least understandable in the light of crude misapplications of quantitative evaluation, such as Sinclair Lewis satirizes in the esthetic taste of George F. Babbitt, for whom one building is more beautiful than another, because it is two stories taller. In associating beauty with bigness, Babbitt clearly misses the point (49).

The only occasion on which Jesus of Nazareth was said to have lost his temper was when he saw religion commercialized.* He saw piety measured by the amount of money a man spent on a "sacrifice."

A Russian I once knew was appalled by an article on the Average American Housewife in one of our picture magazines. The Average Housewife's life was described in strictly quantitative terms, such as the average number of steps she takes in her kitchen throughout the year, the average number of hair-do's she gets, and the average number of soap opera hours she listens to.

"How about her inner life?" the Russian wanted to know. "What does she think about? What does she feel strongly about? There is not a word about that."

"In a way there is," I pointed out. "It says here she has a minor quarrel with her husband on the average of once in six weeks and a

*Matt. 21.

major fight twice a year, the subjects of quarreling being, in the order of frequency, in-laws, money. . . ."

"Ah, that is not what I mean," the Russian sighed.

One feels justifiably impatient with vulgar attempts at quantification, which, incidentally, are especially frequent in American journalism. These attempts smack of introducing the morality of the marketplace into human relations, of making life appear to be "printed on dollar bills," as a character in a play by Clifford Odets put it.

We see, however, that the common denominator of the emotional aversion to quantitative evaluation of human factors is in the feeling that these efforts are *misdirected*. Beauty, it is felt, has nothing to do with size, nor piety with money, nor personality with the minutiae of habits. It is commonplace to attribute this misdirection of effort to an orientation characteristic of "science" and "business," both of which are viewed by many people as de-humanizing enterprises.

However, attempts to describe moral matters quantitatively antedate the age of science and business. Already Aristotle (3) proposed a moral system based on seeking out an optimum between extremes. Generosity, in Aristotle's estimation, appears as midway between stinginess and extravagance; courage is the "golden mean" between cowardice and foolhardiness, etc. A medieval example of "quantitative morality" is found in the writings of St. Anselm. St. Anselm enumerates the sins of sensuousness according to the number of senses involved. There being "five senses," it seems there are five sensuous sins involving one sense each, ten sins involving two senses each (since ten different pairs can be formed of five senses), ten involving three senses (since ten triples can be formed), five of four senses, and just one very grave sin involving all five senses (presumably eating sweets, listening to music, looking at a sunset, and fondling a well-perfumed woman all at the same time).

St. Anselm's quantification of sin appears, of course, as ludicrous as Babbitt's quantification of beauty, but it does not follow that all such attempts must necessarily be ludicrous. Where Aristotle and St. Anselm and George F. Babbitt have failed, others may succeed.[47] We should recall that the failures of crackpot inventors of flying machines from the fifteenth to the nineteenth centuries did not warrant the conclusion that flying is impossible. Furthermore, I submit that the attempts to quantify moral and esthetic matters may arise (consciously or unconsciously) from an extremely praiseworthy motive—the desire to come to agreement. For quality is vague, but quantity is precise. Arguments about the value of a gem are immediately resolved when one measures the amount of precious materials in it. Attempts to quantify "virtue" go back to the most ancient days of Egyptian civilization, where a man's good deeds were imagined weighed against his sins. Such beliefs stem from a desire to resolve controversial matters in terms of verifiable criteria. It may well be that the compulsions toward quantitative evaluations of excellence so widespread in American culture (from batting averages of baseball players to market quotations on Old Masters) have their sources in similar desires.

If this is so, if quantification does afford an opportunity to describe and evaluate human matters on a more objective basis, then operational philosophy must view such attempts seriously (if critically) and must pursue them further.

WHAT IS COMPARABLE?

Perhaps the most serious objection to quantification rests on the argument that there are things which cannot be compared. Suppose, for example, we have quantified the value of a food in terms of the amounts of nutritive components in it. Suppose, further, that we have quantified the value of a garment in terms of its insulating property. How can the two values be compared? One cannot eat the garment, and one cannot wear the food. The two values are values of different *kinds*, it is maintained. There is a *qualitative* difference between them.

This argument appears even more potent when the "values" are on different levels of abstraction. Suppose we can quantify the amount of freedom an individual possesses in a given society and find that he enjoys more of it than an individual in another society, but that he gets less to eat. How can the need for freedom be weighed against the need to eat?

The answer to this objection depends to a great extent on what aims one has when one makes the comparison. It is important to keep in mind that "quantity" is not inherent in the thing quantified but in the operations associated with the quantification. Thus a piece of gold has a number of quantities associated with it, which are all different. There is volume (the space it occupies), weight (the force of gravitational attraction on it), the price (what people are willing to give for it). The need to compare two things is the need to find a common denominator for them. The market of modern commercial society is an extensive system of assigning a common denominator (price) to a multitude of commodities.

It can be maintained, of course, that price does not necessarily reflect other values; that it is ludicrous, for example, to measure the value of a work of art by its price, or the extent of a man's love for a woman by the price tags on the gifts he buys her. That is entirely true. I mention the market only as an *example* of how a common denominator can be found for a specific purpose of comparison, namely, for the purpose of exchanging commodities. The market is a social invention which performs this function. When the practices of the market are applied to things which people feel *ought not to be exchanged* (for example, sexual favors for articles of clothing), sensitivities are offended and the whole process of quantification is felt to be somewhat immoral.

However, the market is by no means the only source of a common denominator of value. To take the example of food *vs.* clothing, they are indeed not comparable if one does not know that food is a source of body heat, which clothing is designed to conserve. If one is concerned with surviving in the arctic, one can profitably think in terms of the relative merits (in terms of heat production and conservation) of certain foods and certain items of clothing.

Even for the abstract values ("freedom," etc.) scales of comparison with other values can sometimes be designed in certain social contexts. In a way, if a man has a choice of working so many hours for so much pay, he is trading a part of his "freedom" for other necessities.

So far, however, all the attempts to provide bases of comparison for seemingly noncomparable quantities have been based on the assumption that the only kind of quantity is one which can be represented as a point on a one-dimensional scale. In modern mathematics such quantities are called "scalars." Thus time intervals, distances, weights, temperatures, and prices are scalars, since each of them can be represented by a single number.

Scalars, however, do not exhaust the quantities of use in modern science. "Force," for example, is not a scalar, because in order to describe a force quantitatively, it is not sufficient to give its magnitude. One must also give its direction, and direction itself (in three-dimensional space) cannot be described by a single number. Quantities like force (which need several numbers to describe them) are called *vectors*. They are operated on by special rules which sometimes are markedly different from the rules of operation on ordinary (scalar) quantities. Besides vectors, there are other multi-dimensional quantities used in modern mathematical sciences and their use has broadened to a very large extent the area of quantifiable knowledge. Many arguments which purport to indicate the limits of quantification really treat only the kind of quantification which is possible with scalars. As an example I will describe a recent attempt to quantify some elementary "social structures."

A QUANTIFIED STRUCTURE

An experimental program recently developed at the Massachusetts Institute of Technology was designed with a view of investigating the ways in which numbers of human beings cooperate to solve a problem (6). The problems were simple. For example, each of a group of five people was given a set of marbles of different colors. One color, however, was common to all five sets. The group problem consisted in determining what the common color was, and the problem was considered solved when every member of the group knew the answer.

Of course, if the five people could come together and compare their marbles, they could quickly solve the problem. But the point of the experiment was that the people had to work under certain imposed conditions. They could communicate only by written messages and furthermore the channels of communication were restricted. Each person could send messages only to specified people and receive them only from specified people. Such rules of communication define the *structure* of the group. The structure of anything is the totality of relations among its parts. Here the relations are the existence or the nonexistence of a communication channel, and the structure is defined by the existing channels.

The group problem-solving experiments were designed to determine whether the structure had any influence on the efficiency with which a group operates. Several factors were examined. One was the speed with which the group learned to solve a particular kind of problem. This was revealed in a characteristic learning curve. That is, if the time that it took to solve the problem each time it was presented was plotted against the number of times it was presented, it was found that the time of solution decreased in a certain regular way, *which was characteristic of the structure rather than of the individuals that composed the group.*

Other factors were also examined, such as the time it took the group to reorganize its procedure in response to a *new* problem, the inventiveness of the group in finding shortcuts to solutions, etc. It was found that groups efficient with respect to one factor may be very inefficient with respect to another. At any rate, it was found that a great many factors entering the group's learning behavior (which could be considered as making up the collective "intelligence" of the group) depended most strongly not on the individuals composing it but on the structure of the group—the way the group was organized.

The question now arises: is structure a *quantity*?

According to a narrow definition of quantity (a number), the structures as defined by the communication channels are not quantities, because they cannot be represented by numbers in the ordinary sense.[48] To see this, let us take two typical structures used in the Massachusetts Institute of Technology experiments. They are shown in Figures 1 and 2.

Fig. 1. The "wheel" structure of a group. The arrows indicate where communication may flow.

Fig. 2. The "chain" structure of a group.

The circles represent the people and the lines the permissible communication channels among them. The numbers obviously associated with each of these structures are the same. The number of people in each case is five. The number of distinct communication lines is four (eight, if we wish to count each one-way channel). Yet the problem-solving behavior of each group is markedly different. The team with the "wheel" type structure (Fig. 1) excels in learning a routine task but lags behind the team with the "chain" type structure (Fig. 2) in readjusting to a new kind of task. In ordinary parlance, the "quality" of each group is different. Yet in some contexts this "quality" can be quantified, not by a number, to be sure, but by a more general mathematical quantity called a *matrix*.

A matrix is an *array* of quantities arranged like a checker board in rows and columns. Such an array can conveniently represent the set of relations between each pair of members in some set. Suppose, for example, we have a set of five members (such as the five individuals in our problem-solving teams). The relation in this case is the possibility of communicating. Let us symbolize this possibility by a "1" and the absence of it by a "0." To signify that team member No. 2 can talk to team member No. 3, we put a "1" in the second row, third column place of the matrix; to signify that member No. 3 cannot talk to member No. 5, we put a "0" in the third row, fifth column of the matrix. In general the existence of a communication channel from member i to member j is denoted by a "1" in the i-th row, j-th column of the checker board array, while the absence of a channel is denoted by a "0." The matrices which represent the wheel and the chain structures respectively are shown in Figures 3 and 4.

1	1	1	1	1		1	1	0	0	0
1	1	0	0	0		1	1	1	0	0
1	0	1	0	0		0	1	1	1	0
1	0	0	1	0		0	0	1	1	1
1	0	0	0	1		0	0	0	1	1

Fig. 3   Fig. 4

Note that in the wheel structure, No. 1 can send to everyone, but everyone can send only to No. 1. In matrix notation, this appears as the "1's" in all places of the first row and the first column and "0's" everywhere else except on the diagonal. The "1's" on the diagonal reflect the assumption that each individual can talk to himself (that is, No. i can talk to No. i). In the chain structure, each can send only to his next-door neighbors (and to himself), and the corresponding matrix says just that.

What makes matrices quantities is the fact that one can reckon with them. There are rules for "adding" and "multiplying" matrices with each other. These rules resemble those of ordinary arithmetic but they are not quite identical with them. They are entirely consistent, however, and their great usefulness lies in providing a "mechanical" procedure for drawing conclusions. It has been shown, for example, that the spread of information in a group characterized by fixed communication channels can be represented by the successive "powers" (in a sense analogous to algebraic powers of numbers) of the matrix which represents the communication structure of the group (53, 54, 91). Other mathematical methods have been worked out which allow one to deduce the structure of a group by noting certain facts about the spread of information within it. In particular, it is sometimes possible to say whether there are "cliques" within the group.

The mathematization of social structure (certainly communication channels are indicative of social structure to a certain extent) is still in a primitive state but is showing increasing promise. Theoretical and experimental work along these lines has expanded rapidly in the years following World War II, and it appears at this writing as if quantification of human behavior (both individual and group) is becoming more and more a reality through the expansion of the meaning of "quantity." This development is in itself an answer to those who do not believe that the language of quantity is sufficiently general. What they mean is that the language of classical mathematics, which deals primarily with scalars, is not sufficiently general. The mathematics of nonscalars, however, goes much further. It provides "rules of reckoning" in situations formerly thought to be describable only vaguely in qualitative terms. We will find more of these rules of reckoning in the next chapter.

This brings us to the final group of objections, raised by those who are sceptical about the possibility of objective description altogether in some areas of knowledge. This is a most difficult objection to meet, because the only proof to the contrary can be made only by exhibiting objective descriptions where none are thought possible. Obviously, this cannot be done in every instance. The belief in the ultimate adequacy of objective (perhaps even quantitative) language is a faith. To what extent this faith will be justified remains to be seen. It can be pointed out, however, that phenomena have been "objectified" and quantified which had been persistently held to be beyond analysis. It would have seemed fantastic to Beethoven that the actual sounds of his violin concerto played by a great master could be frozen into an intricate mold in a piece of wax and that this mold (a structure) could be "brought to life" at will, that is, translated into vibrant and noble sounds.

The idea that perhaps the "feelings" evoked by the music in some individual can also be translated into a structure still seems preposterous to many. To others it seems exciting that the "structure" of human feelings may be associated with space-time configurations of nervous impulses and hormonal secretions. Far from considering such notions degrading, the modern adventurers in science feel them to be romantic, stimulating, and inspiring. The task of transforming these ideas into public knowledge seems as challenging today as the classical problems of exploration and of navigation seemed to the bold ones of yesterday. Some of the labor will certainly be lost (as the attempts to find the Northwest Passage were wasted); some will be crowned with success (as the attempt to circumnavigate the globe has been); and some, like the discovery of the New World, will yield rewards far in excess of original expectations.

Chapter 14. QUANTIFICATION OF VALIDITY, TRUTH, AND CAUSALITY

O VER a century ago George Boole (10) succeeded in quantifying logic. He showed that deductive reasoning is in principle no different from the sort of thing one does in arithmetic or algebra. Algebra is a way of manipulating symbols in accordance with prescribed rule. There are in algebra two basic operations, "addition" and "multiplication."[49] These operations are defined in terms of equivalent ways of writing expressions (combinations of symbols and "operators"). For example, the rule

1. $$x+y \equiv y+x*$$

shows an equivalence between two expressions and implies that "addition is commutative," that is, the result of addition is independent of the order in which the summands are written. A special case of this rule is seen in the equality $5+7=7+5$. Another rule is

2. $$x+(y+z) \equiv (x+y)+z,$$

which says that addition is "associative," that is, the result of adding more than two quantities is independent of the order in which the additions of pairs is performed. For example,

$$(5+7)+2=12+2=5+(7+2)=5+9.$$

Similar rules apply to multiplication. We have

3. $$xy \equiv yx,$$
and
4. $$xy(z) \equiv x(yz).$$

*The sign $\equiv$ indicates "identity," that is, an equality which holds regardless of the values of the variables (cf. p. 41).

An important rule connecting addition and multiplication is

5. $x(y+z) \equiv xy+xz.$

We see this in the equality $5 \times (7+2) = 5 \times 7 + 5 \times 2$. The important thing about these algebraic rules of reckoning is that we can substitute *any* numbers for the symbols x, y, and z and obtain correct results.

Boole was the inventor of the so-called Boolean Algebra. This "algebra" has only two numbers in it, "1" and "0." Its "unknowns" are denoted by letters of the alphabet as they are in ordinary algebra (except that p, q, and r rather than x, y, and z are the favorites in Boolean Algebra). Because of the limited number system, the unknowns can stand only for "1" or "0."

There are in Boolean Algebra, as in ordinary algebra, certain operators and certain rules of operation. The operators are ($'$), pronounced "prime" and denoting "negation"; (v), pronounced "cup" and denoting "addition" or "disjunction"; and (ʌ), pronounced "cap" and denoting "multiplication" or "conjunction." The rules of reckoning are as follows:

1. The negation changes the value of a symbol, that is, if $p=1$, then $p'=0$; if $p=0$, then $p'=1$.

2. Addition and multiplication are "idempotent," that is,

$$p \vee p = p; \quad p \wedge p = p.$$

3. Addition and multiplication are associative and communicative, as in ordinary algebra, that is,

$$p \vee (q \vee r) \equiv (p \vee q) \vee r; \quad p \vee q \equiv q \vee p;$$
$$p \wedge (q \wedge r) \equiv (p \wedge q) \wedge r; \quad p \wedge q \equiv q \wedge p.$$

4. $p \vee p' \equiv 1.$

5. $p \wedge p' \equiv 0.$

6. Multiplication is distributive with respect to addition and vice versa, that is,

$$p \wedge (q \vee r) \equiv (p \wedge q) \vee (p \wedge r)$$
$$p \vee (q \wedge r) \equiv (p \vee q) \wedge (p \vee r).$$

One might wonder why these rules have been chosen and not others. The reason in the choice is apparent in the origin of Boolean Algebra. It originated as an algebra of "sets," in which the operator (v) designated the "logical sum" of two sets, that is, the set formed of the elements belonging to either of two sets, and the operator ($\wedge$) designated the "logical product" or the "intersection" of two sets, that is, the set formed of the elements belonging to *both* sets.[50] The operator (') designated the set formed of elements not belonging to a given set. In this context, the rules of reckoning follow of their own accord.[51] However, our interest here is not in the algebra of sets but in the quantification of logic. The reader will therefore be asked to take the rules of reckoning as simply given. The most interesting thing about them from the point of view of this discussion is that they form a connecting bridge between conventional logic and the theory of probability, as will be seen in what follows.

Boolean Algebra as Algebra

Let us first see whether the rules of Boolean Algebra have anything to do with the rules of ordinary algebra and arithmetic. Some of these rules look "right," and others do not. If (v) is interpreted as "plus," and ($\wedge$) as "times," then Rule 3 says the same thing as the corresponding rules in algebra, namely that addition and multiplication are associative and commutative. Rule 1 makes sense if the operator (') is interpreted as signifying that the quantity it operates on is to be subtracted from 1, since in that case, p' means $1 - p$. Rule 2 is partly all right. Since p can be only "1" or "0," it follows that $p \wedge p \equiv p$, if ($\wedge$) means "times." However, if (v) means "plus," the rule $p \vee p \equiv p$ does not seem right if $p = 1$. Rules 4 and 5 are both all right, as the reader can verify. The first part of Rule 6 is the same as in algebra, but the second is not.

Now *all* of the Boolean rules can be made to agree with the rules of algebra if only the operator (v), which we assumed meant "plus," is given a somewhat different interpretation. If instead of interpreting $p \vee q$ as $p + q$, we take it instead to mean $p + q - pq$, then a perfect agreement between Boolean and ordinary algebra is achieved. We will verify this agreement in one case and leave it to the reader to verify the other cases of discrepancy if he wishes. Take the "idempotency" of addition, which says that $p \vee p \equiv p$. According to our new interpretation of (v), $p \vee p$ means $p + p - p^2$. But p can be only "1" or "0." Substituting either of these values into $p + p - p^2$, we obtain the same value for the answer.

The importance of our interpretation of (v) will become clear when we discuss the relation between Boolean Algebra and probability theory. In the meantime, let us see what relation Boolean Algebra has to logic. Again we translate the Boolean symbols, this time into the language of logic. The unknowns (p, q, etc.) now will stand for *propositions* (assertions). Furthermore,

"1" will stand for "true."

"0" will stand for "false."

(') will stand for "not."

(v) will stand for "and/or."

($\wedge$) will stand for "and."

The equation $p = q$ will mean, "If p is true, q is true; if p is false, q is false and vice versa" (in other words, p and q have the same truth value).

We can now see how Boolean rules of reckoning are really statements of Aristotelian rules of logic. For example, Rule 1 implies that if $p = 1$, $p' = 0$. In Aristotelian language, this says that if a proposition is true, its negation is false. Furthermore, Rule 4 says, "Either a proposition or its negation must be true," which is the Aristotelian Law of Excluded Middle. Rule 5 says, "A proposition *and* its negation cannot both be true," which is the well known Aristotelian Law of Contradiction. These translations are consequences of interpreting (v) as "or" and ($\wedge$) as "and," while substituting "true" and "false" for "1" and "0."

Thus Boolean Algebra covers the whole of Aristotelian logic. But it goes beyond Aristotelian logic, much as algebra goes beyond arithmetic. Boolean Algebra with its formal rules of reckoning can be used to disentangle complicated strands of reasoning, much as the formal rules of algebra can be used to solve problems practically impermeable to the methods of arithmetic.

The following example is facetious, but its facetiousness is in its content, not its form. Similar problems arise in altogether serious situations.

Example: Suppose the following four propositions are given.

1. If a mathematician does not have to wait 20 minutes for a bus, then he either likes Mozart in the morning or whiskey at night, but not both.

2. If a man likes whiskey at night, then he either likes Mozart in the morning and does not have to wait 20 minutes for a bus, or he does not like Mozart in the morning and has to wait 20 minutes for a bus or else he is no mathematician.

3. If a man likes Mozart in the morning and does not have to wait 20 minutes for a bus, then he likes whiskey at night.

4. If a mathematician likes Mozart in the morning, he either likes

whiskey at night or has to wait 20 minutes for a bus; conversely, if he likes whiskey at night and has to wait 20 minutes for a bus, he is a mathematician—if he likes Mozart in the morning.

Question: When must a mathematician wait 20 minutes for a bus?*

The problem seems complicated, but it really is no more complicated than the problems which teen-agers solve in doing their algebra homework. Looked at in another way, algebra problems would be just as complicated if one tried to solve them by ordinary verbal (syllogistic) reasoning instead of by mathematical reckoning rules. We will now proceed to solve this problem in logic.

We will need one or two theorems (Boolean Algebra, like any other mathematical system, has, of course, its theorems which can be deduced from the postulates or rules).

Theorem 1. The assertion "If p, then q" can be written as $p \wedge q' = 0$.

Proof. "If p, then q" means that if p is true, q *must* be true. In other words, we cannot have p true and q false. But $p \wedge q'$ is the assertion which connects p and the *negation* of q. Therefore, this assertion must be false. But this is just what is implied by the equation $p \wedge q' = 0$. Q.E.D.

Example: The assertion, "If John is the husband of Mary, then Mary is the wife of John" can be re-stated as "The assertion 'John is the husband of Mary and Mary is *not* the wife of John' is false." If we denote the assertion "John is the husband of Mary" by "p" and "Mary is the wife of John" by "q," we will have the statement of the theorem.

Theorem 2. The assertion $(p \wedge q)'$ can be written as $(p' \vee q')$, and the assertion $(p \vee q)'$ can be written as $(p' \wedge q')$.

Proof. The assertion $(p \wedge q)'$ says that p and q are not *both* true. On the other hand $p' \vee q'$ says that either p or q (or both) are false, which is saying the same thing. Furthermore $(p \vee q)'$ says that no matter which you are saying, p *or* q, you are lying; while $(p' \wedge q')$ says that p is false and q is false, which is the same thing. Q.E.D.

With these theorems established, we can translate our propositions about mathematicians, Mozart, and whiskey into the language of Boolean Algebra. Just as in solving algebraic problems we assign symbols to quantities, so in solving Boolean problems we assign symbols to propositions. Let, therefore,

*An examination question in a course given by Walter Pitts at the Massachusetts Institute of Technology.

p stand for "He is a mathematician."
q stand for "He likes Mozart in the morning."
r stand for "He has to wait 20 minutes for a bus."
s stand for "He likes whiskey at night."
Then p' must mean, "He is *not* a mathematician," etc. Let us now look at the propositions of the problem. The first proposition says "If p and r', then q or s but not both q and s."

With the aid of our rules of reckoning and our two theorems, we can translate this proposition into the following Boolean equation:

$$p \wedge r' \wedge (q' \wedge s' \vee q \wedge s) = 0 \qquad (1)$$

Proceeding in the same way to the other propositions, we establish additional equations:

$$p \wedge s \wedge (q' \vee r) \wedge (q \vee r') = 0 \qquad (2)$$
$$q \wedge r' \wedge s' = 0 \qquad (3)$$
$$p \wedge q \wedge r' \wedge s' = 0 \qquad (4)$$
$$p' \wedge q \wedge r \wedge s = 0 \qquad (5)$$

Now we translate the question: What conditions imply that when $p = 1$ (someone is a mathematician), then *necessarily* $r = 1$ (he must wait 20 minutes for a bus)? In other words, when must "If p, then r" be a true proposition? According to our Theorem 1, we can write "If p, then r" as $p \wedge r' = 0$. Now $(p \wedge r')$ appears as a factor in equations (1) and (4). This factor *must* be zero, if all the other factors in those products are *not* zero, that is, are equal to 1. This is so if $q' \wedge s'$ or $q \wedge s$ or $q \wedge s'$ is equal to 1. We write this as a Boolean equation:

$$q' \wedge s' \vee q \wedge s \vee q \wedge s' = 1.$$

However, $q \wedge s$ cannot be 1, since, if p, q, r, and s are all 1, equation (2) is violated. On the other hand, if $q \wedge s' = 1$, equation (1) can be satisfied if $p = 1$ and $r = 0$, contrary to the condition of the question. Therefore, we must have $q' \wedge s' = 1$, which implies $q' = 1$ and $s' = 1$, or, in plain English, "A mathematician must wait 20 minutes for a bus if he likes neither Mozart in the morning nor whiskey at night."

We see thus in Boolean Algebra an example of a system which is like an algebra (with a limited number system consisting only of "1" and "0") and which includes the Aristotelian two-valued logic. This sheds light on the equivalence of two-valued logic with a *very small* portion of algebra (namely, one dealing with a limited number system).

Theory of Probability as an Infinite-valued Logic

It is natural to ask what would happen to logic if its underlying algebra were extended to a broader number system. Some such logics have actually been constructed (for example, three-valued logics, where there are three values of truth instead of just "true" and "false"). One such more general logic is of the utmost importance in the theory of knowledge, namely, one where the number system is allowed to range all the way from 0 to 1 inclusive over all the intervening values. This system can be called the logic of probability.

Much has been written on the logical, psychological, and mathematical foundations of probability theory (16, 82). It is not my purpose here to treat or criticize these foundations. I only want to give a rough description of the first elements of the theory with a definite aim which pertains to the study of quantification of logic: to show how the theory of probability is an *extension* of ordinary two-valued logic. The implication is that the probability theory is a more sophisticated logic (because you can do everything with it that you can with logic and more). Probabilistic logic assigns *fractional* truth values to propositions. An assertion is absolutely false only if its truth value is zero; it is absolutely true, if its truth value is one. A truth value between zero and one denotes the degree to which a proposition is *probable*.

Knowledge of probabilities is indispensable as a guide to action. The reason people get along without any formal knowledge of probability theory is because they have some intuitive knowledge of it. The reason a "reasonable" person will refuse to cross an express highway blindfolded is not because he knows he will be killed but because "it is dangerous," that is, the *chances* of getting killed are substantial. The same "reasonable" person, taking "reasonable" precautions crosses many streets every day, even though it is not perfectly safe to do so either. He weighs his chances, that is, he roughly calculates the probabilities involved. In industry, business, warfare, and other activities where taking chances is part of a work-aday reality, the probabilities are sometimes mathematically calculated. Decisions are based on some accepted way of comparing the risk of failure with the desirability of success.

Let us now see how the elements of probability theory are derived from those of logic. Suppose a coin is tossed three times in succession. There are eight possible outcomes. If H stands for heads, and T for tails, the eight outcomes are

$$HHH \quad HHT \quad HTH \quad THH \quad TTH \quad THT \quad HTT \quad TTT$$

We suppose that all the outcomes are equally likely, so that each has one chance out of eight of occurring. In other words, the probability of each outcome is $\frac{1}{8}$.

Let now p stand for the proposition, "The first throw results in heads." Let q stand for, "The second throw results in heads." Let r stand for, "The third throw results in heads." Then, of course, p' must stand for, "The first throw results in tails," and similarly for q' and r'. Now all eight outcomes can be written as combinations of these propositions connected by "and." In Boolean notation, they look like this:

$$p \wedge q \wedge r; p \wedge q \wedge r'; p \wedge q' \wedge r; p' \wedge q \wedge r;$$
$$p' \wedge q' \wedge r; p' \wedge q \wedge r'; p \wedge q' \wedge r'; p' \wedge q' \wedge r'.$$

We can also form other combinations of propositions. For example, "The first throw results in heads *or* the second throw results in tails"; "The first two throws heads or first heads and the last two tails." In Boolean notation, these assertions would be denoted respectively by $p \vee q'$ and by $(p \wedge q) \vee (p \wedge q' \wedge r')$.

How are we to evaluate the probabilities of such events described by compound propositions? Any such evaluation hinges, of course, on our definition of such probabilities. A natural way to define the probability of an event is by a fraction which denotes the ratio between the number of ways the event can happen and the total number of possible events. Thus $p = \frac{4}{8} = \frac{1}{2}$, because a head on the first throw occurs in four cases out of eight. Similarly $q = \frac{1}{2}$, and $r = \frac{1}{2}$. Now how about "$p \vee q$"? That is, what is the probability that there is a head on the first *or* a head on the second throw? This occurs in six cases: $HHH, HHT, HTH, THH, THT, HTT$. Therefore $(p \vee q)$ must be $\frac{6}{8}$ or $\frac{3}{4}$. Similarly, we see that $p \wedge q$ must be $\frac{1}{4}$, and so on for all possible combinations of p, q, and r and their negations p', q', and r' connected by $(\vee)$ and $(\wedge)$.

We are now ready to extend the Boolean rules to the logic of probability. We let the values of p, q, etc., range over the whole interval from zero to one. (In the case we are considering, all the variables have the value $\frac{1}{2}$.) We further translate the Boolean operations into algebraic ones. We recall that the Boolean expression $(p \vee q)$ means in the language of algebra $(p+q-pq)$, and $(p \wedge q)$

means pq. It is now obvious that the "truth value" of $(p \vee q)$, which, we recall, stands for "A heads on the first or second throw," is given by $\frac{1}{2} + \frac{1}{2} - \frac{1}{4} = \frac{3}{4}$, which is the answer obtained previously. Likewise, the truth value of "A heads on both first and second" $(p \wedge q)$ is given by $\frac{1}{2} \times \frac{1}{2} = \frac{1}{4}$, as before.

To see that this extension holds more generally, take the result of our Theorem 2 (cf. p. 172), which states that

$$(p \vee q)' \equiv p' \wedge q'.$$

In algebra, this would have to mean (since negation means subtracting from 1),

$$1 - (p + q - pq) = (1 - p)(1 - q),$$

and it does, as can be verified by removing the parentheses.

The reader can verify all the other Boolean rules that way, keeping in mind, however, that the idempotent rule of multiplication $(p^2 = p)$ must hold.[52]

Thus by treating the Boolean rules of logic as ordinary algebraic rules and by applying them to the truth values of propositions, we can calculate the truth values of any logical combination of propositions. In complicated problems there is more than arithmetic involved in the calculations. One must sometimes disentangle the known from the unknown quantities (as one does in algebra), take limits of variable quantities (as in the calculus), etc. Quantification of truth by means of the probability theory thus involves the use of complicated mathematical machinery and makes available the power of that machinery in the pursuit of truth.

PREDICTIVE CONTENT AND THE QUANTIFICATION OF CAUSALITY

We have seen (cf. p. 37) that the truth content of an assertion is related to its predictive content. How can we quantify predictive content?

Suppose you go to a fortune teller, and she tells you that sometime in the near future you will get a letter, and you do. If you ordinarily receive on the average two letters per week, you will probably not be impressed by the clairvoyant powers of the fortune teller. Now suppose the fortune teller informs you that during the coming week you will receive one letter on Monday, three on Tuesday, none on Wednesday and Thursday, and one each on Friday and Saturday, and it happens just so. Your scepticism could then be justifiably shaken.

The difference between the two predictions is, of course, in the relative probabilities of the two events. The first event (getting a letter on some unspecified day) is probable. The second (getting specified numbers of letters on specified days) is improbable, so that its prediction contains a great deal of "information."

Predictive content, then, is related to the probability of the events predicted. The smaller the probability, the greater the predictive content. The probability is here a subjective matter. It is measured by our expectation of the event *a priori* (that is, in the absence of any information).

Quantification of causality involves the difference between probabilities expected *a priori* and the actual frequency of an event. For example, if "heads" is ordinarily expected to occur once in every two throws (on the average) and actually occurs once in every ten throws, we look for a "cause." We turn our attention to other events associated with the throws such as possible peculiarities of the coin or the peculiar flips of the wrist employed by the thrower.

Strictly speaking, the question, "Is X the cause of Y?" cannot be answered by yes or no. It is clear that if in some cases Y does not follow X, we cannot definitely say "Yes." On the other hand, we cannot with absolute assurance say "No."

For example, if a man smokes excessively and does not contract a cancer of the lungs, we cannot conclude that "Smoking has nothing to do with lung cancer." A great number of observations may show that more smokers get lung cancers than nonsmokers. To answer the question, "Does smoking cause lung cancer?" is to disentangle the possible causes of lung cancer so that smoking as a possible factor can be studied in isolation. This is a problem in statistics, which is based on the theory of probability.

Ignorance of the ideas underlying quantification of causality makes people prey to a variety of rackets. Suppose, for example, a man comes into a community, sets up an office, and declares that he can influence the sex of unborn children. He can by means of a simple, harmless treatment make pregnant women deliver boys or girls to order. The fee for this service is $100, payable in advance. To forestall any suspicion of a swindle, an ironclad guarantee is offered: in case of failure not only will the fee be refunded but also a bonus of $50 will be paid as a compensation for the waste of time.

The ordinary "logic" of the situation is such that if one is willing to pay $100 to have a child of a desired sex, the offer is attractive.

If the man succeeds, well and good, if not, there is nothing to lose, even $50 to gain.

According to the logic of probability, however, the charlatan is getting two-to-one odds on a bet where the chances of the two outcomes are practically even! It may be that no American community would fall for a trick like that, but many do fall for water-dowsing, which works on the same principle, except that in case of failure bonuses are never paid and the fees are but seldom returned.

Medicine based on scientific knowledge is less than a century old. It has, however, commanded the confidence of people for scores of centuries, because by far the greater portion of the people who get sick get well anyway (sometimes in spite of what the doctors do), and the question is seldom raised as to whether it was the doctor who cured the disease (that is, whether the activities of the doctor made the probability of recovery higher than the *a priori* probability).

We see that the answer to the question "Why is X?" often has to be couched in mathematical terms. For this reason such questions as "Do bad roads cause accidents?" "Does irreligion cause crime?" "Does capitalism cause wars?" "Does frustration cause aggression?" "Has mass production improved the standard of living?" have very little meaning operationally speaking, until they can be translated into such terms as to allow us to observe how one set of variables is correlated with another.

There is no question that in some cases such translation can be made (in fact, this is one of the principal tasks of theoretical social science). The answer then appears not as a "Yes" or a "No" but as a *measure* of the causal relation involved.

Chapter 15. QUANTIFICATION OF ORDER, OF LIFE, AND OF ETHICS

As a final example of the modern trend towards giving precise meaning to what used to be exceedingly nebulous philosophical concepts, I would like to discuss some recent thinking on the meaning of life and intelligence.

"Life," says E. Schroedinger in his little book *What Is Life?* (88), "feeds on negative entropy."

I submit that here indeed is a striking metaphor to be added to all the other answers to the chronic question which is the title of Schroedinger's book. That which has been called a prison, a bed of roses, a thorny path, a lottery, not an empty dream, etc., now becomes something that "feeds on negative entropy"! To make sense of this, we must examine the experiences which have led to the notion of entropy, and those which have given the notion of life its meaning.

ENTROPY

The concept of entropy first appeared in connection with problems in the construction of heat engines. A heat engine is a device for transforming heat into work, for example, a locomotive. In a locomotive, the heat of burning fuels is used to make steam, and the force of expanding steam is harnessed to push levers, which turn wheels. Suppose we have decided to construct a locomotive. We put water in a vessel and build a fire under it. The water will eventually boil and turn into steam. We allow the steam to expand into a cylinder, one end of which is a movable piston. The expanding steam moves the piston, to which is attached a lever, which moves the wheel. Now suppose everything has taken place; the water has boiled, the steam has expanded, the piston has moved to the far end of the cylinder, and accordingly our wheel has moved a few feet. What happens next?

If the engine is to *keep on* working, the piston has to be brought back to its original position. This can be done in different ways. If a system of valves is synchronized to open and close with the movement of the piston, the steam can be let in alternately from both sides of the piston, so as to move it back and forth. Or else the inertia of the wheel can carry it forward, so that after half a turn, the lever will be moving in the opposite direction and so bring the piston into the original position. In both of these cases, there will be either a waste of steam (if it is allowed to escape) or a waste of energy in compressing the steam (if it remains in the cylinder).

In the third decade of the nineteenth century engineers found out that the best possible arrangement of the working parts of a heat engine working in a cycle cannot utilize more than a certain fraction of the heat obtained from the fuel in converting heat into work. It was found that such an engine must operate "between two temperatures," receiving heat from the boiler at one temperature and giving up heat to a cooler at another, and that the most efficient heat engine possible (not practical, but *possible*, that is, conceivable) must waste a fraction of the available heat equal to the ratio of the lower temperature to the higher (measured from "absolute zero," that is, about 460° below zero Fahrenheit). Only if the cooler were at absolute zero would an ideal heat engine operate with 100 per cent efficiency. All this is in consequence of the universally observed fact that heat can flow spontaneously only from a hotter body to a colder one and not vice versa.

Now these facts about heat engines do not in themselves shed much light on the question "What is life?" But experience with these facts, if coupled with an orientation of inquisitiveness expressed in a constant desire for making meaningful generalizations, *has led* to a chain of reasoning which gives us an insight into such questions. It is not preoccupation with heat engines and their "practical" applications which has led to such insights but rather a concern with what is behind the principles on which heat engines work. In other words, questions about heat engines can be generalized and made to yield scientific "dividends."

The general principles are now known as the first and second laws of thermodynamics. They are often stated in a negative way, asserting what *cannot* be done. They thus illustrate the paradoxical definition of freedom as the "recognition of necessity" (cf. p. 125): once we know the "laws of nature," that is, what cannot be done in violation of these laws, we acquire the freedom to make use of the laws. Our entire technology is based on the principles of thermo-dynamics.

The first law of thermodynamics states that we cannot build a perpetual motion machine of the "first kind," that is, one that operates without being fed energy in some form from an outside source. The positive implication of this law, and the foundation of all our technology, is that continuously operating machines are pos-sible if energy is fed into them. The discovery that heat is a form of energy made possible the construction of heat engines which transform heat (energy fed into them) into useful work.

The second law of thermodynamics says that we cannot build a perpetual motion machine of the "second kind," that is, one which completely transforms an amount of heat into work without any other changes taking place in the environment. Heat engines are possible because in the process of turning heat into work *other* changes also take place in the environment, such as the flow of heat from the boiler to the cooler. Now these "other changes" are shown to result in the increase of a certain physical quantity (related both to heat and to temperature) called *entropy*. Another way of stating the second law (roughly), then, is this: if things are left to them-selves entropy will increase.

What is this entropy, which keeps increasing "by itself"? Its precise definition involves sophisticated concepts of physics and mathematics. But an idea of entropy can be formed without refer-ence to precise concepts. Entropy is the *unavailability* of energy for specific purposes. For instance, if we have two bodies at different temperatures, we can rig up a heat engine between them, using one for a "boiler," the other for a "cooler." Thus some of the heat of the hotter body will be available for being transformed into work. But if the bodies are left alone, say in contact with each other, eventually the hotter one will cool off and the cooler one warm up, and they will settle down to the same temperature. Then no heat engine can be rigged up between them because a heat engine must work between two temperatures. No heat has disappeared; it was only redistributed. But now no heat is available for doing work, because of this distribution. The physicist says, "The entropy of the system has increased," and he can calculate by how much.

The second law of thermodynamics is a sort of a yes-but modifica-tion of the first law. The first law says that the energy of the universe remains constant (is conserved). One form can be transformed into another, for example, heat into work. The second law, however, says, "Yes, but less and less energy becomes *available* for being transformed into work. The energy is there, but it is becoming 'degraded' —useless."

According to the second law, if all the temperature in the universe were equalized, nothing else would ever happen. There would be no discernible "events," and certainly no life of any sort. The universe is slowly but surely going toward that state, "running down," says the relentless second law.[53]

We are still far from anything that seems to have much bearing on the question "What is life?" But we have got a glimpse into a process which in principle makes life more and more difficult—the increase of entropy in the universe. Perhaps life is something that resists that process? But how? The next development in the science of thermodynamics brings us a little closer to a possible answer.

This next development is the so-called "kinetic theory of matter." According to this theory, the minute particles of which all matter is composed (atoms and molecules) are in constant motion. What we perceive as the "temperature" of a body and assume to be a measure of its heat content is, according to the kinetic theory, the energy of motion of its particles. The faster the particles move, the hotter the body is and the more energy it contains. Here the connection between heat and work (energy) becomes apparent.

Suppose now that a gas is hotter in one half of a container than in the other. This means that there are more fast flying molecules on the hotter side and more slower ones on the cooler side. What will happen now if the gas is left alone? There is really no way of knowing without tracing the paths of all the molecules and recording their collisions. But there is a way of "guessing" what will happen. The guessing has to do with estimating the chances each molecule has of bumping into a slower molecule or a faster molecule at various collision angles. These bumps will determine whether a molecule will gain or lose speed. These estimates of chances lead to the conclusion that in all *likelihood* (that is, practically certainly) the average speed of the molecules will tend to be equalized throughout the container, which means that temperature will become equalized, and consequently the entropy will increase. There is still a question of what one means by "in all likelihood." Since an involved mathematical argument is beyond the scope of this book, let us resort to analogy.

Quantification of Order

Take a deck of cards and arrange them so that the first twenty-six are red and the other twenty-six black. Now shuffle the cards. If you shuffle them long enough, the reds and the blacks will "diffuse" through each other, so that finally there will be cards of both colors throughout the deck. If you continue shuffling, the equipartition of cards will "in all likelihood" persist. Occasionally, there may be a sizable preponderance of one color in one half of the deck or the other. But it will not last. It is exceedingly unlikely that through shuffling alone we can make the cards resume their original order. The reason for it is that an "orderly" arrangement of the cards is an "improbable" arrangement, while disorderly arrangements are more "probable."

This explanation can in no way be considered satisfactory unless we define the terms "orderly" and "probable" more precisely. The reader's patience is earnestly solicited.

Suppose we throw a coin eight times. Ordinarily the heads and tails will be haphazardly mixed up in the outcome of the eight throws. But it may happen that the first four throws result in heads and the last four in tails. Intuitively we feel that this is an "orderly" arrangement of heads and tails. But why do we feel that way? Why is the arrangement *HHHHTTTT* more "orderly" than, say, *HTTHTHTH*? I suspect we define the amount of order in a situation by the amount of talking we have to do to describe the situation. Where the first four throws are heads and the last four are tails, we need only say "Heads on first four throws only." But to describe the situation *HTTHTHTH* we have to say, "Heads on first, fourth, sixth, and eighth throws only."

Similarly with cards. To describe the "orderly" arrangement, we need only say, "First twenty-six red." To describe some random arrangement completely, we must specify where in the deck the red cards appear. Between the notions of complete order (least number of words necessary) and complete disorder (or randomness), there are gradations. Suppose, for example, that the orderly arrangement is disturbed by just one card out of place in each half of the deck. We can describe the arrangement by saying, "The first twenty-six red except card number so and so; the last twenty-six black except card number so and so." Here more words are required than in the case of complete order, but still far fewer than in the case of an arbitrary arrangement.

The notion of order has thus been "quantified." Now why does an orderly arrangement appear less probable than a disorderly one? Let us go back to our coin experiment (because there are fewer coins than cards, so that the probabilities of the arrangements are easier to calculate).

Actually, the arrangements *HHHHTTTT* and *HTTHTHTH* have an equal chance to occur. This is so because the outcome of each head and each tail is assumed to have the probability of $\frac{1}{2}$. The probability of every outcome of eight throws (in whatever order the heads and tails appear) is therefore $(\frac{1}{2})^8 = \frac{1}{256}$. How then does it appear that the disorderly arrangements are more probable? This appears so only because we describe the disorderly arrangements only *partially* and thus we really lump many such arrangements into one. For example, we can refer to the arrangement *HTTHTHTH* as "four heads and four tails." This describes the outcome somewhat but not completely, since many other arrangements with four heads and four tails can occur, for example, *HHTTHTHT* and *THTHTHTH*. In fact, it can be easily calculated that there are 70 arrangements with exactly four heads and four tails, so that the probability of four heads out of eight throws is $\frac{70}{256}$, or seventy times more probable than that of any *completely* specified outcome. It is because we associate completely specified outcomes with "order" (because ordered arrangements are those which are easy to specify completely) that orderly arrangements appear to us less likely; not because of any preference by the "laws of chance" for disorderly arrangements. Similarly a hand of poker consisting of the ace, the king, the queen, the jack, and the ten of hearts is not less likely to occur than the hand consisting of the two of hearts, the seven of diamonds, the three of clubs, and the queen and the jack of spades. It is only because poker players see a special significance in the first hand (and thus give it a special name, Royal Flush, which specifies it completely), while they see no significance in the second hand (and thus tend to lump it with many others) that the probabilities appear to be very different.

Exactly the same considerations apply to our card shuffling experiments. The number of ways in which the reds and the blacks can be haphazardly scattered through the deck is much greater than the number of ways the reds can arrange themselves among the first twenty-six. Thus the "orderly" arrangements appear far less likely.

It is clear, therefore, that if each shuffling is considered as a random rearrangement of the cards, the "disordered" arrangements will appear much more frequently than the "ordered" ones. However, the point of the whole discussion is that the notion of order is not quite an objective notion. It depends on our ability to describe situations, that is, on our ability to *recognize* situations.

When we say, "The temperature of a gas is uniform throughout the container," we have described the situation only in a very general way (like saying "four heads" without specifying which throws came out heads). Thus a great many possible distributions of molecular speeds fall under that description. That is why this situation is "more probable" than others. Simply more possible cases are included in it.

The increase in entropy of a system means that the system passes from a less probable to a more probable state, but it must be borne in mind that the probability of a state depends on how precisely or how loosely we describe it. In general, the more loosely a state is described, the more "probable" it is.

MAXWELL'S DEMON

Let imagination take over now, because the situation we are about to describe is utterly fantastic.

Suppose we put a partition into our box filled with gas (whose temperature is uniform throughout the box) and fix a little trap door in the partition, just big enough to let one molecule pass from one side to the other. Imagine now a little demon sitting at the trap door and watching the molecules go by. Some of them will hit the trap door, so that if it is open they will pass to the other side. Some of the molecules are slow, some are fast. Uniform temperature means only that the average speed of the molecules is the same in all parts of the box.

Suppose now the demon operates the trap door so that each time a fast molecule approaches it from the east side of the box, he lets it through to the west side, and each time a slow molecule approaches from the west side, he lets it through to the east side. But he does not let the slow molecules go to the west side, nor the fast ones to the east side. In due time, the fast molecules will accumulate on the west side and the slow ones on the east side, and the temperature will have gone from a uniform distribution to a nonuniform one. While this process was going on, we would actually observe the warmer side getting warmer and the cooler one getting cooler in contradiction to the second law of thermodynamics.

The argument that this is only fantasy, that there are no such demons, is not relevant. The laws of physics are presumably such that a violation of them is unthinkable even in an imaginary experiment. If a violation can *in principle* occur, the law must be revised —it does not tell the whole story. That the law of increasing entropy does not tell the whole story is evident in the card-shuffling experiment. Here, as in the case of the gas, entropy means disorder. Even though it is unlikely that by shuffling we can pass from a disorderly arrangement to an orderly one, it is not *inconceivable*. Therefore in this case "entropy" may spontaneously decrease instead of increase as the second law demands.

To be sure, the laws of thermodynamics were not stated about the behavior of cards in shuffling. But the reasoning, by which the second law is derived from the kinetic theory of matter, is exactly the same kind of reasoning we have used in estimating how tossed coins and shuffled cards will behave—it is reasoning by laws of chance. If the statistical foundations of thermodynamics are sound (and the overwhelming evidence is that they are), then the laws of thermodynamics are nothing but gross expressions of the laws of chance.

Now we *know* we can violate the "laws of chance" in the case of card shuffling, simply by interfering with the process. We can cheat. That is, we can shuffle the cards to suit our purpose, for example put all the red ones on one side. We can do this *if we watch what we are doing* and if we can discriminate between a red and a black card. But this is exactly what the demon is doing in our imaginary experiment: distinguishing between fast and slow molecules and separating them so as to decrease the entropy and thus violate the second law.

The usual argument against this allegation that the second law can be violated goes as follows. You must include the demon in the physical system you are considering. Even though the entropy of the gas does decrease through his activities, the demon's *own* entropy may be increasing in the process, so that the *total* result will still be a net increase in entropy.[54]

However, this argument makes the tacit assumption that the total entropy of some system can be defined without specifying the observer. In any physical definition, however, measurements are involved (for example, measurements of temperatures), and these measurements are the "observers," and it is with respect to *their* discriminating powers that entropy is defined. A thermometer, for example, does not distinguish between the velocities of single molecules. It responds only to the average velocity of a tremendous number of molecules. It is the same with the statistical definition of entropy (in terms of the probabilities of the various states). The probability of a state depends on how many situations we have lumped into that state, and this, in turn, depends on our ability to discriminate the situations.

Therefore, the question whether the total entropy of the system including both the gas and the demon actually increases cannot be answered without specifying the discriminatory power of the observer with respect to whom entropy must be defined.

In statistical physics, entropy is associated with the "amount of disorder." We must modify this concept by adding "with respect to certain instruments or observers with certain discriminating abilities."

"Negentropy" is entropy with its algebraic sign reversed. Therefore negentropy increases when entropy decreases and vice versa. It may therefore be said that negentropy measures the amount of order (again with respect to an observer). The definition of negentropy as the amount of order is more precise than we have given it. It was discovered in recent investigations in the mathematical theory of communication that the quantity which communication engineers call "information" has the same mathematical form as the negative of entropy (in the physical sense).

LIFE, KNOWLEDGE, AND PURPOSE

Even aside from the remarkable discovery linking entropy with the "amount of information," the intuitive notion that "order," "entropy," and "intelligence" are somehow connected has moved physicists to speculate on the relation between these concepts and life. It was known for some time that in all living things there are chemical reactions taking place which *ordinarily* (spontaneously) do not take place. For example, plants are able to synthesize sugars from carbon dioxide and water. This synthesis never happens by itself. On the contrary, the reverse process, the oxidation of sugars into CO_2 and H_2O is easy to accomplish and does take place spontaneously. To take another example, an animal in digesting food synthesizes the specific proteins needed to sustain its own integrity (rebuild its cells, etc.). Where there is no life, just the opposite occurs: the specific proteins of a dead organism break down into their simpler component parts.

In chemistry, the second law of thermodynamics is applied to determine the direction of chemical processes. If left alone, the reaction will always proceed in such a way that the total entropy of the system in which it takes place will increase. Life seems to be able to reverse the process. It is self-sustaining. And this self-sustaining activity can be loosely described as the creation of order from disorder—a decrease of entropy, at least locally within the living organism. This is the conjectured meaning of Schroedinger's remark that life feeds on negative entropy.

Again the usual argument of the physicist demolishes our hopes that life is the answer to the relentless working of the second law. Entropy may be decreased locally, says the physicist, but this happens only at the expense of entropy increasing elsewhere. The total entropy of the universe is still increasing. We are headed toward chaos.[55]

I have already implied that the total entropy of the universe is a concept whose objective meaning is open to doubt, since an observer must be tacitly postulated. Moreover, we are especially interested in what a decrease of entropy can do *locally*. The understanding of this local behavior of entropy enables us to predict the direction of chemical reactions, to build heat engines; and now this concept is entering our understanding of the processes of communication. That is to say, other problems than the ultimate fate of the universe command our attention. Our primary concern is not with what will ultimately happen to distant nebulae, but what will happen in the not too distant future to us—to our bodies and minds, to our children and our society. It is in problems such as these that the connection between order and information, between entropy and intelligence, between knowledge and life may become of paramount importance. These problems revolve around a central problem—the quantification of concepts in terms of which activities peculiar to life, particularly what we call "intelligent" life, are described.

To take an example, let us turn once again to the bothersome question of "freedom." The relation between freedom and purposefulness has been discussed on the conventional verbal level by philosophers for centuries. The quantitative notions derived from "operationalizing" the notion of purposefulness give us a much more rewarding approach to this subject.

A. Rosenblueth, N. Wiener, and J. Bigelow (84) have described a scale on which forms of behavior are listed beginning with those which appear to us least purposeful to those which appear most purposeful. One can subdivide all behavior, say these authors, into two large categories, passive and active. A dog running would under this classification appear as an instance of active behavior, but the motion of a dog hurled through the air would appear passive. In passive behavior, we think of the causes of behavior being outside, in active behavior inside the object concerned.

Now active behavior can again be subdivided into nonpurposeful and purposeful. For example, the frog lashing his tongue out to catch a fly appears to us to be acting purposefully, but the same frog convulsively jerking his limbs in response to an injection of strychnine seems to be behaving without purpose, even though such behavior is active (originates within the frog).

Purposeful behavior can be divided still further, namely into behavior with and without "feedback." Feedback is correction of behavior as it goes along. There is probably no feedback in the frog's lashing out at a fly. Once the aim is taken and the "trigger" released, there is no stopping or changing the course of action. A fly quick enough to dodge will get away. But a dog running after a quarry is an instance of feedback-corrected behavior. The dog runs *after* the quarry and shifts his course according to what the quarry does. In other words, feedback-corrected behavior is purposeful behavior governed by signals which indicate the *discrepancy between the actual and the desired state of affairs*. When we reach out for something, our movements are so governed—we manipulate our muscles —so as to move our hands in the general direction of the object to grasp (even if the object is moving). Once our hand is within grasping distance, other muscles come into play and the object is taken hold of.

Feedback-corrected behavior can be predictive and nonpredictive. Consider a child chasing another around a tree. The behavior is active, purposeful, and feedback-corrected (because the direction of running keeps changing in such a way as to keep the pursuer after the "quarry"). But once the pursuer gets the brilliant idea to turn around suddenly and meet the "quarry," he exhibits a behavior of still higher order. He has made a correction not merely on the basis of present data (the relative positions of himself and the quarry) but on the basis of *predicted* data, namely, where the quarry is *going* to be.

There is evidence that higher animals are capable of predictive behavior of this sort. It is often observed that a cat leaping at a running mouse leaps not directly at the mouse but so as to intercept the mouse; that is, the cat leaps at an empty spot where the mouse is going to be (in the estimation of the cat). This is active-purposeful-feedback-corrected-first-order predictive behavior.

It is called first-order predictive, because there are higher order predictive behaviors. The cat predicts only to a "first approximation." In other words, she seems to estimate the speed of the mouse and on the basis of that estimate she seems to guess where the mouse is going to be at the moment of collision.

The estimate involves an "assumption" that the velocity of the mouse will remain constant. By rapidly changing its speed or direction (as ships do to foil submarines) the mouse could frustrate the cat, but not if the cat could predict these changes and make proper corrections. But if she could, she would be exhibiting behavior of a still higher order, where corrections depend not only on the rate of change of the position of the mouse, but also on the rate of change of velocity (that is, on the rate of change of the rate of change of position), on "higher derivatives" in the language of the calculus.[56]

By defining the higher orders of purposefulness in terms of the *flexibility* of behavior, Rosenblueth, Wiener, and Bigelow have called attention to something which may be at the basis of biological intelligence. We thus have ways of quantifying "order" and "purposefulness" (and hence biological intelligence and, perhaps, "freedom"), factors which have long been recognized to have an important relation to life. Perhaps in this approach lies a basis for a quantification of ethics.

Quantification of Ethics

In Chapter 13 I described various early attempts to quantify moral values. These attempts have persisted to our own day, culminating in the nineteenth-century notion of "progress." The notion of progress implies a quantification of values since it implies a *direction* toward the achievement of a better state and thus at least a rough scale on the basis of which one can make choices.

The nineteenth-century notion of progress had two aspects. There was social progress, which was generally equated with increase in technological potential and, since technology was predominantly a cultural trait of the Western civilization, "progress" came to mean becoming more and more like Western Europeans. There was, besides, biological progress, also an idea which came to full fruition in the nineteenth century. According to this notion, man's position as the crown of creation was seen as a result of progress (evolution) rather than of divine decree (as it had appeared before).

We have also seen how the whole notion of progress was challenged in our own century by relativism, which questioned the existence of universal measuring sticks for values. We also have biological relativism. This view denies that the notions of "higher organism" and "lower organism" have any meaning. Evolution, say the biological relativists, is a process in which species progressively adjust to their environment. A well-adjusted species survives, and survival is the only measure of its adjustment. Thus, since a tapeworm is as admirably adjusted to its environment as man is to his, there is no reason to consider man in any way superior to the tapeworm.

We see that the argument of biological relativism is a replica of that of cultural relativism. Both stress adjustment to environment (physical in one case, "traditional" in the other).

However, the classification of behavior by Rosenblueth, Wiener, and Bigelow shows that "adjustment" is a many-storied affair. Translating the "orders of purposefulness" into the terminology of adjustment, we see that we may have first-order adjustment (the adjustment to conditions *as they are*), and higher order adjustments (that is, potentialities for adjustment under changing conditions). Thus, the ability to *learn*, a characteristic largely confined to higher vertebrates, amounts to an ability to adjust under changing conditions. But the ability to symbolize and transmit the results of learning (peculiar to man) is an ability of still higher order, because it involves the ability to predict the changes and to prepare for them.[57]

The whole difficulty in quantifying values is in the choice of an appropriate variable. What is the quantity which we should always choose to increase? We see how the wrong choice of this quantity leads to frustration. We need food. Hence food is a value. But we cannot increase our food consumption indefinitely. We need certain standards of comfort. But concentrating on comfort (as has been the case in Western civilization) leads to the neglect of other important values. Likewise the denial of comfort (the course chosen by adherents of various ascetic philosophies) leads nowhere. The quest for power (the present guiding principle of national policies) is inevitably frustrating, because it inevitably leads to conflict and destruction.

Only one direction seems promising—the acquisition of the higher adjustment faculties. This direction can be taken by individuals, groups, and the whole of mankind. It implies a struggle; not a competitive struggle against potential allies, but a struggle against the chaotic tendency of nature, a struggle of creating order out of chaos, knowledge out of ignorance, insight out of illusion, freedom out of compulsion. It implies a quantitative evaluation of social orders and of cultures—someday we will be able to measure the information-absorbing capacities of various societies and groups, hence their potentialities for high-order adjustment. It implies an evaluation of man's position in the biological world, in fact it seems to vindicate man's claim for being the highest form of life. It indicates the fruitful direction of social evolution—toward increasing freedom from the old crippling compulsions. And it may even indicate the direction of biological evolution to our descendants, should they ever possess the power of guiding their biological destiny.[58]

SUMMARY OF CHAPTERS 13, 14, AND 15

Quantification is an attempt to reduce statements about the world to statements about quantities and relations among them. Attempts at quantification are old in Western culture. The early attempts were mixtures of science and mysticism. A rapid advance in quantifying our knowledge of the physical word began with systematic measurements and the generalization of measurement to quantities which are expressible as ratios of directly measured quantities. Further advances came with the generalization of the notion of quantity itself.

At present the domain of quantified description of events is rapidly increasing and spreading into the very areas which have traditionally been considered as unyielding to quantitative (or any kind of objective) description. The importance of this trend is that it indicates a possibility of coming to terms in any discussion by translating the discussion into a language in which evaluations are least influenced by subjective states and emotional commitments.

Chapter 16. THE EXTENSIONAL BARGAIN

So FAR I have presented operationalism as an outlook which views meaningfulness and truth in terms of analysis, that is, an attempt to understand the whole in terms of its parts, the abstract in terms of the concrete, the qualitative in terms of the quantitative. It is an assumption of operational philosophy that such analysis is a means of improving communication by sharpening its tools and by relating the means of communication to basic, invariant experiences.

However, when the operational philosophers of our century (4, 17, 113) applied their tools—logical analysis—to the formidable output of traditional philosophy, which was principally couched in generalities, "absolutes," moral judgments, and unanswerable questions, most of this output was revealed to have no operational content. Accordingly, man's preoccupation with philosophical questions was mercilessly criticized. It was shown to be a preoccupation with largely meaningless assertions. Outstanding examples of such criticism are Ayer's *Language, Truth and Logic* and Wittgenstein's *Tractatus Logico-philosophicus*. The first book demolishes the meaningfulness of value judgments, and the second performs the same service for all the remaining judgments of philosophy.

Significantly, however, Wittgenstein's statement at the end of the book reveals his awareness of the fact that he has been sawing off the limb he is sitting on, for he raises the following question: "What sort of assertions have *I* made in my book? Are *they* operationally meaningful?" And he finds that they are not. Hence he too has been talking non-sense, no less than the philosophers whom he has criticized. What to do?

Faced with this difficulty, Wittgenstein finally achieves the humility which is as necessary to a serious thinker as discipline and insight. He admits that he has been talking non-sense and, in effect, begs the reader to disregard what he has said. He compares his dissertation to a ladder which one pushes away after one has climbed through a window. He means, I suppose, that the *act* of communication has occurred (the reader has been introduced to a certain orientation), after which the vehicle of communication (Wittgenstein's thesis) serves no purpose. In effect, this is an admission that communication can occur through other than operationally meaningful assertions. One can put it in still another way: Wittgenstein's thesis is useful but self-defeating. It makes sense to someone who has not yet acquired the operationalist (in this case the logical positivist) point of view, and it helps one attain this point of view: but once the point of view is attained, the thesis becomes meaningless.

Wittgenstein's self-criticism has had repercussions in subsequent discussions of logical positivism (107). The argument of logical positivism has been summarized as follows. Logical positivists distinguish two kinds of meaningful assertions, "analytic" and "synthetic." The first kind are assertions about assertions such as were described in Chapter 4. They have no "truth content" but only a validity content. The second are assertions about the world and do have truth content. Assertions in the form "X ought to be" (value judgments) are at most assertions about how people behave or about what they say and feel when certain actions occur. For example, "One ought not kill" has no operational meaning as it stands. It acquires meaning in the form "People who kill are punished" or "When someone kills, I become angry."

The investigation of the truth content of assertions, say the logical positivists, ought to be left to science. Logical analysis (investigations of the validity and the meaningfulness of assertions) is, on the other hand, the proper task of philosophy.

So runs the argument of the logical positivists. But it appears that the tables can be turned on the logical positivist, because he has just made an "ought" statement himself, namely what the task of philosophy ought to be. One can now tell *him* that the only meaning of his prescription for philosophy is that he is saying that he feels bad when philosophers do something other than logical analysis.

The difficulty can be avoided if sharp distinctions between operationally meaningful and meaningless assertions are *not* made. One does not then have to face embarrassing questions of the kind that plagued Wittgenstein. One can view operationally completely meaningful assertions as the ideal vehicles of communication. But like noise-free channels in communication theory, they are only ideals. The point is that communication is possible even if the channels are not noise-free. Sometimes communication goes on in spite of enormous amounts of noise. To be sure, the chief task of philosophy remains, as it has been defined by the logical positivists, to reduce the amount of noise. But philosophers should recognize that one can achieve this aim only by skillfully utilizing the channels of communication at one's disposal and these are never noise-free.

Discursive and Nondiscursive Languages

In Chapter 1, I started with the notion of meaning as a relation between language and experience. I pointed out that a theory of language based on the role of meaning would classify languages into categories different from those established in linguistics. Let us call this classification a semantic classification as distinguished from a linguistic one. We may recall that in view of this interpretation of language, it appears that "in the long run" people speaking the same "semantic" language will understand each other more fully than people who speak the same "linguistic" language but different semantic languages. All that semantically co-lingual people need to do in order to understand each other is to make formal translations from one vocabulary to the other (for example, generals talking about military tactics or mathematicians talking about group theory or anyone talking about primitive physiological functions). Coming to an understanding is more difficult for people who talk languages semantically remote from each other, because there it is not a matter of translation but of acquiring new experience.

The fundamental terms used in chess, for example, are easily related to their referents. The meaning of "rook," "bishop," etc., can be easily learned. But it is much more difficult for a chess master to explain to a beginner why one game was "brilliant" and another "dull," why one player's style is "audacious," and another's "pedantic," or why at a certain point a player evaluates his position as hopeless and concedes the game in spite of having material superiority. A chess master can talk of these things freely (with assurance of being understood) only to another chess master.

The same can, of course, be said of musicians, stamp collectors, polar explorers, and other people who face and solve similar problems and share similar aspirations.

It is stressed in many works dealing with the methods and significance of science (including this one) that scientists understand each other and are able to arrive at agreements because the concepts of science have operational meaning and the criteria for truth are operationally defined. However, the scientists' area of mutual understanding usually extends beyond operationally meaningful discourse. It includes all "shop talk," and shop talk is by no means operationally meaningful throughout.

To return to our example of the chess master, he will not confine his shop talk to the operationally definable chess terms (check, mate, exchange, castling, etc.). He will also talk of such matters as mobility, pressure, development, tempo, style, etc. Few, if any, of these terms are operationally defined. But they do have meaning for chess players. I am sure that readers who are intimately acquainted with sculptors or golfers, or aviators can supply similar lists. It must be emphasized, however, that we are not talking now about jargon or slang equivalents of technical terms (such as "snake eyes" and "box cars" in craps, which *are* operationally defined) but of that fringe of metaphorical haze that surrounds every area of definable experience and adds to it the elements of zest and adventure.

Once the extension of the operationally precise to the vague but *intimate* fringe area is understood, the act of communication acquires an entirely new meaning. The intimacy between happily married couples, the funniness of family jokes, the spice of dialect humor, the *raison d'être* of the *New Yorker*, and the exclusiveness of the argot of teen-agers and of jazz enthusiasts can be properly understood only in terms of this meaning, which rests on shared but not yet systematically articulated experience.

Where one starts a discussion of communication depends on one's purpose. Our purpose is to show the act of communication on the operationally meaningful level as the solid core of operational philosophy in a dual role:

1. As the foundation of the operational theory of knowledge (operational definition, operational criteria for truth, etc.); and

2. The foundation of operational ethics (since the value placed on inquiry in this ethics makes the act of communication on the operationally meaningful level the primary ethical act).

Therefore the "vague" areas appear in this treatment as extensions and border regions of operational knowledge. On the other hand, if this had been a book on language or communication, especially if it had been written from an evolutionary point of view,

the logical beginning would probably have been from the opposite
end, that is, from the sort of "knowledge" that has no logic and
the sort of "language" that has no grammar—the unanalyzable
kinds of knowledge and language.

That such exist and operate is well known. Birds "know" aerodynamics, that is to say, they behave in such a way that aerodynamic
principles keep them aloft. This "knowledge" is quite different from
man's knowledge of aerodynamics, which enables him to design a
flying machine. Yet the two kinds cannot be wholly unrelated, because intermediate kinds of knowledge of aerodynamics exist.

If the bird with his built-in knowledge stands at one end, and
the physicist with his equations at the other, then the aviator, the
mechanic, and the engineer are in between. For the aviator (who, let
us assume, has little "formal" knowledge), flying is still partly, as
for the bird, a matter of muscle coordination, but not entirely, because he can analyze what he does to some degree (for example, he
can explain what each of the controls does). The mechanic and the
engineer have more analytical knowledge and perhaps less "intuitive" knowledge of flying principles than the aviator. The physicist
has still more analytical knowledge about the why's and wherefore's
of flying, but very probably he could not design, build, or fly an
aeroplane.

The same gradation from the intuitive to the highly abstract and
systematic exists in communication. On certain levels, communication is unanalyzable—it consists of primary communicative units
and has therefore no "grammar." Such are the so-called "micro-
languages" of animals and children. True languages appear with
grammar, that is, with the possibility of analyzing the meaning of
utterances in terms of component parts, which bear definite relations to each other. But grammatical analysis is still not semantic
analysis, in which the meaning of the primary components themselves (words) is related to even more fundamental carriers of meaning, namely, experience (58).

A most interesting development in the philosophy of language
is the discovery (most articulately expressed in the writings of Ernst
Cassirer and Susanne Langer) that certain symbolic systems have
complex grammatical structure without having a semantic structure. These symbolic systems are the *nondiscursive* languages, of
which the most outstanding example is music (18, 47).

It is meaningful to say that music has a grammar, because the
relations between the parts of a musical utterance are unambigu-

ously analyzable. Anyone versed in the theory of Western music can give a formal analysis of a musical composition which will agree with the analyses given by others equally trained. Terms like phrase, cadence, sequence, period, variation, development, etc., as well as the names of harmonies and of contrapuntal devices are certainly analogous to the grammatical terms of spoken language. But musical utterance has no "semantic" meaning in the narrow sense of the term, that is, it is impossible to point to unambiguous referents for which the musical symbols stand.

There is, therefore, still another way to classify languages (symbolic systems), that is, by the degree of their "discursiveness." At one end would be the purely discursive, "information-transmitting" languages (science, especially designed signal systems, codes for computing machines, etc.). At the other end would be the least discursive languages of ritual, dance, art, and music. Between them would range poetry, prose, and everyday speech.

The discursive languages are characterized by a complete arbitrariness of symbolization. That is why their translation from one set of symbols to another presents no formal problem. The directions on a soap package written in six languages are all "equivalent." Translation is practically "one-to-one," that is, words of one language are simply substituted for the words of another with only minor modifications to conform to the grammatical peculiarities.

Translations from a strongly discursive language to a more weakly discursive one can still sometimes be made, but such translations are "artificial." They are possible only if the repertoire of the weakly discursive language has been extended to include the symbols corresponding to those of the strongly discursive one. Formally, the translation conveys the same "meaning" but not psychologically. To take an example, consider the following translation. In mathematics (the most strongly discursive language) one writes

$$d^2x/dt^2 + a \ dx/dt + bx = 0$$

In English, this reads: the rate of change of the rate of change of one variable with respect to another increased by a constant times the rate of change and another constant times the value of the dependent variable adds up to nothing.

Of course, this sounds like gibberish. It sounds like gibberish even to a mathematician who has to translate this statement into his own symbols (the equation) before its "meaning" becomes clear.[*]

*Cf. the exercise in logic on p. 171.

The meaning of the equation is definite, however, and immediately brings to the mind of the mathematician a certain class of curves and even a certain class of physical problems (for example, harmonic motion with damping or an alternating current circuit with resistance, inductance, and capacitance) associated with the equation. The English translation is only "formally" a translation. It is possible only because common English words exist which *by agreement among mathematicians* can be substituted for the mathematical symbols. It is not a translation in a functional sense, where one set of symbols calls forth the same kind of experience as another.

When one deals with nondiscursive languages, translation becomes impossible altogether. For example, music cannot be translated into English. The translation of poetry from one language into another is notoriously difficult especially if the languages are those of widely dissimilar cultures. A most meticulous description of a dance or a ritual will miss the whole "point" of what it describes.[50]

The reason for this dissimilarity between discursive and nondiscursive languages lies in the fact that the nondiscursive symbols are not arbitrary like the discursive ones but are more or less bound up with the meaning to be conveyed. The referents of the nondiscursive symbols (if they can be so called) are not "out there" in the world. The connection between symbol and referent is not arrived at by explicit agreement among the communicants as in the case of discursive symbols. Rather, the referents of nondiscursive symbols are inside the communicants. Hence they have meaning only if the communicants are somehow attuned to each other.

An assertion like "Music is a universal language" has a limited truth content. What is meant by such an assertion, I suppose, is that a Frenchman, a German, and a Russian can all "understand" the music of Beethoven, even though they may not understand each other's speech. The reason a Frenchman, a German, and a Russian can all "understand" the music of Beethoven is because the musical histories of France, Germany, and Russia were sufficiently intermingled. Most of the people of Europe *learned* to understand the same musical language, just as all railroad engineers in Europe learned the meaning of the same railroad signals. A Turk once told me of his first impressions of a Beethoven symphony. All *he* could hear was a lot of noise through which he could discern only the strokes of the kettle drums. To put the universality of musical language to a good test, it is suggested that the Western reader

listen to recordings of, say, Chinese music and try to determine
the various moods which it is undoubtedly supposed to convey. In
most cases, his score will not be much better than if he had made
random guesses.[60]

I have implied that the symbols of nondiscursive languages do
have referents; that the referents, however, are not "observables"
but the inner states of the communicants. The function of nondiscursive languages is also entirely different from that of discursive
ones. The latter point out relations among referents (the sky is
blue; five is greater than three). The former aim at reproducing the
referent within one communicant inside the other. In the last analysis, the discursive languages have this aim too. When I say, "The
sky is blue," I am calling attention to my inner state (my feelings
of the blueness of the sky) and seek to reproduce it in you. But in
the case of the discursive language, I depend on your being "attuned"
not to me personally but to the objective world in order for you
to "understand" me. On the other hand, the nondiscursive languages
also have in the last analysis "objective" (in principle observable)
referents. It is only that they are hidden from view. They consist of
nervous impulses, hormonal secretions, and what not. The search
for tools which would enable us to observe "subjective" states the
way we observe, say, chemical reactions, is an outstanding task of
the next development in the science of man. Some such tools have
been developed in experimental psychology and in psychiatry.
The so-called "lie detector" is nothing but a crude indicator of
certain inner states. Psychoanalysis is an attempt to infer inner
states which are not indicated in ordinary observed overt behavior.

Probably a great deal could be learned in this area if the techniques were applied in more "neutral" situations than those associated with serious behavioral problems. It would be most instructive, for example, to develop a "psychoanalysis" of musical esthetics
(as suggested by Susanne Langer). Devoid of urgency which is always present in emotional disturbances, the application of psychoanalytic methods in areas where extensive experimentation is possible may shed light not only on the referents behind the symbols
of art but on the methods themselves.

Thus the "semantics" of art, ritual, and other nondiscursive languages promises to become a rich field of future investigations. The
semantics of the discursive languages (mathematics and the exact
sciences) is relatively simple because its terms are least ambiguous
and the operational meaning of its assertions is the most complete.

The semantics of semi-discursive languages (that is, the language of everyday life, of politics, ethics, of philosophy, and esthetics) is the intermediate case. Operational analysis can be applied to its terms and assertions to a certain extent. But all such analysis is limited, because it can go only so far. Sooner or later the level of undefinable terms and "self-evident truths" is reached. It is on this level that agreement takes place among people who speak the same language (in the semantic sense).

THE LEVEL OF AGREEMENT

Wendell Johnson (43) has coined a fortunate term to describe the agreement among people who speak the same semantic language: *extensional bargain.* You and I make an extensional bargain when we agree not to go beyond a certain point with our analysis. You know what I mean, and I know what you mean. If it were not for the fact that disagreements *do* occur and that groups speaking different languages (in the semantic sense) *do* clash, the need for analysis would never be felt. *Analysis is an attempt to reach a level at which extensional bargains can be struck.* The ideal of physical science is to reduce the description of the world to terms derivable entirely and exclusively from undefined symbols and structure relations among these symbols. This ideal is inspired by the observation that on that level an extensional bargain can be struck most easily under the most general conditions. That level is the rock bottom of conceptual invariances. Everyone knows the meaning of "larger than," "smaller than," "before," "after," "between," etc. The ideal of operational ethics is analogous: it is to reduce "ought" assertions to "if so, . . . then so" assertions after the extensional bargain has been struck on the meaning of "good." This ideal is inspired by a *conjecture* that such a bargain is possible.

Analysis, therefore, is a means, not an end. There is no harm in pursuing it beyond the point where understanding has occurred, but it is no misfortune if an unanalyzed or even an unanalyzable fringe area occurs in one's outlook or discourse, as long as those with whom one has to communicate share the same area.

It appears, therefore, that the weak spot in logical positivism is a weak spot only from the strict logical positivist point of view. It ceases to be a "weak spot" if the limitations of analysis are frankly recognized. Philosophy cannot confine itself to operationally meaningful assertions if it aspires to make the area of operationally meaningful assertions as wide as possible, because the very need to broaden the operationally meaningful area arises from a realization that it is sometimes *necessary* to talk non-sense. They who wish to carry the word of God to the heathen must speak the language of the heathen. Wittgenstein's severe admonition, "Whereof one cannot speak, one must remain silent" should be replaced by a more indulgent one, "Before one has learned to speak, one must babble."

The philosopher may (in fact, must), therefore, leave the haven of operationally meaningful discourse without apology but not without apprehension. For he must view his departure as a venture. He can wander only so long as his extensional bargain with his listeners or readers holds. When things become too fuzzy or when new listeners come, with whom the philosopher has not made the bargain, he must go back and start from somewhere where communication is still possible. This is what the "analytic" philosophers have tried to do—Aristotle, Descartes, Hume, Kant, Locke. They tried to start with concepts which (they thought) were common property. That is why their contributions seem (to a "liberal" operational philosopher) sincere and constructive. And this is what the "synthetic" philosophers, who began with eternal magnificent verities, have not done—Plato, Hegel, Nietzsche, Fichte, and Schelling—and that is why their contributions to thought seem (again to an operationalist) at best simply creations of poetry.

The way of fruitful philosophy, then, is not unlike the way of fruitful science—from the known to the unknown; from proof to conjecture; from the obvious to the controversial. How does one make this transition? One uses the characteristic device of human thought—imagination. One generalizes.

Generalizations go under many names. The generalizations of science are made consciously with awareness of the abstracting processes involved. They are formulated as hypotheses, theories, laws, abstract models, and analogies. Science, however, has not always been science. Its intellectual roots are in scholastic dissertations and in the frustrating quests of the alchemists, yes, and in literature and in law, where the habit of generalization has been practiced until it was harnessed to the task of fathoming and changing the world. For this reason, it behooves modern philosophy which has discovered the secret of success of the scientific method to approach the analysis of the older attempts with sympathy and understanding. Before science learned to talk, it babbled. Where there is an extensional bargain, babbling too can be richly communicative, as every mother knows.

Chapter 17. METAPHORS AND MODELS

GENERALIZATION depends on the discovery of analogous structures in dissimilar things. We have seen (cf. p. 61) how such discoveries underlie all explanations. Something is explained when it is shown to be like something familiar to us. The difference between a naive explanation and a scientific one is that the naive explanation is complete when a similarity has been pointed out, but a scientific explanation is expected to yield "dividends," to go beyond the event "explained."

Long before the perception of similarities between seemingly unrelated things was molded into the scientific outlook, such similarities were pointed out for the sheer pleasure of perceiving them. In literature and poetry, this matching of widely dissimilar things according to some perceived similarity is called "metaphor." It seems, however, that this form of *linguistic* behavior merits attention not only as a literary device but as an instance of a more fundamental form of human activity. Magic is essentially metaphorical. So are dreams. So is most artistic activity. Finally, theoretical science is essentially disciplined exploitation of metaphor.

The metaphors of magic induce a belief in an ability to manipulate events by manipulating their metaphorical representation. To stick a pin into a wax figurine in the belief that it will harm the person represented, to eat a lion's heart in the belief that it will make one brave, to eat bread in the belief that one thus enjoys a mystic union with the deity are all instances of magical metaphor. So are talismans, charms, potions, invocations, prayer, blessings, and curses.

The discovery that dreams are metaphorical enactments of one's desires is one of the foundations of psychoanalysis. A similar analysis applied to the arts, particularly to music, may reveal the bases of their emotional appeal. In all of these activities—magic, dreaming, artistic pursuits—the metaphor appears as a compulsive expression with little or no awareness of the logical relations between the representation and the thing represented. In literary metaphor, this awareness emerges, and in scientific metaphor it becomes explicit and conscious.

Edwin Loeb (52), attempting to re-establish the evolutionary point of view in anthropology (against which a reaction still persists), calls attention to a process of intellectual development as reflected in the passage from "play-thinking" to the use of proverbs, then to the use of deductive logic, and finally to inductive reasoning. Play-thinking corresponds to magical metaphor. Underlying both is the inability to distinguish between the wish and the fact, the imagined and the real as, for example, with very young children who often confuse dreams with real events.

From play-thinking, however, emerges the expressive metaphor of the ritual (and perhaps of the arts). Here a separation between the wish and the fact becomes recognizable. The ritual is a well-circumscribed act performed at a specific time. Characteristically, it serves to introduce or merely to symbolize the real act instead of to substitute for it. Having performed the war dance (to insure victory in battle), one still makes sure that the weapons are in good condition. Having offered a sacrifice (to insure the fertility of the soil), one still takes pains to plow, to sow, and to fertilize the fields. A partial separation of function thus takes place between "religion" and "science."

Primitive science now develops its own metaphors embodied in the recognition of analogies and in generalizations. These are the basis of "folk wisdom," most clearly expressed in proverbs but found also in myths and in literary works. Proverbs may be primitive psychological observations, such as "A new wife is well treated in the beginning." They may be ethical prescriptions in metaphorical garb, such as, "A messenger in service is never harmed" (do not confuse the content of information with its bearer). Or they may be crude statements of biological laws: "Like father, like son" (characteristics are hereditary); or social observations stated as biological metaphor: "Birds of a feather flock together" (people are united by common interests).[61]

The metaphors of literature are less obviously utilitarian and "scientific" but in a sense are seen to satisfy a basic need, the need to create order. It is significant that some poetic formalizations of metaphor are remarkably widespread among widely separated cultures.[62]

On a still more sophisticated level are the metaphors of individually created literary works. Greek and Shakespearean tragedies are full of them. They reflect a conscious *search* for analogy as a means for effective description of relations inherent in phenomena, especially in human affairs. The search is often deliberate and discriminating. The similarities noted are far-reaching rather than accidental and, significantly, the *implications* of the metaphor are often worked out.

The metaphors of poetry and literature merge imperceptibly with those of philosophy. "Life is a prison" might have been said by a pessimistic poet or by a Schopenhauer. Goethe, in picturing Mephistopheles as the enemy of life and a champion of chaos, unwittingly (or, perhaps, with uncanny intuitive insight) anticipated the modern conjecture which pictures the life process as a struggle against increase in entropy (cf. Chapter 15). Schiller, whom most people would classify as a poet, gave expression to the importance of predictive content in his famous lines,

> Mit dem Genius steht die Natur in ewigem Bunde
> Was der Eine verspricht, leistet die Andre gewiss.*

A fact of prime importance is that metaphors are not only symptoms of the way events are perceived but also factors in the shaping of perception. Metaphors are fixers of ideas. They enable particular perceptions to perpetuate themselves. This is especially true of the metaphors which describe the nature of man and society and thus implicitly incorporate value judgments (30).

In the heydays of absolute monarchy, when a state was thought of as a body whose "head" was the monarch, the notion of doing away with absolute monarchy appeared as terrible as beheading. In our day, when the predominant view of society still stems from Herbert Spencer's biological metaphor, "the struggle for existence and the survival of the fittest," competition appears as a beneficent selection process which assures that the best men win. Accordingly, interference with competition appears as interference with the "natural state of affairs." If the symbol of virginity is a white dress, the biological concomitant of sexual love assumes the connotation of uncleanliness. If honor is pictured as a possession, it seems natural

---

*Nature and genius have made an eternal pact: whatever the latter predicts, the former fulfills.

to "guard" it, to fear its loss, to try to "regain" it when it is "lost," etc.

The power of the metaphor was well known to the orators of antiquity, and it is well known to the political cartoonists of our day. The personification of states and of political ideologies has done its work in channelizing (and thus making easier to control) the political thinking of populations, which had been threatening to get out of hand with the spread of literacy.

The metaphor, then, like language itself works both ways. It serves to clarify and to confuse, to open new vistas and to perpetuate existing myths, to organize thinking so as to make it fruitful and to regiment thinking so as to make it sterile. The abuse of language occurs when its metaphorical nature is hidden, if the representation is *identified* with the thing represented. Therefore the linguistically hygienic use of metaphor depends on the full recognition of its limitations, that is, on critical consciousness of the generalizations, analogies, and abstractions involved.

Exact science is characterized, then, not by the absence of metaphor but by their abundant use with full recognition of their limitations. Scientific metaphors are called "models." They are made with a full knowledge that the connection between the metaphor and the real thing is primarily in the mind of the scientist. And they are made with a clearly definable purpose—as starting points of a deductive process. There is an "as-if-ness" about the models of exact science which "insulates" the model from reality and prevents a false identification. Like every other aspect of scientific procedure, the scientific metaphor is a pragmatic device, to be used freely as long as it serves its purpose, to be discarded without regrets when it fails to do so. The scientist, therefore, if he is completely a scientist, is unique among the users of metaphors in that he does not become an "addict" of a particular way of perceiving.

A MODEL

Let us examine a scientific metaphor.

"Think of a gas," says any textbook in physics, "as consisting of billions and billions of tiny perfectly elastic billiard balls, each having a mass but no volume, flying every which way throughout the container in which the gas is enclosed, so that nothing deflects them from straight line paths except collisions among themselves and with the walls."

What poetry or magic could invent anything more fantastic? A

ball with mass but no volume! Balls colliding in spite of having no
size! And perfectly elastic!

"Nevertheless," says physics, "think of a gas *as if* it were so."

We are thinking.

"Now," says physics, "think of the *consequences* of this metaphor.
Apply the laws of motion to the paths of the molecules (the 'billiard balls'). They will strike the walls of the container with a certain average frequency, which depends on their speed, their number, and the size of the container. . . ."

If we follow the argument based on the laws of motion and certain statistical considerations, we will arrive at the conclusion:

"The pressure exerted by a certain mass of gas on the walls of
the container will be inversely proportional to the volume of the
container." This conclusion is known as Boyle's Law.

This law was known before the "billiard ball" metaphor was
invented. But it was known as a "brute fact," not as a conclusion
of a deduction. The scientific metaphor (or model) explains the
fact.

Karl Deutsch (22) speaks of this function of models (to explain
facts) as the *organizing* function. It is the function which the scientific metaphor shares with all other metaphors. By pointing out
similarities among events it organizes our world view and satisfies
the need for order. The scientific model, however, has, as Deutsch
has lucidly pointed out, several other functions which were only
dimly or not at all perceived in pre-scientific metaphor. These functions yield the "dividends" of the scientific explanation mentioned
on page 49.

There is the *heuristic* function which leads us to ask new questions suggested by the model.

There is the *predictive* function which enables us to predict events
on the basis of the assumptions implied by the model.

There is the *measuring* function which enbles us to quantify notions which had been only qualitative.

To take another example, light is explained in physics by means
of a model where its propagation is pictured as the propagation of
electromagnetic waves in a certain frequency range.

The heuristic function of such a model is such that it leads to
many questions about light phenomena, such as "If light is waves,
is it subject to interference effects like sound waves (analogous to
the 'beats' heard when two tones close together are heard simultaneously)?" The answer is yes.[63]

The predictive function enables us to predict that there is "invisible" light (that is, electromagnetic waves of frequencies above and below those which affect our eyes). We now know high-frequency light as ultraviolet and x-rays, and low-frequency light as radio waves and radiant heat.

The measuring function of models enables us to establish an exact quantitative scale for color, which otherwise appears only as a "quality."

Thus the criteria by means of which the worth of a scientific model can be evaluated are more objective than those applied to the pre-scientific metaphor (such as literary elegance or an emotional commitment to the origin or the implications of the metaphor).

Models of Society

The making of social science (in other words, the elimination of social superstitions) depends on the creation of scientific models to replace the metaphors in which so much discourse about social matters is still couched. Such models are now emerging and replacing the old metaphorical models of religion and of traditional (literary) philosophy.

When the making of a model is a conscious and critical process (as it must be in science), one is always faced with the question, "What is to be abstracted? What are the important features of the subject matter which should be included in the model?" For obviously the model cannot include everything about the subject matter: if it did, there would be no point in making it; one could simply study the subject matter.

To the *laissez-faire* economist, society appeared as a market, and classical economics is an outgrowth of this metaphor. If society were truly a "market" (that is, a collection of individuals buying and selling goods and services, each determined to maximize his gains), then the theories of classical economics would be sufficient to account for all social phenomena. It is well known, however, that the market model cannot even account for purely economic phenomena satisfactorily. Society, then, is not just a market. One is almost tempted to ask, "If it is not a market, what is it?" It is not, however, a wise question to ask, since it simply invites another metaphor for an answer. The traditional way to answer such questions was to ransack one's experience to find something which human society is like. It may, however, be unlike anything in our experience, in which case the search is a waste of time.

The modern theoretical scientist proceeds differently. He *constructs* models. To say that society is a market means that the individuals in society are governed in their behavior by certain motivations, that is, they behave in accordance with certain rules. The construction of a model is a specific description of the rules. Once the rules have been explicitly stated, alternative sets of rules can be easily imagined. This means that the model can be modified or replaced by another. To investigate the implications of a model means to make predictions about the gross effects of the rules on the behavior of the society represented. To test the model means to compare its predictions with the actual behavior of the society.

With the present means at our disposal we cannot hope to fit all social behavior into a simple model. But we can hope to fit parts of it. Outside of pure economics (producing, consuming, buying, and selling) a great deal of inquiry is currently carried out about the goal-seeking and decision-making behavior of human groups (particularly small ones). I have already mentioned the studies of problem-saving groups (p. 103). It was assumed in that work that the essential feature of a problem-solving group is its communication net. Generalization of these models involves as an important feature the channelization of goals.

A classification can be made of human groups in accordance with the degree to which their goal-seeking behavior is consistent and integrated. Thus we can speak of a collection of "rational" individuals, if the choices of each in a given situation are self-consistent. That is to say, given a range of choices, each individual will always arrange them in some order of preference which remains fixed, at least for some time. If the preferences of the individuals are not correlated or are altogether incompatible with each other, and if each individual can manipulate the environment (in accordance with prescribed rules) so as to try to make a preferred situation come about, we are dealing with a "game."

Ordinary games are good examples. In checkers, for example, each player prefers to capture as many of the opponent's men as he can and to prevent the opponent from capturing his. Here the preferences of the two players are incompatible. Moreover, each tries to make his preferred situations come about within a framework of rules. Therefore checkers is a "game" according to our definition. The situation depicted in classical (completely competitive) economics is also a "game."[64]

There are, however, other formations discernible in social behavior. One can, for example, consider "coalitions." Here the members can cooperate in the direction of common goals *to a certain extent*, but beyond a certain point these goals become incompatible. An example of a coalition is the relation between labor and management with regard to wages. Although it appears that it is always in the interest of management to cut wages and in the interest of labor to boost them, this is not quite correct. It is not in the interest of "rational" management to cut wages below prevailing rates in a tight labor market, since they may lose their workers. Even in a flooded labor market, wages must be at a certain subsistence level, otherwise the efficiency of labor will be seriously impaired. Therefore, up to a certain level, it is in the interest of both labor and management to raise wages. But beyond that level, wages become a controversial issue. It is characteristic of coalitions that they give rise to *bargaining* procedures (also found in political coalitions).

On another level of organization we have "foundations," that is, organizations which have their own goals apart from the goals of the members. An industry which must perform certain services regardless of whether they are profitable (such as utilities with charters where certain conditions of minimum service are specified, or foundations engaged in supporting certain activities in which the members are not engaged) is an example. Questions of policy in such organizations will necessarily involve the consideration of *incentives*, whose purpose is to harmonize the goals of the members with those of the organization.

Finally, we have the most integrated form of organization conceivable—a "team"—in which the preferences of every member coincide with each other and with those of the organization itself. For example, a basketball team which is a team in the coach's sense of the word (that is, where each player has only one goal—to help win the game) is also a team in our sense of the word. But if the desire of an individual player is to try to score as many baskets as he can even if his tactics jeopardize the team's chances of winning the game, then the team is not a "team" but only a "foundation."[65]

All these are "constructed" models, fictitious structures that are never realized in their pure form in real life. But they serve an important heuristic purpose. When investigated, they give indications of how groups *would* behave if they had structures similar to those of the models.

In a way the investigation of constructed models is a thought process which reverses the usual creation of a metaphor. Shakespeare could say, "All the world's a stage and all the men and women merely players," because he noticed that people tend to act out roles. The modern theoretical social scientist investigating models would have said, "If men behaved in real life according to the rules of theatrical performance (which I hereby define), such and such consequences would follow." He would then match such consequences with observed behavior and decide to what extent life resembles a stage.

Another important characteristic of scientific models is that their implied predictions are often quantitative. The predictive content of such models is therefore high. For example, the relation between pressure and volume predicted by the kinetic model of the gas is a mathematical relation. It says not only that the smaller the volume of the container the greater will be the pressure of the gas in it but also *by how much*. To the extent that the quantitative predictions agree with the observations, the model is a good one. However, when the observed quantities depart from the predictive ones (even though they still agree *qualitatively* in the sense that pressure increases as volume decreases), the inadequacy of the model is apparent and modifications must be sought. Thus even in its failure the quantitative model serves a useful purpose in stimulating new investigations. The same considerations apply to the market models of classical economics. Their inadequacy is shown not so much in qualitative discrepancies between observation and prediction as in quantitative ones. Thus a search for other factors in economic activity besides the maximization of gains under competitive conditions is indicated.

ANALYSIS VS. SYNTHESIS

A scientific model is thus a result both of synthesis and of analysis. Its synthetic nature is in the opportunity it gives for contemplating a class of events *as a whole* (which is what all metaphors do). Its analytic nature is in the specific description of the structure (the totality of relations) of the situation studied. The model therefore serves as a bridge between the analytic and the holistic approaches to phenomena. Conscious model building (a recent development in psychology and in social science) came at an opportune time when the controversy between the positivists (who are analytic and behavioristic) and the holists (who march under the slogan, "The whole is greater than the sum of all its parts") was reaching a climax.

In psychology the gestaltists were criticizing the behaviorists on the ground that perception could not be put together out of minute sense data like a mosaic. In sociology the conceptualists were attacking the statisticians on the grounds that man is not a statistical unit. In anthropology the functionalists were chiding the gatherers of "cultural traits" on the grounds that no matter how carefully one examines every brick of a house one cannot thereby understand the house.

One of the leading philosophers of our age, A. N. Whitehead, tried to bring the spirit of holism into the general philosophy of science on the grounds that the ideal of describing the universe in terms of structure involving times and places has outlived its usefulness (109).

The entire argument of holistic philosophy may be summarized thus.* There are different levels of organization in the occurrence of events. You cannot explain the events of one level in terms of the events of another. For example, you cannot explain life in terms of mechanical concepts, nor society in terms of individual psychology. Analysis can only take you *down* the scale of organization. It cannot reveal the working of things on a higher level.

To some extent the holistic philosophers are right. Their point can be illustrated in a most trivial example. We can know all the properties of a circle. But there is more to be said about two circles than the totality of their properties. For example, the distance between the centers appears as a *new* relation, in no way inherent in the properties of the circles themselves. Similarly, behavior has aspects apart from stimulus-response patterns with which the behaviorists are concerned; relations among people are entities which cannot be perceived by studying individuals apart from each other, etc.

The proponents of holistic methods, therefore, advise scientists to try to contemplate wholes rather than parts. The contemplation of wholes, however, at least as it is practiced today, is primarily metaphorical thinking, because those wholes in order to be understood (in fact, in order to be perceived at all) must be related to something in the past experience of the perceiver. In fact, the metaphors of metaphysics are based on such relations of the perceived to the known—for example, "The Cosmos is a mechanism," or "The Cosmos is an organism," or "The Cosmos is a game of chance." The

*I am giving the argument as I understand it, which is none too well.

metaphysical metaphor establishes the keynote of perception, the spirit in which knowledge will be sought.

The strongest argument of the holists is that there arrives a time when it is necessary to change the key. The analyst, however, can interpret this poetic way of speaking in his own prosaic terms: the time has come to try out a new model. That is not to say that the metaphors of the holists are useless to the analyst. On the contrary, they can serve as an inspiration for the construction of new models. In fact, the dissatisfaction with the atomistic, chaotic models of society which were the concomitants of the market metaphor and the growing insistence of the holists on developing "organismic" theories of society have already led to the construction of models based on communication nets rather than on the chaotic interplay of self-seeking individuals.

There is still another useful function performed by holistic conceptualists. They venture into areas where analysts fear to tread. They often establish new "feelings" for a subject about which one cannot speak intelligently except by striking an extensional bargain. In a way, such extensional bargains are "extensions of credit" to concepts which cannot pay off in operational definitions but which seem like good investments. One treats such concepts *as if* they were operationally definable without placing too strict demands on their meaningfulness. Even a strict operationalist with an analytic orientation can afford such departures into the vague areas of speculation if his faith in the ultimate reduction of all useful concepts to specifically defined relations among operationally definable entities is sufficiently strong.

After all, the laws of thermodynamics *have* been shown to be derivable from those of mechanics and statistics. The direction of biological evolution *has* been shown to be derivable from the simpler notions of random variation and natural selection. The notion of purposefulness *has* been shown to be derivable from principles governing the construction of robots and servo-mechanisms. The notion of creative intelligence *has* been shown to be derivable from the simpler notions of "learning," "learning to learn," etc. Until the time is ripe for analysis, one has to work with unanalyzable concepts.

The founding fathers of science took the concepts that seemed useful without worrying about their operational definitions. Operational definitions of "force," "space," and "time" are recent acquisitions. For some centuries the physicists worked with them *as if* they knew what they were talking about. Only when the lack of operational definitions got them into difficulties (toward the end of the nineteenth century), did it become necessary to provide such definitions and to overhaul the foundations of science. Today, to my knowledge, an operational definition of the "gene" has not yet been given. Yet it is a concept of unquestioned usefulness in biology. The "id," the "ego," and the "superego" of Freudian psychology are still more vague, but they are or were of *some* use. To make what use one can of what one has and to be constantly looking for opportunities to improve one's conceptual foundations is essentially the attitude of the operationalist.

The tolerance of the operationalist, however, is not unlimited. In the first place, he recognizes a hierarchy of concepts and methods ranged according to the degree of meaningfulness and precision embodied in them. He tolerates nonoperational concepts and methods, but only tolerates them. He does not give them equal status with the operational ones. In his opinion, the attempts to "operationalize" the concepts and to establish links between lower order events and higher order "emergent phenomena" should be constantly pursued. He believes in provisional autonomy of disciplines but stresses the provisional character of this autonomy. The ultimate fate of all science in the opinion of the operationalist is a system of deduction, by means of which every observed event on whatever level of complexity or organization is shown to be derivable from fundamental laws of structure involving only the simplest relations on whose nature every normal human being can agree.

Thus, the dream of the rationalists, Descartes, Leibnitz, and Kant still lives. The possibility of *a priori* knowledge, however, has been abandoned, as Reichenbach has so clearly shown (81). Rather a circularity of knowledge is conceded. The general principles of structure are deduced from observation of particulars; the totality of particular truths is deduced from the general principles of structure.

Chapter 18. THE PHILOSOPHER'S JOB

J OHN DEWEY saw the coming reconstruction of philosophy as the fusion of theory and practice. One might think that his outlook reflected the spirit of the age and of the land that nurtured him—the age and land of "practical" men. Yet it would be a disservice to his memory to identify his outlook with what has come to be considered "practical" in common parlance. Practicality in the world of politics and competitive enterprise has come to mean a "know-how" in the business of getting one's own way. In popular conception, this sort of practicality is usually the antithesis of "theory" or of "idealism" or of the "philosophical attitude," so that the dichotomy between doing and knowing *still remains*. But this is precisely the dichotomy which Dewey sought to erase! It can be erased only if creative thought becomes rooted in action and if action becomes rooted in thought.

I have tried to show in this book that such a fusion of thought and action is reflected in what I called operationalism. In my description of this outlook I have devoted considerable attention to logical positivism, because its central notions of meaning and truth were operationally oriented, that is, defined in terms of experience. Dewey's views on meaning and truth were practically identical with those of the logical positivists. It ought to appear, therefore, that the logical positivist views on the tasks of philosophy and those of Dewey would be similar. However, they are not. The prevalent logical positivist view, as expressed, for example by Ayer (4) or Carnap (16), is that philosophy should confine itself to logical analysis, in other words, become a purely analytic discipline (like logic and mathematics). Philosophy should abandon, so say the logical positivists, any attempts to say something factual, for that is the business of science. Philosophy should also jettison its metaphysical baggage (inherited from theology), which has been cluttering up its conceptual frameworks. Ethics and esthetics, formerly considered to be integral parts of philosophy, should also be left alone. Empirical or descriptive ethics and esthetics (which are little more than records of what various people in various societies hold good and beautiful) are said to be properly the business of psychology and social science, while metaphysical ethics and esthetics (which presumably delve into the "real" nature of good and beauty) are declared to be meaningless. In short, logical positivists advise philosophers to stick strictly to linguistic matters.

This was certainly not Dewey's conception of the "reconstructed" philosophy. "It must undertake," he writes in the introduction to the 1948 edition of *Reconstruction in Philosophy* (25), "to do for the development of inquiry into human affairs and hence into morals which the philosophers of the last few centuries did for promotion of scientific inquiry in physical and physiological conditions and aspects of human life."

In this sentence appears not only the hope of what philosophy can do in the future but also a recognition of its role in the past as the instigator of scientific inquiry. Few logical positivists see the role of traditional philosophy in this light.

How does it come about that starting with identical conceptions of the central philosophical ideas (meaning and truth, both pertaining to the theory of knowledge) the logical positivists and Dewey have come to such divergent conclusions on what ought to be the role of philosophy?

One is tempted to seek an explanation in the sociology of knowledge. A similar situation comes to mind in the comparison between the Hellenic era and the Renaissance. Both centered around a rational, "naturalistic" view of the world. In both, there were the beginnings of genuine scientific spirit. Yet Hellenic science remained just talk, and Renaissance science transformed the world. Why? Perhaps because in the Greek mind knowing and doing were separated and for the Renaissance mind they were intimately connected. One need only compare Plato with da Vinci to see the enormous difference in outlooks.

Perhaps there is something of this difference in the way operationalism developed on European and on American soil. Intellectual life in Europe in the 1920's and 1930's (the culminating decades of logical positivism) was on the defensive. Its only hope was to preserve itself against the onslaught of social insanity. Escape into academic sanctuaries seemed to be the only course. In America, however, intellectual life was awakening during this same period. And its seeds were being sown outside the secluded "academic" circles and the leisure classes. Perhaps future history will compare twentieth-century America to eighteenth-century France, where steadily worsening political conditions went hand in hand with a democratization of rational knowledge.

The democratization of knowledge is, I think, what distinguished Renaissance intellectual life from Hellenic intellectual life and more recently American operationalism from its European counterpart.

An example of how a certain word acquired different meanings in Europe and in America will illustrate my point further. The emphasis placed in operationalism on linguistic theory has brought the obscure word "semantics" into the limelight. Among the European logical positivists, semantics is practically co-extensive with philosophy. Semanticists are concerned with what people can do with language. Logical analysis is their stock in trade. Much of the work done in this field is written in a special code (the notation of symbolic logic) which, like mathematics, only specially trained people can read.

In America, semantics has become a newspaper word. The central concern of American semanticists is with what language can do to people. Hence semantics naturally extends into psychology, sociology, and anthropology. In fact, interest in "semantics" has spread to the world of business and of public and industrial relations, where "practical" questions are asked such as, "What can people, using language as a tool, do to other people?" There is also a "defensive" interest in semantics among educators, group workers, and others, who want to know how people can protect themselves from "being done to" by clever manipulators of symbols. Finally, a fashionable preoccupation with semantics has reached that vast amorphous field of activity connected with "personal adjustment," ranging from clinical psychiatry to various self-improvement cults. (78).

Some "academic" semanticists have seen fit to dissociate themselves from this activist approach to semantics. Tarski, for example, in one of his papers calls semantics "a sober and modest discipline which has no pretensions of being a universal patent-medicine for all the ills and diseases of mankind."

"You will not find in semantics," Tarski assures the reader, "any remedy for decayed teeth or illusions of grandeur or class conflicts" (98).

Tarski reflects the strict logical positivist view on the tasks of philosophy, which we described above. Korzybski, on the other hand, an exponent of the "activist" school, was equally quick to dissociate himself from the linguistic kind of semantics.

"My work," he writes in his preface to the third edition of *Science and Sanity*, "was developed entirely independently of linguistic 'semantics'. . . . General semantics turned out to be an empirical science" (46).

If he meant by this statement that the assertions in *Science and Sanity* are synthetic rather than analytic, he was right. His repeated use of the words "science" and "scientific," however, have caused serious concern. By science one understands nowadays a more or less coherent system of assertions about observable events some of which at least are capable of verification by properly trained workers.

The factual assertions of general semantics have to do with the effects on the human nervous system of certain linguistic habits. The assertions are interesting and sometimes plausible, and their consequences appear of immense importance for mankind. Yet one can take issue with Korzybski's claim of scientific status for general semantics by asking where, when, and how its factual assertions have been verified, and who are the trained workers in the field.

The writings of Korzybski have drawn heavy critical fire because of their persistent claims to scientific validity. But Korzybski is by no means alone in his speculations on what language has done and is doing to man. Ernst Cassirer, Susanne Langer, Charles Morris, Benjamin Lee Whorf (to name a few) have all contributed to the philosophy of language, and in their writings (18, 47, 63, 31) language appears not as a system of rules (as it is usually conceived by logical positivists) but as an immensely important part of human behavior, as the subject matter of "neuro-linguistics."

Similarly, for Dewey the theory of knowledge is not merely a system of rules for distinguishing true assertions from false, valid from invalid, meaningful from meaningless (as theory of knowledge appears to the logical positivists and as it has been developed in Part I of this book) but a culturally conditioned fountainhead of action and of morals.

In this anthropological and psychological, perhaps even physiological (as Korzybski thought it to be) approach to language lies, I think, the possibility of linking the rigorously analytic linguistic philosophy of the "classical" semanticists to the activist socially applicable philosophy of operationalism. Just as science became both rigorous and practical through the application to the pressing human problems of yesterday (which were technological), so, perhaps, philosophy can become both rigorous (as the logical positivists want it to be) and practical (as Dewey and his co-operationalists want it to be) through application to the most pressing problems of today (which are social). Pure, technical sophisticated philosophy need not be "degraded" in the process any more than pure mathematics was degraded through the yeoman service it performed in helping solve "practical" problems.

The task of philosophy, in my opinion, is to become a science of language, not only an analytic science but also an empirical one. In its analytic aspects, philosophy should include logical analysis, as it is understood by logical positivists. There is one aspect of logical analysis, however, which is not often stressed in the literature of that discipline, namely the task of reducing the concepts of one level of abstraction to that of another. In some areas this task has been carried out. A classical example is statistical mechanics, in which the concepts of temperature, entropy, and others are shown to be statistical concepts, arising from those of classical mechanics and probabilistic rules. This sort of approach may settle once for all the problem of "emergent phenomena" and "autonomous fields" to which holists and gestaltists and philosophers like Whyte (110) and Whitehead attach so much significance. The analysis of "purpose" by Rosenblueth, Wiener, and Bigelow (cf. p. 188) is another example of this approach.

It is conceivable that emergent social phenomena have a similar basis. How, for example, is the welfare of an individual connected with the welfare of the community? To take a simple case, what does it mean to Mr. A that the burglary rate of A-ville, where he lives, has been reduced? If Mr. A considers his personal situation, it means nothing. His house is either robbed or it is not. The number of houses robbed does not reflect in his fortune at all. Yet in thinking this way, Mr. A is sure to miss the point. He *should* feel more comfortable when the rate of burglary is reduced, in the sense that the *probability* of his house being robbed decreases. This probability is a *social* concept, since it means nothing in the individual case. It is felt only if Mr. A. somehow identifies his fortunes with those of the community.

No matter how individualistic we are, we all feel this identification. We feel "safer" traveling on wide, well-graded roads. We feel "safer" in healthy, sanitary localities, etc. This feeling of safety is the reflection in our personal feeling of the reduced probabilities of misfortune, and it has a meaning only in the sense that we feel to be a part of the aggregate. The logical analysis of such matters (coupled, perhaps, with psychological investigations) is a legitimate field of philosophy.

In its empirical aspect, philosophy of language should be linked to anthropology and psychology. However, in so becoming linked, philosophy would not be simply encroaching on the territory of "factual science" (as logical positivists suppose), because its subject matter (language) is not a "natural" entity like the subject matter of most factual sciences, about which one simply discovers "facts."

Language does not "stay put" as one studies it, as do stars, mountains, animals, and even to a certain extent human beings. The peculiar thing about language is that it is studied by means of itself and thus becomes transfigured in the process at a rate comparable to the "rate of study." There is thus a powerful "feed-back" in the philosophy of language. Language analysis radically changes the potentialities of the language analyzed, and these, in turn, lead to new methods of analysis.

There is another reason why an empirical study of language is not like an ordinary empirical science. Ordinarily "empirical science" designates a discipline that looks at facts or experiments with concrete situations rather than one that pursues abstract speculations. But the pursuit of abstract speculations is tantamount to experimenting with the potentialities of language!

One of the most widespread methods in this sort of experiment is the pursuit of analogy. Analogical thinking is not confined to the "naive" explanations of events. Fruitful scientific conjectures are essentially pursuits of analogies. A famous example is the bold conjecture of de Broglie (who is properly classed as a philosopher rather than a physicist) concerning the wave aspect of matter. The conjecture was a "verbal experiment." "If wave phenomena exhibit characteristics of particles in some aspects," reasoned de Broglie, "can it be that particles exhibit wave characteristics too?" The answer was yes. Answers to such questions are not always "yes," of course, but it seems worthwhile to ask such questions. The statement of an analogy is, then, a linguistic experiment. One puts words together in an assertion, whose structure is similar to another assertion known to be true, in order to see what is asserted as a result.

The sterility of purely analogical methods of primitives, ancients, scholasticists, etc., was in their failure to go beyond the linguistic experiment. They believed linguistic coherence to be equivalent to fact. Or, perhaps, they were not even aware of the difference between linguistic coherence and fact, as young children are not aware of the differences between things and their names (69, 70) or between dreams and reality.

Empirical study of language, therefore, leads naturally to what is ordinarily called "speculation," the traditional task of philosophy. A philosophy rooted in scientific practice, however, should attain sufficient maturity to distinguish fruitful speculation from idle fancy. Fruitful speculation is essentially a search for fruitful concepts. A fruitful concept is one about which questions are suggested which lead to answers pregnant with new questions. The fruitful concepts of physical science have for the most part acquired strict operational meanings (e.g., energy, mass, temperature, flux, etc.). But not all fruitful concepts have achieved this maturity. Even some firmly established ones, such as "atom," "electron," and "gene," cannot be unequivocally defined in terms of specific operations. They are, however, extremely useful linguistic devices for talking about operationally meaningful things. They are "idea fixers." One uses them *as if* one knew what one is talking about and in the process one does arrive at meaningful assertions. The concepts of social science (culture, society, personality, class structure, etc.) are even further removed from operational meaning, but even these terms seem to have some use as "idea fixers."

There is no way of knowing *a priori* just when abstract concepts cease to be fruitful. But this is precisely the philosopher's job—to find out. He should not, however, in testing the meaningfulness of a term, apply to it the severe objective tests of operational and logical analysis. If he did this, then indeed he would come to the conclusion that most of philosophy (and a goodly part of theoretical science) is meaningless. Rather, his task is to see what sense can *possibly* be made of the verbal output of the human race without neglecting the nondiscursive, expressive uses of language, the analogical significances of metaphor, the existence of extensional bargains among people who understand each other, and the possibility of meaning emerging through new experience where no meaning had been.

If the philosopher accepts this job, then the traditional problem of ethics, "What is good?" falls within his sphere. To be sure, there is still the "factual" research to be done by anthropologists, sociologists, etc., in recording the actual observations which people in various circumstances make in answer to this question. But there the job is only begun. The philosopher (and he, of course, can also be the anthropologist or the sociologist) must make "sense" of these answers. He must construct theories about the sort of social action which will actually lead people to say, "Yes, this is what we meant—that is good."

The social action which leads to the *recognition* that it is desirable is not necessarily the social action deemed desirable by the majority *a priori*.

It is this discrepancy between what is deemed desirable and what will be found desirable which has led some philosophers (like Dewey and Korzybski) to an activist position. For merely to announce the findings of an investigation: "This is deemed desirable, but in all probability not this but that will be found desirable" already amounts to a value judgment. But it is also a synthetic statement capable of verification! Hence the sharp distinction between value judgments and propositions does not always exist (as logical positivists suppose). An ethics naturally follows from *any* philosophical position, even from the position that ethics should not be a part of philosophy.

Operational philosophy is the philosophy of action-directed goals. It *starts* with logical analysis. But logical analysis is not conducted in a social vacuum by electronic computers. It is conducted by men and women with beliefs, prejudices, and convictions. The results of logical analysis must inevitably produce an impact on these beliefs and convictions and induce to further action. This further action may be nothing more than further logical analysis, but there may enter a selection of concepts to be analyzed. Or the action may be speculation, but again there may enter a selection of topics to speculate about.

As an illustration, consider the logical analysis involved in the discovery of the probabilistic foundations of entropy (cf. Chapter 15 and any text on statistical mechanics). We have mentioned the fact that the similarity between negative entropy and information was noted as a result of the logical analysis of the concept of information. On the other hand, speculation on the nature of life processes has led Schroedinger and others to postulate an intimate connection between negative entropy and life. All this leads to a philosophical question which appears almost in metaphysical garb: "Life, knowledge, and order (negative entropy)—what do they have in common?"

The question is not a strictly meaningful one (by operational criteria). But to people who have pondered on the facts of life, the theory of knowledge, and the criteria of order, the question is full of "meaning." Such a metaphysical looking question is not at all like the questions of old-fashioned metaphysics, because the chain of abstractions leading from the question to operationally meaningful definitions and assertions is discernible. However, there may be links missing in that chain. It is the philosopher's job to forge these links and to extend the chain.

Norbert Wiener, for example, extends the chain to questions about what meaning could be assigned to the entropy of a society. He invents a metaphor in which a "closed" society (that is, one which has shut off sources of information outside its own conceptual framework) is compared to a closed physical system (one which does not exchange matter or energy with the outside environment). Now according to the second law of thermodynamics, the entropy of such a system is bound to increase, that is, its energy, though conserved, will become degraded, unavailable for useful work. Can similar reasoning, Wiener wonders, be applied to a "closed" society, by substituting decrease of information for increase in entropy with a consequent degradation of whatever it is that corresponds to energy?

From such questions it is but a step to the sort of problems that worried Spengler, who saw whole cultures exhibiting what seemed like a life cycle with maturation, senescence, and death. Why the resemblance? Is it superficial or profound? What does it mean to say that it is profound? Modern philosophy can, at least, answer this last question. The similarity between two phenomena is profound if there exists a *single* underlying theory from which the laws of both phenomena can be deduced. Spengler believed in the existence of a unified theory governing the life cycles of civilizations. It is the modern philosopher's job to seek, formulate, develop, criticize, and demolish such general theories.

There are two important differences between such speculations and those of the old metaphysicians. One we have mentioned. In the new philosophical speculations there is at least a partial chain of abstractions connecting the language of speculation to operationally meaningful concepts, while there was not such a chain in traditional metaphysics. The other difference is even more important. The old metaphysical speculations were offered as answers, but the new ones are offered as questions. They are points of departure, not of arrival. They spur thinkers and investigators to action.

This, then, is the job of operational philosophy:

1. To extend the analytical tools of rigorous linguistic philosophy —logic, logical analysis, mathematics, and other deductive systems which may be invented—and to make them into powerful machinery of inquiry.

2. To establish the chain of reduction wherever possible, showing how the concepts at one level of abstraction emerge from those of another level.

3. To use the power of human imagination to experiment with ideas in the search for new fruitful concepts.

4. To translate the findings of abstract inquiry into formulations having a bearing on the ethical and moral problems with which humanity is faced.

GLOSSARY

The definitions offered here indicate only the context in which the terms have been used in this book.

Absolute zero: the lowest theoretically possible temperature, about $-273°$ Centigrade.

Action-directed goals: goals which become apparent in the light of experience obtained from solving specific problems.

Analytic assertions: assertions which are valid as a consequence of their own structure, such as, "All mortal beings die." All assertions of mathematics are held by most modern mathematicians to be analytic.

Animism: a conceptual framework in which causes of events are attributed to the wills or whims of sentient beings.

A priori: without previous knowledge.

Atomic theory: a theory (at present firmly established) according to which all matter consists of minute particles called atoms. The atoms of an element are all alike (except for slight differences among the isotopes of the element). There are less than one hundred kinds of atoms known (1953).

Behaviorism: a direction in psychology, where attention is focused on the overt behavior of organisms only and where the usefulness of introspective and holistic methods is questioned or denied.

Boolean Algebra: (1) the formalization of a two-valued logic as a mathematical system; (2) the algebra of classes or sets, where the operations denote the determination of new sets from given sets. For an elementary treatment see (9).

Boyle's Law: the volume of a mass of gas is inversely proportional to the pressure it exerts (the law is accurate only at high temperatures and low pressures).

Causality: a relation assumed among two events in order to explain one in terms of the other.

Classical mathematics: usually applied to the calculus and its derivative disciplines (function theory, differential equations, and other branches of analysis) developed in the seventeenth, eighteenth, and nineteenth centuries in connection with the problems of Newtonian physics. The number systems of classical mathematics are usually either the real or the complex numbers (q.v.), and the operations are those of algebra and the calculus. Modern mathematics (as distinguished from classical) is marked by the generalizations of the concept of "number" (or "quantity") and of "operations."

Communication: any process involving an encoding, a transmission, and a decoding of a signal. Examples: (1) Telegraph: a rhythmic pattern beat out by the transmission key is encoded into a succession of electrical impulses, transmitted over a wire, and decoded into a corresponding pattern of the receiving key. (2) Spoken language: mental images are encoded into words, transmitted as sound waves, and decoded back into mental images.

Communism: (1) (as defined by Communists): a social system in which no restriction is placed on the individual's consumption and no obligation governs the individual's production ("From each according to his ability, to each according to his needs"). (2): the socio-economic system of the U.S.S.R. and her allies. (3) (as defined by professional anti-Communists) the holding of an opinion resembling one held by a Communist or Socialist.

Complex number: a quantity symbolized by $a+bi$, where a and b are real numbers (q.v.) and i is defined by the equation $i^2 = -1$. Complex numbers can be represented on a two-dimensional scale (real numbers can be represented on a one-dimensional scale). They are usually the most general quantities of classical mathematics.

Compulsion: in this book the term is used both in its psychological sense (as an inner irresistible drive to perform some act) and in the sociological (as the compulsion of law, public opinion, etc.).

Conjecture: a hunch.

Constant: a quantity whose value is assumed fixed during an investigation.

Construct (noun): a term which can be defined by operations on symbols alone, for example, mathematical entities (see also Note 25).

Cultural matrix: the totality of influences at work in a given culture.

Culture: a pattern of ideas or behavior within which people understand each other's actions, preferences, aspirations, etc. See also *language.*

Deduction: the process of drawing conclusions in accordance with specified rules, as in logic or in mathematics.

Determinism: (1): a presumed principle in nature according to which the future is already "on record" and cannot be changed, because all our efforts to change it are parts of the "record." (2): in classical physics, a principle according to which having observed a system in a certain state, one can predict all future states provided no outside influences impinge on the system. Example: the prediction of future positions of heavenly bodies from observed positions.

Dialectical materialism: a direction in philosophy which is an adaptation of the evolutionary views of Hegel to a materialistic outlook. For an interesting discussion see (73).

Dichotomy: sharp distinction.

Discursive language: a language whose assertions serve to inform, that is, have a verifiable meaning.

Divine right of kings: a doctrine according to which monarchs derived their power from God.

Ecology: the study of the relations among species and between species and environment.

Emergent phenomenon: a phenomenon which cannot be described or understood in terms of its component parts alone, as, for example, the behavior of a mob cannot (presumably) be understood from the knowledge of its constituent members alone.

Empiricism: an outlook in philosophy which holds that information obtained from sense data is the only source and content of knowledge (exponents: Bacon, Berkeley, Locke, Hume).

Essence: the totality of essential properties of a thing (in modern parlance, an abstraction of its characteristics). In Platonic philosophy, the "essences" (or Forms or Ideas) were supposed to be the "perfect" origins of things from which actual things have degenerated. In Aristotelian philosophy, on the contrary, the essences were supposed to be within the things themselves and were thought of as the ultimate goals of all that happens to the things.

Ether: a hypothetical substance presumed at one time to pervade all space and to be the medium through which electromagnetic waves (in particular, light) are transmitted.

Ethics: in this book an ethics is taken to mean any system of rules for choosing courses of action. Thus, even the rules of chess strategy constitute an ethics according to this definition. More pertinent examples are the various policies of action, such as legal codes, educational systems, and political ideologies. What is ordinarily called "ethics," that is, more specifically theories of conduct and attitude, also falls within the sphere of this definition.

Evaluation: the process presumably going on within an individual which "translates" the stimuli impinging upon him into patterns of action; for example, the interpretation of a question and the formulation of an answer or the response to a work of art or to an insult.

Extensional bargain: a level of understanding at which definitions are not necessary.

Extensional definition: a definition which lists the referents to which the term applies.

Fact: that to which a true assertion refers.

False: an assertion is false if it is meaningful and determinate but not true.

Feed-back: a principle according to which an action is controlled by its own results. Examples: (1) Technological: the furnace heats the house and, as the temperature rises, the action of the thermostat shuts off the furnace. (2) Biological: increased carbon dioxide concentration in the blood results in increased respiration rate, which lowers the carbon dioxide concentration, which, in turn, decreases the respiration rate. (3) Social: legislation influenced by public opinion on existing legislation.

Free will: a presumed principle according to which man has "control" over his actions; a denial of determinism in human affairs.

Frustration: inability to fulfill a strong drive or desire.

Gene: the postulated unit of heredity.

Gestalt psychology: a direction in psychology which seeks to understand the reactions of the organism-as-a-whole to "gestalts," that is, shapes, forms, complexes, etc., instead of analyzing the action of the environment and the response of the organism into constituent units (as behaviorism does, q.v.).

Holism: the view that analysis is inadequate as a method of cognition, because certain entities or phenomena can be understood only if viewed in their entirety.

Hypothesis: the initial assumptions of any investigation; something assumed to be true for the purpose of tracing the consequences of the assumption. If the deduced consequences are verified, the belief in the truth of the hypothesis is strengthened. In modern scientific philosophy, all synthetic assertions of science are considered hypotheses in the broadest sense of the term, although in ordinary usage the most firmly established hypotheses are called "facts."

Hypothetico-deductive method: the method of a science with a highly developed theoretical basis. The starting point is a hypothesis on the basis of which predictions are deduced. If the predictions are verified, the hypothesis is retained; if not, the hypothesis is modified or discarded.

Idealization: the abstraction of certain features presumed to characterize an experience and the conception of the experience in terms of those features alone. Examples: (1) A pendulum is imagined to consist of a weight concentrated at a point and suspended by a perfectly rigid weightless rod. (2) A society in economic theory is imagined to consist of identical individuals behaving in accordance with certain rules governing the exchange of goods and services.

Ideology: a basis of a political ethics.

Indeterminate: an assertion is indeterminate if it is meaningful but if its truth value has not been determined by verification.

Induction: the rule which allows the forming of a general conclusion on the basis of observations of particular cases.

Intensional definition: a definition which lists the properties by which the thing defined is to be distinguished.

Intuitive knowledge: knowledge which cannot be easily (or at all) transmitted by language. Example: the knowledge of what garlic smells like. The impossibility of transmitting such knowledge is not inherent. It is conceivable, for example, that odors can be completely analyzed, described, and synthesized from the description. Then what had been intuitive knowledge becomes analytic.

Invariance: something which remains constant as other things change. Examples: (1) The size of a rigid object as it moves in space. (2) The I.Q. of an adult over a period of years. (3) The total energy of a closed physical system as its inner structure changes.

I.Q. (intelligence quotient): a score made by an individual on a certain test, presumably a measure of linguistic proficiency and of reasoning ability.

Kinetic theory: a theory about the motions of molecules or atoms (particularly of a gas), from which thermodynamic laws are derived.

Language: (1): a pattern of signs and symbols, together with rules for combining them, by means of which inner states of one individual (knowledge or feelings) can be reproduced in others. Examples: Italian, Morse code, algebra, music. (2): More generally, a system of abstracting and symbolizing experience; a system of evaluation.

Logic: (1): a self-consistent system of rules for drawing conclusions; (2) a habitual pattern of evaluation, as, for example, the logic of paranoia.

Logical analysis: a study of the meaning of assertions with reference to the relations between the terms and their (presumed) referents; the analysis of the predictive content of assertions.

Logical positivism: see Note 2.

Magic: practices designed to influence the course of events with no systematic provisions to test the effectiveness of such practices.

Magnitude: a quantity which can be represented on a one-dimensional scale; also called a scalar or a real number.

Materialistic: in this book the term is used as "pertaining to the mechanistic outlook."

Matrix: a rectangular array of quantities or other symbols, convenient for representing relations between each pair of an aggregate. Example: a mileage chart which gives distances between each pair of a list of cities. Strictly speaking such an array can be called a matrix only if it itself can be treated as a generalized quantity, that is, subjected to certain rules of calculation. The matrices of modern higher algebra are such quantities (9). Recently matrix mathematics has been applied to theories dealing with group dynamics.

Meaning: the correspondence between a term and its referents or between an assertion and the relations among the referents of its terms.

Mechanics: the science comprising the laws of motion and their consequences with regard to events which can be described in terms of forces acting on matter.

Mechanistic metaphysics: a conceptual framework seeking to explain all events in terms of classical mechanics.

Mental rehearsal: imagining the performance of some act before actually going through it.

Metalinguistics: see Note 3.

Metaphor: a linguistic identification of something with something else because of (presumed) similarity. Example: "You blocks, you stones, you worse than senseless things!" (*Julius Caesar*, Act I, Scene 1.)

Metaphysics: a conceptual framework in terms of which the world is perceived and explanations of events formulated; for example, the Newtonian system of the universe. Traditionally metaphysics was the branch of philosophy which (presumably) inquired into the nature of "being." The reader is cautioned not to confuse the two meanings.

Micro-language: a language without grammar, that is, in which each utterance is complete in itself, such as the languages of animals and infants.

Model: in theoretical science a fictitious representation of the state of affairs under consideration to allow the application of deductive reasoning. Example: the earth considered as a perfect sphere.

Motivation: an assumed cause of behavior not directly associated with a stimulus.

Natural selection: a principle assumed in biology according to which individuals better adapted to their environment have more progeny than the others. The principle purports to account for the progressive adaptation of species to their environments without resorting to postulating special mechanisms within the organism to accomplish this.

Nominalists: see Note 1.

Nondiscursive language: a language whose assertions do not seek to inform (e.g., lyric poetry, music) and hence do not necessarily have verifiable meaning.

Objectivity: invariance with respect to different observers.

One-dimensional scale: a scale on which each value is specified by a single number, such as a ruler. Not all quantities can be so specified. For example, position of the earth's surface must be specified by two numbers (latitude and longitude).

Operational definition: a definition which describes operations to be performed so that the thing defined (or its effects) will be observed.

Operationalism: an attitude which views thought and action inseparable; which defines "truth" in terms of the predictive content of assertions, and ethics in terms of action-directed goals.

Opportunism: the pursuit of immediate advantage to the disregard of larger principles.

Order: structure of which one is aware, especially structure which can be described comparatively easily. Example: the alphabetical arrangement of the words in a dictionary; the arrangement of black and white squares on a chess board.

Organismic metaphysics: a conceptual framework seeking to explain events teleologically.

Parsimony: a principle in the philosophy of science according to which one strives to keep the number of concepts and assumptions at a minimum. Hence, of two theories explaining a phenomenon equally well, the "simpler" one is to be preferred. (The "simpler" one does not necessarily mean the one easier to understand in terms of previously accepted concepts but rather the one which uses fewer independent concepts and assumptions.)

Phenomenological psychology: a school of psychology which places at the center of interest the restoration of balance within the organism following a disturbance.

Phlogiston: a hypothetical substance which was supposed to impart the property of combustibility to matter containing it and which was consumed in combustion.

Physiologus: a collection of allegories about animals (many of them mythical) purporting to represent various creatures as embodiments of various moral qualities. These stories were widely read in the Middle Ages.

Pi: the ratio of the diameter to the circumference of a circle (approximately 3.14159).

Positivism: see Note 24.

Post hypnotic suggestion: a suggestion made to a subject under hypnosis and acted upon when the subject is no longer apparently under hypnosis.

Postulate: an assertion whose validity is assumed throughout a discussion, especially in a mathematical system.

Pragmatism: an early designation of what we call operationalism. The meaning of pragmatism is sometimes perverted to practical synonymity with opportunism.

Predictive content: the range of predictions which can be derived as logical consequences of an assertion. Examples: (1) The predictive content of the assertion, "The sun is bright" is in the prediction, "Every time you look at the sun, you will experience brightness." (2) The predictive content of the law of gravity is in the totality of predictions that can be made about the behavior of terrestrial and celestial bodies on the basis of that law.

Premises: the assertions of a syllogism upon whose validity the validity of the conclusion depends.

Probability: a measure of the subjective expectancy of an event expressed as a fraction, which usually denotes the ratio of the number of ways an event can occur to the number of all possible outcomes of the situation in question.

Pseudo-explanation: an "explanation" which merely gives another name to the phenomenon to be explained. Example: Mr. Q is afraid of the number 13, because he has triskaidekophobia.

Pseudo-purpose: a purpose which is simply another name for the act whose purpose is inquired into. Example: Mr. L wants to marry Miss M, because he wants to be her husband.

Quantification: describing an event in terms of quantities and relations among them. Example: "The opening of Beethoven's *Fifth Symphony* consists of three sets of interrupted sound wave trains, having frequencies of 384 vibrations per second and lasting about 0.2 seconds each, and a set having a frequency of 308 vibrations per second and lasting about 4 seconds."

Quality: a property which has not been quantified.

Quantity: a property expressible by a number or more generally by any symbols which can be operated on according to specified mathematical rules.

Quantum theory: a physical theory which rests on the assumption that energy is emitted and absorbed in minute "packets" (quanta) rather than continuously.

Quantum mechanics: a section of theoretical physics dealing with sub-atomic events on the basis of the quantum theory. Quantum mechanics represents a departure from classical mechanics in that in it the variables (position, momentum, energy) of the latter are replaced by probability distributions of the values which may be assumed by those variables.

Rationalism: an outlook in philosophy which holds that the totality of knowledge can be won by the deductive process alone (or predominantly). (Exponents: Descartes, Leibnitz, Kant.)

Realists: see Note 1.

Reality: an assumed carrier of an invariance (q.v.). Example: I see a two-headed man. To determine whether what I see is "real," I ask my companion, "Do you see what I see?" Here I am testing the invariance of the impression made by the thing I see on my companion. Similar tests are applicable to physical concepts (distance, mass, etc.), psychological constructs, and others. The extent of the reality is measured by the extent of the predictions that can be based on the invariance in question.

Real number: a quantity that can be represented on a one-dimensional scale.

Reductionism: a view that the concepts of various scientific disciplines can be ultimately reduced to a few fundamental ones, as, for example, many concepts of chemistry have been reduced to those of physics.

Relativism (ethical): a view that what is "desirable" can be defined only in terms of preconceived notions; hence that no universally human ethics is possible.

Scholasticists: typical representatives of medieval thought characterized by an overwhelming emphasis on theology, logic, and other purely verbal disciplines.

Security: a feeling that things will continue to be "all right." Freedom from fear.

Self-extension: the feeling that one's self is a part of some entity which includes it; hence the transference of the self-feeling to that entity, for example, the family, tribe, nation, humanity, a cause, a business, etc.

Self-identification: the recognition of one's self as distinct from the rest of the world.

Self-realizing assumptions: assumptions which themselves influence the outcome of the results deduced from them.

Socialism: social control of economic processes; more specifically, a system of production and distribution in which the consumption of the goods and services produced rather than the profits derived from the process of production constitute the principal motivation for production.

Sociology of knowledge: a study of how social structure influences what is likely to be selected for inquiry and what is likely to be defined as "knowledge."

Structure: the totality of relations among the parts of a system. Examples: (1) A family has a structure consisting of the various kinship relations among its members: husband, wife, father, mother, son, daughter, brother, sister. (2) The system of whole numbers has a structure determined by the relation "greater than," which is fixed between any two numbers.

Subjectivity: totality of impressions confined to a single observer.

Syllogism: the simplest act of deduction in Aristotelian logic.

Symbolic logic: logic developed by formalized rules of operation on symbols, analogous to the method of mathematics.

Synthetic assertion: an assertion which cannot be established by deductive methods alone, one which needs experimental verification, such as, "All women are beautiful." Likewise, the assertions of empirical science.

System: a portion of the world sufficiently well defined to be the subject of study; something characterized by a structure, for example, a social system.

Teleology: a presumed principle of purposefulness in nature.

Theology: a discipline which presumes to conduct inquiries on the nature of God.

Theory of relativity (special): a reformulation of classical mechanics in which the speed of light rather than distances between points in a fixed spatial framework or intervals of time measured on an absolute scale is taken as the absolute invariant.

Time-binding: the process of transmitting accumulated knowledge and experience to future generations. As far as we know, this process is confined to the human kind.

True: an assertion is true if it is synthetic and if verifiable predictions can be made on the basis of it or its consequences. In some discussions I have used true and valid interchangeably.

Valid: an assertion is valid if it is analytic and self-consistent or if it can be deduced from another assertion assumed to be valid.

Value (1): in logic and mathematics, the particular meaning assigned to a variable; (2): in ethics, that which is desirable.

Variable: a quantity whose value is not fixed in an investigation, for example, the position of a moving particle.

Vector: a quantity which can be represented on a many-dimensional scale and is subject to certain rules of mathematical operation.

Vital force: a principle presumed to exist in living things which is not explainable in terms of physical principles. Fewer biologists today than formerly believe in the usefulness of this concept.

NOTES

¹ The argument was between the "nominalists" and the "realists," two opposing schools in scholastic philosophy. The realists maintained that only "universals" were real, that is, what existed primarily were categories, such as House, Man, or Tree, and that the individual houses, men, and trees were only secondary manifestations of the universals. The nominalists, on the contrary, held that the individual things only were real, the universal categories being mere names applied to classes of things (hence the label "nominalists"). The nominalists thus were already leaning toward what is known in general semantics as the "extensional orientation." References to the latter are found in (20, 35, 43, 46).

² Logical positivism (or logical empiricism, as some of its adherents prefer to call it) is a direction in modern philosophy which stresses the analysis of meaning of assertions. It is, for the most part, sharply critical of the traditional philosophical methods of inquiry. The outlook of logical positivism has inspired much of what now goes under the name of semantics (16, 36, 78).

I call the extreme logical positivist position "conservative" because of its uncompromising attitude toward meaning. Elsewhere (p. 154) I also call it "radical." Both terms simply mean "extreme," in contrast to the "liberal" logical positivist attitude which is more lenient in its critical analysis of philosophic thought. Ayer, in his second edition of *Language, Truth, and Logic* (4), manifests a leaning toward the liberal view as opposed to his original position (cf. first and second editions of *op. cit.*).

³ Metalinguistics (as the term is used by some anthropologists) deals with those aspects of language which reflect (and, perhaps, influence) a certain world view, that is, a certain way of selecting portions of one's environment for special attention and a certain way of reacting to them. For articles on metalinguistics and references to further literature see (31).

⁴ S. I. Hayakawa (37) illustrates this point by an incident which occurred in his home. He was hanging an abstract painting by the late L. Moholy-Nagy. A woman visitor, apparently not able to keep her mind on the conversation, kept turning to stare at the painting. Finally she broke down

and approached the painting to read the label, *Space Modulator*. This piece of information seemed to pacify her completely, and she never glanced at the painting again.

[5] "Whereof one cannot speak, one must remain silent" (113).

[6] However, already Kant (1724–1804) in his *Critique of Pure Reason* (44) distinguished between analytic and synthetic assertions and thus virtually discovered the difference between truth and validity. Analytic assertions are tautologies; for example, "All women are females." Synthetic assertions, on the other hand, cannot be verified just by being examined. To verify "Grass is green" you must examine grass, not the assertion. Kant missed the full significance of his distinction in that he stuck to the conviction that the assertions of mathematics are synthetic (that is, they say something about the world). This belief (entirely excusable in his time) led him to assume his famous, though mistaken, theory of *a priori* knowledge. As will appear, I use the term "valid assertion" in a broader sense than "analytic assertion." A valid assertion is valid only with reference to other assertions, of which it is a logical consequence (cf. p. 39). An analytic assertion is valid as a consequence of the meanings of its own terms.

[7] Here we are talking about the validity of an analytic assertion.

[8] For a discussion of all the variations of the syllogism, see (50).

[9] Students of metalinguistics especially (see Note 3) view logic as a function of language structure. In this connection, see Benjamin Lee Whorf's article in (31). In fact, they make little distinction between grammar and logic. Thus, it is often implied in metalinguistic literature that questions dealing with grammatical representation of events ("Should every verb have a subject?" "What is the relation between time and tenses?") are questions of logic. As will appear, I will not usually speak of logic in this sense, and when I do, I will say so.

[10] These two mathematicians were Nicolas Lobachevsky (1793–1856), a Russian, and John Bolyai (1802–1860), a Hungarian. Gauss (1777–1855), considered by some as the greatest mathematician of the nineteenth century, also made this intellectual experiment, but he did not dare publish the results. It seems it takes more than genius to launch an intellectual revolution. It takes courage. A similar situation occurred in the early years of our century when Max Planck made the first step in the development of the quantum theory but did not dare see the implications. It remained for Albert Einstein and Niels Bohr to carry the ball.

[11] Georg Friedrich Riemann (1826–1866), the creator of Riemannian or "elliptic" geometry, which became the basis of the relativistic theory of space.

[12] This point was stressed already around 1870 by William Kingdon Clifford (1845–1879), an English mathematician who entertained ideas strikingly similar to those of the theory of relativity. "The geometer of today," said Clifford, "knows nothing about the nature of actually existing

space at an infinite distance; he knows nothing about the properties of this present space in a past or future eternity . . ." (quoted from [66]).

[13] To quote Clifford again, "Remember then that [scientific thought] is the guide to action; that the truth it arrives at is not that which we can ideally contemplate without error, but that which we may act upon without fear" (66).

[14] Actually, Newton deduced the inverse square law from the motions of the planets as described by Kepler. However, he deduced the motions of the moon from the inverse square law, thus demonstrating that the deduction could go both ways.

[15] As Einstein put it in his *Sidelights on Relativity*, "As far as the laws of mathematics refer to reality, they are not certain; and as far as they are certain, they do not refer to reality" (quoted from [46]).

[16] Yet in his penetrating analysis of the notion of causality, David Hume (1711–1776) confined himself pretty much to examining this notion in the light of observed correlations among events (39). Although the principle of *post hoc—propter hoc* (after it, therefore because of it) has long been recognized as faulty reasoning, Hume tried to show that all our notions of causality reduce to that unconvincing principle. Hume's scepticism concerning the "reality" of the principle of causation can, perhaps, be attributed to the following limitations of his outlook.

1. Throughout he assumed a *passive* observer, who simply watched things happen instead of actively manipulating the world about him.

2. He neglected the explanatory aspect of causality, in which this notion is frankly defined as an *assumed* relation among events which enables us to fit events into patterns. That is, Hume did not see the importance of the heuristic value of this concept.

3. He expected too much from the empiricist approach to knowledge. He expected to find the same degree of certainty in induction as appears in deduction. Only when the certainty of empirical (inductive) truth was forever given up, did its value become wholly apparent.

For further discussion of Hume, see (81).

[17] Reichenbach (81) uses the term "pseudo-explanation" to refer to any argument by naive analogy, such as those on page 53 of this book. I use the term "pseudo-explanation" in another sense, namely to refer to explanations which are verbal only. Examples are given on p. 56.

[18] This interchangeability appears most clearly in "functional causality," as it is treated in mathematical physics. Consider the expression for the centripetal force acting on a mass revolving around a circle: $F = mv^2/R$. The equation says that this force is proportional to the mass and to the square of its speed and inversely proportional to the radius of the circle. Certain predictions can be immediately deduced from this relation. For example, other things being equal, we can say, "If the radius is doubled, force will be halved," or "If the mass is tripled, so will the radius be," or "If the force is quadrupled, velocity will be doubled." All these relations

seem to indicate cause-effect relations. But in every case, the "cause" and the "effect" can be interchanged, that is, experiments can be easily performed where *any* of the quantities can be changed at will, while the others will follow as predicted. Clearly the question which is "really" the cause and which the effect has no meaning in this case.

[19] This example was given (whether seriously or facetiously I do not know) by A. Standen in his book *Science Is a Sacred Cow* with a view of depreciating the validity of scientific reasoning.

[20] When these pages were already written, I found that Michael Polanyi (in an article published in *The British Journal for the Philosophy of Science*, November, 1952) used almost identical examples (of Zande and Soviet reasoning) to illustrate his discussion of the stability of beliefs. However, Polanyi's implied definition of causality is confined to the postulational, without reference to the predictive content of assertions. It is the emphasis of predictive content and of manipulability that sets scientific reasoning apart from the mystical. For this reason, it seems somewhat misleading to subsume the convictions of the scientist and those of a "primitive" under the single term "belief."

[21] For especially illuminating discussions of organismic philosophy see (33) and (73).

[22] Kant's philosophy of nature is, perhaps, the clearest expression of mechanistic metaphysics. For further discussion, see (81).

[23] If light consists of ether waves and if the earth is moving through the ether, then the speed of light measured relatively to a point on the earth's surface ought to vary with the direction in which the beam is sent. Michelson and Morley in 1881 set out to measure this difference. In spite of the fact that the theoretically predicted difference in the speed of light along two directions perpendicular to each other should have been clearly detected by the apparatus, no such difference was observed.

[24] The term "positivism" has been used rather loosely. It is applied among other things to the philosophy of social science introduced by Auguste Comte (1798–1857). It is sometimes applied to the outlook of the behaviorists in psychology. The modified term "logical positivism" is applied to a certain direction in modern philosophy (see Note 2). While it is wise to bear in mind the various meanings of "positivism," yet there is a common referent pertaining to all of them: positivism stresses the importance of talking about *observables* in any scientific discussion. In its extreme form it recognizes no other categories.

[25] Margenau (59) points out that many of the most powerful concepts in the physical sciences cannot be operationally defined in the strictest sense of the term "operational," that is, in terms of unambiguous operations and observations. Even "time" figures in the equations of physics as not necessarily "something measured by the clock" (operational definition) but as a "construct," simply defined as the independent variable in the differential equations of motion. This is certainly so. However, when the

physicist works with "constructs," he really leaves the area of truth and enters the realm of validity. His methods become analytic and logical rather than synthetic and empirical. To get back to "truth," he must link his mathematical constructs to operations and observations. Often, to be sure, this connection is made in a complex and roundabout way. The emphasis on constructs as the principal conceptual tools was made by H. Poincaré (72).

[26] Cf., for example, the remarks of Felix S. Cohen: "Our legal system is filled with . . . concepts which cannot be defined in terms of experience and from which all sorts of empirical decisions are supposed to flow. . . . Against these unverifiable concepts modern jurisprudence presents an ultimatum. Any word that cannot pay up in the currency of fact, upon demand, is to be declared bankrupt, and we are to have no further dealings with it" (quoted from [36]).

[27] For an account of Hegel's discussion, see (73).

[28] The clearest view of this remarkable approach to biology can be obtained from the actual stenographic report of the discussions (100); see also (74).

[29] For further elaboration of this theory of art and poetry, see (35).

[30] Some authors explicitly deny the "need for order" origins of pure science and prefer to trace it exclusively through utilitarian channels. This point of view (close to the Marxist) is developed in Lancelot Hogben's fascinating book *Mathematics for the Million* (38). I disagree with Hogben on this point without, however, discounting the importance of utilitarian incentives in the development of "pure" science. It is easier to imagine both factors operating—the esthetic "need for order" and the utilitarian survival drive. Perhaps they operate most effectively when they happen to affect the same field of inquiry.

[31] George Herbert Mead, for example (61), develops a somewhat different theory of self-identification and extension based on the concept of the "generalized other."

[32] In this connection, see the terrifying notion of the "un-person" in George Orwell's novel *Nineteen Eighty-four* (67).

[33] For an example of a "logic" (in its metalinguistic meaning) governing the ethics of redemption and to a large extent the ethics of retribution see St. Anselm's *Cur Deus Homo* (2).

[34] Popper (73) describes Plato's philosophy as completely dominated by this attitude.

[35] In this connection, see Charles Morris' more detailed classification of ethical systems and the corresponding types of personality in his book *The Open Self* (63).

[36] Dewey's philosophy of education is analogous to this attitude. Learning is supposed to be motivated by interest, but interest emerges only in the process of an activity of some sort. The goals of education thus appear as "action-directed goals" (23, 24, 25, 26).

[37] Inasmuch as this ethics emerges from the philosophy of science (sufficiently liberalized to include the "frontier areas" discussed in Part III) it seems to me to be the reconstructed philosophy recommended by Dewey (25).

[38] All these are examples of pseudo-purposes analogous to the pseudo-explanations discussed on p. 56. To see the analogy, let us rephrase the directive, "You must not marry your sister, because it is incestuous" as "You must avoid marrying your sister, because you must avoid incest." Suppose, then, one asks what incest is. An operational definition of incest would list all incestuous acts, including (among others) that of marrying one's sister. Hence the prohibition actually states, "You must avoid marrying your sister, because you must avoid (among other things) marrying your sister." This is an example of an analytic, not a synthetic assertion since it involves only giving two labels to the same act. It is altogether another matter if one says, "You must not marry your sister, because the marriage may result in defective offspring." Here a connection is established between an act and a consequence which is not inherent in the definition of the act.

[39] For a discussion of this topic from the sociologist's point of view, see (28).

[40] See, the example, the description of "scientific method" by R. Meyers (62) or W. Johnson (43). Excellent as these descriptions are for the purpose of emphasizing the rigorous and objective aspects of scientific cognition, they fail to take into account the role of self-predictive assumptions. Both authors, are, of course, aware of the importance of such assumptions, but they discuss them largely in connection with nonscientific, inadequate evaluations and behavior patterns. Our point is that operational philosophy, in contrast with the older strictly deterministic scientific philosophy, recognizes that these assumptions may play a part in any cognitive process, including science.

[41] The only serious objections to this view come from the neo-Malthusians and some ecologists (105). The first warn that the introduction of technology and medical improvements into backward overpopulated areas will aggravate the problem, because they will result in a still greater increase of population (at least initially) which will more than offset the rise of productivity. One school of ecologists warns that many natural resources are nearing exhaustion and cannot withstand more intense exploitation. Whatever the merit of these arguments, the problems raised in them are still "technological," that is, call for solution by invention of techniques directed, say, to finding other sources of food supply in one case or to mass propaganda for birth control in the other. The difficulty of the problems is not the point. The point raised here is that such problems are of technological character.

[42] In 1907 V. I. Lenin wrote a philosophical essay, *Materialism and Empirio-criticism*, which has subsequently channelized philosophical dis-

cussions in the U.S.S.R. into an attitude of uncompromising hostility toward any formulation suspected of the slightest deviation from established dogma. For further discussion, see (75).

[43] See discussions of the "audience determined" entertainment market by Seldes (89) and Maloney (56).

[44] See, however, Vyshinsky's contention that the U.S.S.R. is "a million times more democratic" than the U.S. (106). A U.S. controlled radio in Tokyo caught the spirit of this sort of quantification when it declared the (alleged) holding of U.N. prisoners as hostages by the Communists to be ". . . blackmail . . . a *thousand* times more repulsive than kidnapping by the lowest form of gangster." (Quoted by Irving Pflaum in *Chicago Sun-Times,* December 12, 1951.)

[45] The school of philosophy founded by Pythagoras placed number at the center of interest. Universal realities were supposed to reside in numerical relations. Much of this teaching was interlaced with mysticism and superstition, but its core—the belief that many relations are reducible to relations of magnitude—has been a fruitful hypothesis in modern science.

[46] In general, a musical tone is a combination of different vibration frequencies called overtones, all multiples of a fundamental frequency. The "quality" or timbre of the tone is completely determined by the relative intensities of the overtones.

[47] N. Rashevsky has proposed a theory of neural activity which correlates the intensity of esthetic gratification with the intensity of activity in certain centers of the brain. The theory was tested in an evaluation of certain geometric figures for their esthetic value and was found to give good agreement with experimental findings (80). Earlier, G. Birkhoff (8) had developed another mathematical theory of esthetic measure, also applied to polygons, among other things. There were, however, wide discrepancies between Birkhoff's results and observations.

[48] In a trivial sense, a structure can always be associated with a number. In any real situation, we deal with only a finite number of structures. If we choose simply to number them, we can call each structure by its associated number. This numbering, however, does not associate a *magnitude* with a structure, except artificially. We cannot draw any conclusions from our numbering, and we cannot operate on the numbers so as to deduce further relations among the structures.

[49] The "inverse" operations, subtraction and division, need not be considered separately, if the number system includes negative numbers and fractions, because subtracting a positive number is equivalent to adding a negative one and vice versa; similarly, dividing by a number is equivalent to multiplying by its reciprocal and vice versa.

[50] For example, if p stands for "all females" and q for "all children," then $(p \text{ v } q)$ stands for all persons who are *either* female *or* children (in common parlance, "women and children") and $(p \wedge q)$ for all persons who are *both* female *and* children (that is, little girls). Note that the "and"

of ordinary language is used loosely to mean also "or." In the algebra of sets, the set "women and children" is denoted by "females and/or children." The "and" is reserved to denote the application of both properties. According to that usage, "females and children" would mean only those who are both females and children (that is, little girls).

[51] Take, for example, the rule $p \wedge (q \vee r) \equiv (p \wedge q) \vee (p \wedge r)$. Let p stand for "children," q for "Americans," and r for "Chinese." Then the left side represents all persons who are children *and* either American or Chinese, while the right side all those who are either (American and children) or (Chinese and children). Both sets are the same: American and Chinese children. For complete discussion of these rules, see (9) and (50).

[52] The interpretation $p+q-pq$ is valid only if p and q are "independent events," that is, if the occurrence or nonoccurrence of one in no way influences the chances of the other. In our example, p, q, and r were all independent, and so their probabilities could be multiplied. If events are not independent, more complicated rules apply in the calculation of the probabilities of joint events. Obviously the event p is not independent of *itself*. Therefore, we cannot interpret the probability of the joint event $(p \wedge p)$ as p^2. The joint event "p and p" is identical with p. This is the reason for the strange looking rule $p^2=p$.

[53] This is the "classical" deterministic statement of the second law. It involves the concept of the "total entropy of the universe." The meaningfulness of this concept has been recently challenged. However, all experimental evidence has so far confirmed the inevitable rise in entropy in any "closed system," that is, one which does not exchange any energy with its environment.

[54] For a discussion of this problem, see (12, 13).

[55] It must be kept in mind that a living organism is never a closed system. It always exchanges energy and matter with its environment. In fact, a sure way to kill an organism (and thus to increase its entropy) is to shut it off completely from the environment.

[56] The reader need not conclude that the cat "knows calculus." Her nervous system *does* "calculations" just as the spider's nervous system does geometric constructions and just as our digestive organs do fancy chemistry. This "built-in" knowledge differs fundamentally from "symbol-manipulating" knowledge, which is peculiarly (probably exclusively) human. The built-in calculating abilities of the human nervous system have been tested in recent experiments (29). The high degree of predictability of which the human nervous system is capable resides not in the more or less automatic responses of the nervous system to immediate events impinging on it but on a translation of these events into symbols by means of which accumulated past experience can be "re-lived."

[57] For a discussion of so-called deutero-learning (higher order learning), see G. Bateson's article in (65).

[58] Theories implicitly based on the quantification of ethics, where the

"variable" appears to be the *potentiality* of adjustment, the development of the learning capacity, are especially clearly presented in the works of J. Huxley (41, 42) and in the writings of K. Deutsch (21, 22).

[59] For a striking example, see the description of an opera performance as it appears to an "extensionally-oriented" girl, Natasha Rostova, whom Tolstoy pictures as an Epicurean in *War and Peace* (102).

[60] I once asked a well-educated Indian what in his opinion was the mood Beethoven attempted to convey in the last movement of the *Moonlight Sonata*. He said it must have been "joyful exuberance"!

[61] For many more interesting examples and their origin, see (52).

[62] In many widely separated cultures we encounter a literary form known as the "proto-sonnet," an eight-line poem, in which the first four lines are a metaphor and the last four the concrete situation depicted. For examples, see (52). Resembling the proto-sonnet is the "negative metaphor" of the Russian saga (bylini), in which the metaphorical part is put in the negative to indicate presumably that the resemblance between the metaphorical and the concrete situation is so strong that identity has to be denied.

[63] If a beam of light is passed through a pinhole and then through two other pin holes, so as to illuminate two overlapping areas on a screen, the overlapping region will show thin dark bands. These bands are attributed to "interference." They can be explained if it is assumed that light consists of waves. Then the dark bands are interpreted as the regions where the crests from one set of waves coincide with the troughs from the other, so as to "cancel" each other. The assumption that light consists of streams of particles (Newton's theory) does not offer an analogous explanation.

[64] An extremely far-reaching attempt to develop a theory of behavior based on the "game" model is found in the *Theory of Games and Economic Behavior* by Von Neumann and Morgenstern (64).

[65] This classification of groups in accordance with their goal-seeking behavior was presented by Jacob Marschak in a lecture at a meeting of the American Statistical Association held in Chicago on December 28, 1952.

BIBLIOGRAPHY

The numbers in parentheses throughout the text refer to the entries in this list. The editions indicated are those consulted by the author and are not necessarily the original publications.

1. Allee, W. C., Emerson, A. E., Park, O., Park, T., and Schmidt, K. P. *Principles of Animal Ecology.* Philadelphia and London: W. B. Saunders Co., 1949.
2. Anselm, St. *Cur Deus Homo.* Edinburgh: John Grant, 1909.
3. Aristotle. *The Nichomachean Ethics.* New York: G. P. Putnam's Sons, 1926.
4. Ayer, Alfred Jules. *Language, Truth, and Logic.* London: V. Gollancz, 1936; (2nd ed.) New York: Dover Publications, 1950.
5. Bacon, Francis. *Novum Organum.* Oxford: The Clarendon Press, 1889.
6. Bavelas, Alex. "Communication patterns in task-oriented groups." *The Journal of the Acoustical Society of America.* Vol. 22, No. 6 (Nov., 1950).
7. Berkeley, George. *The Principles of Human Knowledge.* Chicago: The Open Court Publishing Co., 1920.
8. Birkhoff, G. *Aesthetic Measure.* Cambridge, Mass.: Harvard University Press, 1933.
9. Birkhoff, G., and MacLane, S. *A Survey of Modern Algebra.* New York: The Macmillan Company, 1941.
10. Boole, George. *The Mathematical Analysis of Logic.* New York: Philosophical Library, 1948.
11. Bridgman, P. W. *The Logic of Modern Physics.* New York: The Macmillan Company, 1927.
12. Brillouin, L. "Life, thermodynamics, and cybernetics." *American Scientist.* Vol. 37, pp. 554-568 (1949).
13. ———"Thermodynamics and information theory." *American Scientist.* Vol. 38, pp. 594-599 (1950).
14. Burke, Kenneth. *Permanence and Change.* New York: *The New Republic,* 1936.

15. Butler, Samuel. *Erewhon.* New York: E. P. Dutton & Co., 1917.
16. Carnap, Rudolf. *The Logical Foundations of Probability.* Chicago: The University of Chicago Press, 1950.
17. ———*Philosophy and Logical Syntax.* London: K. Paul, Trench, Trubner, & Co., 1935.
18. Cassirer, Ernst. *An Essay on Man.* New Haven: Yale University Press, 1944.
19. Chase, Stuart. *The Tyranny of Words.* New York: Harcourt, Brace & Co., 1938.
20. Chisolm, Francis P. *Introductory Lectures on General Semantics.* Lakeville, Conn.: Institute of General Semantics, 1945.
21. Deutsch, Karl W. "Mechanism, organism, and society." *Philosophy of Science.* Vol. 18, No. 3 (July, 1951).
22. ———"On communication models in the social sciences." *Public Opinion Quarterly.* Vol. 16, No. 3 (fall, 1952).
23. Dewey, John. *Interest and Effort in Education.* Boston and New York: Houghton Mifflin Co., 1913.
24. ———*Logical Conditions of a Scientific Treatment of Morality.* Chicago: The University of Chicago Press, 1903.
25. ———*Reconstruction in Philosophy.* New York: Henry Holt & Co., 1920; enlarged ed., Boston: The Beacon Press, 1948.
26. Dewey, John, and Tufts, James H. *Ethics.* New York: Henry Holt & Co., 1932.
27. Dodd, Stuart C. "On classifying human values: a step in the prediction of human valuing." *American Sociological Review.* Vol. 16, No. 5 (Oct., 1951).
28. Eliot, Thomas D. "Reactions to predictive assumptions." *American Sociological Review.* Vol. 2, No. 4 (Aug., 1937).
29. Ellson, D. G. "The application of operational analysis to human motor behavior." *Psychological Review.* 1949.
30. Embler, Weller. "Metaphor and social belief." *ETC.: A Review of General Semantics.* Vol. 8, No. 2 (Winter, 1951).
31. *ETC.: A Review of General Semantics* (special issue on metalinguistics). Vol. 9, No. 3 (Spring, 1952).
32. France, Anatole. *Thais.* New York: Illustrated Editions, 1931.
33. Frank, Philipp. *Einstein, His Life and Times.* New York: Alfred A. Knopf, 1947.
34. Fromm, Erich. *Man for Himself.* New York: Rinehart & Co., 1947.
35. Hayakawa, S. I. *Language in Thought and Action.* New York: Harcourt, Brace & Co., 1949.
36. ———"Semantics." *ETC.: A Review of General Semantics.* Vol. 9, No. 4 (Summer, 1952).
37. ———"What is meant by Aristotelian structure of language?" *ETC.: A Review of General Semantics.* Vol. 5, No. 4 (Summer, 1948).

38. Hogben, Lancelot. *Mathematics for the Million.* London: G. Allen & Unwin, 1937.

39. Hume, David. *Enquiry Concerning Human Understanding.* Chicago: The Open Court Publishing Co., 1927.

40. Huxley, Aldous. *Brave New World.* Garden City, N. Y.: Doubleday Doran & Co., 1932.

41. Huxley, Julian. *Man Stands Alone.* New York: Harper & Brothers, 1941.

42. ———*On Living in a Revolution.* New York: Harper & Brothers, 1944

43. Johnson, Wendell. *People in Quandaries.* New York: Harper & Brothers, 1946.

44. Kant, Immanuel. *Critique of Pure Reason.* London: Bell and Daldy, 1855.

45. Korzybski, Alfred. *Manhood of Humanity.* New York: E. P. Dutton, 1921.

46. ———*Science and Sanity.* Lakeville, Conn.: Institute of General Semantics, 1948 (3rd ed.).

47. Langer, Susanne K. *Philosophy in a New Key.* Cambridge, Mass.: Harvard University Press, 1942.

48. Lee, Irving J. *Language Habits in Human Affairs.* New York: Harper & Brothers, 1941.

49. Lewis, Sinclair. *Babbitt.* New York: Harcourt, Brace & Co., 1922.

50. Lieber, Lillian. *Mits, Wits, and Logic.* New York: W. W. Norton & Co., 1947.

51. Locke, John. *Essay on the Human Understanding.* Oxford: The Clarendon Press, 1894.

52. Loeb, Edwin. "Proverbs in the intellectual development of primitive peoples." *Scientific Monthly.* Vol. 74, No. 2 (Feb., 1952).

53. Luce, R. D. "Connectivity and generalized cliques in sociometric groups." *Psychometrika.* 15, pp. 169-190 (1950).

54. Luce, R. D., and Perry, A. D. "A method of matrix analysis of group structure." *Psychometrika.* 14, 95-116 (1949).

55. Lundberg, George A. *Can Science Save Us?* New York, London, Toronto: Longmans, Green & Co., 1947.

56. Maloney, Martin. "The unknown god." *ETC.: A Review of General Semantics.* Vol. 9, No. 2 (Winter, 1952).

57. Mannheim, Karl. *Ideology and Utopia.* New York: Harcourt, Brace & Co., 1949.

58. Mannoury, G. *Les fondements psycho-linguistiques des mathematique.* Bussum (The Netherlands): F. G. Kroonder, 1947.

59. Margenau, Henry. "The methodology for integration in the physical sciences," published in *The Nature of Concepts, Their Interrelation and Role in Social Structure.* Stillwater, Oklahoma: Oklahoma Agricultural and Mechanical College, 1950.

60. Mayo, Elton. *The Human Problems of an Industrial Civilization.* Boston: Division of Research, Graduate School of Business Administration, Harvard University, 1946 (2nd ed.).

61. Mead, George Herbert. *Mind, Self, and Society.* Chicago: The University of Chicago Press, 1934.

62. Meyers, Russell. "The aims of general semantics and the method of science." *ETC.: A Review of General Semantics.* Vol. 5, No. 4 (Summer, 1948).

63. Morris, Charles. *The Open Self.* New York: Prentice Hall, 1948.

64. Neumann, John von, and Morgenstern, Oskar. *Theory of Games and Economic Behavior.* Princeton: Princeton University Press, 1947.

65. Newcomb, T. E., and Hartley, E. L. (eds.). *Readings in Social Psychology.* New York: Henry Holt & Co., 1947.

66. Newman, James R. "William Kingdon Clifford." *Scientific American.* Vol. 188, No. 2 (Feb., 1953).

67. Orwell, George. *Nineteen Eighty-four.* New York: Harcourt, Brace & Co., 1949.

68. Overstreet, Harry W. *The Mature Mind.* New York: W. W. Norton & Co., 1949.

69. Piaget, Jean. *The Child's Conception of the World.* New York: Harcourt, Brace & Co., 1929.

70. ———*The Language and Thought of the Child.* New York: Harcourt, Brace & Co., 1926.

71. Plato. *Five Great Dialogues.* New York: Walter J. Black, 1942.

72. Poincaré, Jules Henri. *The Foundations of Science.* New York and Garrison, N. Y.: The Science Press, 1913.

73. Popper, Karl R. *The Open Society and Its Enemies.* Princeton: Princeton University Press, 1950.

74. Rapoport, Anatol. "Death of communication with Russia?" *ETC.: A Review of General Semantics.* Vol. 7, No. 2 (Winter, 1950).

75. ———"Dialectical materialism and general semantics." *ETC.: A Review of General Semantics.* Vol. 5, No. 2 (Winter, 1948).

76. ———"Music and the process of abstraction." *ETC: A Review of General Semantics.* Vol. 4, No. 3 (Spring, 1947).

77. ———*Science and the Goals of Man.* New York: Harper & Brothers, 1950.

78. ———"What is semantics?" *American Scientist.* Vol. 40, No. 1 (Jan., 1952).

79. Rashevsky, Nicolas. *Mathematical Biology of Social Behavior.* Chicago: The University of Chicago Press, 1948.

80. ———*Mathematical Biophysics.* Chicago: The University of Chicago Press, 1948 (2nd ed.).

81. Reichenbach, Hans. *The Rise of Scientific Philosophy.* Berkeley: University of California Press, 1951.

82. Reichenbach, Hans. *The Theory of Probability*. Berkeley: University of California Press, 1949.
83. Riesman, David (in collaboration with Reuel Denney and Nathan Glazer). *The Lonely Crowd*. New Haven, Conn.: Yale University Press, 1950.
84. Rosenblueth, Arturo, Wiener, N., and Bigelow, J. "Behavior, purpose, and teleology." *Philosophy of Science*. Vol. 10 (1943).
85. Rousseau, J. J. *The Social Contract*. New York: G. P. Putnam's Sons, 1893.
86. Russell, Bertrand. *Introduction to Mathematical Philosophy*, London: Allen and Unwin, 1920 (2nd ed.)
87. Schopenhauer, Arthur. *The World as Will and Idea*. London: K. Paul, Trench, Trubner, & Co., 1907-1909 (6th ed.).
88. Schroedinger, E. *What Is Life?* New York: The Macmillan Company, 1945.
89. Seldes, Gilbert. *The Great Audience*. New York: Viking Press, 1950.
90. Shannon, Claude E., and Weaver, Warren. *The Mathematical Theory of Communication*. Urbana, Ill.: University of Illinois Press, 1949.
91. Shimbel, Alfonso. "Applications of matrix algebra to communication nets." *Bulletin of Mathematical Biophysics*. Vol. 13, No. 3 (Sept., 1951).
92. Simpson, George Gaylord. *The Meaning of Evolution*. New Haven, Conn.: Yale University Press, 1950.
93. Sophocles. *Oedipus Rex* (English version by D. Fitts and R. Fitzgerald.) New York: Harcourt, Brace & Co., 1949.
94. Spencer, Herbert. *Principles of Ethics*. New York: D. Appleton & Co., 1898.
95. ———*Principles of Sociology*. New York: D. Appleton & Co., 1892.
96. Spengler, Oswald. *Decline of the West*. New York: Alfred A. Knopf, 1939.
97. Stromberg, Gustaf. "The autonomous field." *Journal of the Franklin Institute*. Vol. 239, No. 1 (Jan., 1945).
98. Tarski, Alfred. "The semantic conception of truth." *Philosophy and Phenomenological Research*. Vol. 4 (1944).
99. Thackeray, William Makepeace. *Vanity Fair*. New York and London: Harper & Brothers, 1898.
100. "The situation in biological science." *Proceedings of the Lenin Academy of Agriculture Sciences of the U.S.S.R.* Moscow: Foreign Language Publishing House, 1949.
101. Tolstoy, L. N. *Gospel Stories*. New York: Thomas Y. Crowell & Co.
102. ———*War and Peace*. New York: The Modern Library, 1931.
103. Toynbee, Arnold. *The Study of History* (abridged version). New York: Oxford University Press, 1947.
104. Vaihinger, Hans. *The Philosophy of As If*. New York: Harcourt, Brace & Co., 1924.

105. Vogt, William. *The Road to Survival*. New York: William Sloane Associates, 1948.

106. Vyshinsky, Andrei. *The Law of the Soviet State*. New York: The Macmillan Company, 1948.

107. Weinberg, Julius Rudolph. *An Examination of Logical Positivism*. London: International Library of Psychology, Philosophy, and Scientific Method, 1950.

108. Whitehead, Alfred North. *Adventures of Ideas*. New York: The Macmillan Company, 1933.

109. ———*Science and the Modern World*. New York: Pelican Mentor Books, 1948.

110. Whyte, L. L. *The Next Development in Man*. New York: Henry Holt & Co., 1948.

111. Wiener, Norbert. *Cybernetics*. New York: John Wiley & Sons, 1948.

112. ———*The Human Use of Human Beings*. Boston: Houghton Mifflin Co., 1950.

113. Wittgenstein, Ludwig. *Tractatus Logico-philosophicus*. New York: Harcourt, Brace & Co., 1922.

INDEX

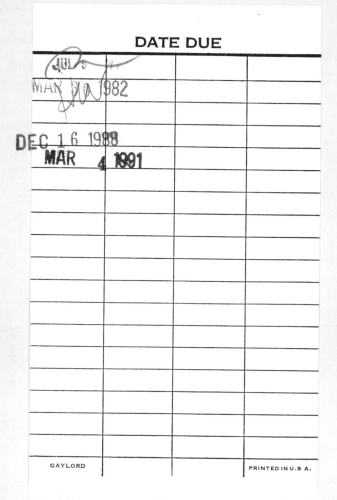

DATE DUE

JUL			
MAR 30 1982			
DEC 16 1988			
MAR 4 1991			